A Guide to
Library Research in Music

Pauline Shaw Bayne

The Scarecrow Press, Inc.
Lanham, Maryland • Toronto • Plymouth, UK
2008

SCARECROW PRESS, INC.

Published in the United States of America
by Scarecrow Press, Inc.
A wholly owned subsidary of
The Rowman & Littlefield Publishing Group, Inc.
4501 Forbes Boulevard, Suite 200, Lanham, Maryland 20706
www.scarecrowpress.com

Estover Road
Plymouth PL6 7PY
United Kingdom

British Library Cataloguing in Publication Information Available

Library of Congress Cataloging-in-Publication Data
Bayne, Pauline Shaw.
  A guide to library research in music / Pauline Shaw Bayne.
    p. cm.
  Includes bibliographical references and indexes.
  ISBN-13: 978-0-8108-6148-0 (cloth : alk. paper)
  ISBN-10: 0-8108-6148-8 (cloth : alk. paper)
  ISBN-13: 978-0-8108-6211-1 (pbk. : alk. paper)
  ISBN-10: 0-8108-6211-5 (pbk. : alk. paper)
 eISBN-13: 978-0-8108-6240-1
 eISBN-10: 0-8108-6240-9
 1. Musicology. 2. Library orientation for college students. 3. Music
librarianship. I. Title.
 ML3797.B29 2008
 780.72–dc22   2008025088

To Chuck,
my wonderful and supportive husband

To Laurel Whisler, Margaret Kaus, and Chris Durman,
among the best of colleagues in the music library world

Contents

Figures

Preface

This textbook on library and computer-based research for music is based on sixteen years of teaching a graduate course in Music Bibliography. It is directed not only to students of music history and theory but also to those pursuing public or private music teaching and performance.

Critical preparations for research include learning the literature and methodology of the field, coming to understand its issues and having an interest in bringing clarity to them, and grasping the reality that, like practicing a musical instrument, research requires regular, iterative applications of time and mind. A practical aim of a music research course for graduate students is to help them develop an arsenal of strategies for identifying and gathering resources. Another is to help them learn to plan a research project and to intelligently and efficiently apply the strategies they are learning.

My preparation has been in piano performance, music education, and musicology on the music side and in library science. As a professional music librarian, I have assisted students, faculty, professional musicians, and interested amateurs in their searches for information and knowledge of musical matters. I have been challenged to explain and help them use the organizing systems of libraries, the burgeoning universe of digital materials, and published resources of music.

A Guide to Library Research in Music has three goals:
- To explain the research process and provide concrete examples of types of writing about music;
- To offer instruction in a variety of information-searching techniques and library-based organizational systems, especially for those who wish to prepare themselves for independent learning;
- To introduce the array of music resources, highlighting electronic and print resources available since the 5th edition of *Music Reference and Research Materials* in 1997.

Who should use this book? It is addressed first to graduate students in music, but motivated undergraduates and independent learners will benefit just as easily. The three parts of the book are somewhat independent tracks available to be explored as needed.

How to Use This Book

Part 1 is called "The Short Course" because it treats essentials of the research process; explains the most basic sources—library catalogs, dictionaries, and bibliographies; addresses scholarly documentation, the use of style manuals, and the basics of copyright; and provides samples of typical written research products. Read this part sequentially, and take time to read one or more of the books on research recommended in Chapter 1.

Part 2 gathers "How To" instruction for developing skills and strategies to find the things you need. Search strategies range from rather "low-tech" browsing of subject-arranged collections to discovering published bibliographies on a topic to the many techniques available for success in the world of computer databases and Internet resources. One special learning topic in Part 2 focuses on thematic catalogs for in-depth information and identification of individual composers' works.

Part 3, "Resources," takes a combination of approaches to introduce the literature of music. It combines a traditional "type-of-literature" approach examining directories, biographies, histories, etc., with brief explanations of how these materials are arranged on the shelf. That is, it explores the logic behind the arrangement of music materials using the *Library of Congress Classification* system. Unlocking the mysteries of those call numbers can result in an efficient approach to intelligent browsing of the books themselves. A special learning topic in Part 3 investigates musical editions.

HINT: It may be helpful to move between the overview chapters of Part 1 and the skill-development chapters of Part 2. More resources of Part 3 could follow the starting-point resources of Part 1.

Alternative Order:

Chapters 1–4	The nature of research and initial discovery resources
Chapters 8–13	Techniques of browsing and database searching in catalogs and indexes using headings (authors, titles, subjects) and keywords
Chapter 5	Summary: A case study to review the research process, resources, and essential search techniques
Chapters 6–7	Scholarly documentation, copyright, and examples of writing about music. Refer to these examples as you begin classroom or real-world writing projects.
Chapters 14–15	Other discovery methods: experts, Internet, using thematic catalogs
Chapters 16–18	More resources by type: scores (M), music literature (ML), instruction and study (MT)

Organization of Chapters

Preview. Read these summary statements as an introduction to chapter content. For concepts that seem completely new, pay careful attention to the explanations and examples in the chapter. For those that you already understand, just skim the information to look for anything that might be new to you.

Content. Subheadings will guide you through the information and instruction in each chapter.

Review Questions. Brief review questions supply a test of your understanding of content presented. If you can't answer a question, reread appropriate parts of the chapter.

Learning Exercises. These are "laboratory" exercises for learning by doing. Your laboratory is the library and the computer. Remember that real comprehension comes through practice.

Appendices

The appendices provide students with shortcuts to resource discovery by using the organization of many research libraries in this country: the *Library of Congress Classification* system. The most helpful list may be that of Appendix 3, which offers access to class numbers for scores and books on music literature and instruction and by topic such as choral music, band, violin, piano, percussion, music education, liturgy and religion, and music therapy. Students may wish to use the appropriate list of classification numbers for their area of study in exploring the music library and as they begin to choose areas of research. Some online catalogs may be "browsed" through classification number searching, also facilitated by these tailored lists.

Bibliography

The bibliography is organized by chapter and subheadings as an easy reminder of print and online sources discussed throughout the book. Refer to it for full bibliographic information. The double asterisk (**) identifies sources recommended as particularly useful.

For Teachers

Choose among the "Learning Exercises" to structure learning activities for your students. Note, however, that projects in Chapter 7, "Writing Samples," are designed to make use of the strategies and resources explored throughout this textbook. One or more of them might be assigned as major course projects.

All books discussed in the chapters are listed in the bibliography at the end of the text. A double asterisk (**) identifies those recommended for their particular value.

Acknowledgments

This book is the product of many years of interactions with students engaged in music research; therefore, it is appropriate to include student work as writing examples for other students. Chapter 7 includes several samples of work by outstanding students. I wish to express my gratitude to them for agreeing to inclusion of their work as writing samples in this book.

Program notes for Debussy's *La Cathédrale Engloutie* is used by permission of Elizabeth Gaile Stephens.

Program notes for *We Shall Overcome* is used by permission of Sean McCollough.

The literature review portions and outline from her thesis are used by permission of Kathy Forester Adkins.

Selections from her annotated bibliography on Chopin chamber music are used by permission of M. Nathalie Hristov.

Bonna Boetcher's review of *Baker's Biographical Dictionary of Musicians* is reprinted from *Notes: Quarterly Journal of the Music Library Association*, vol. 58, no. 3 (March 2002) by permission of the Music Library Association.

Excerpts from the *Library of Congress Subject Headings* and *Library of Congress Classification* are used by permission of the Library of Congress, Cataloging Distribution Service.

Examples of subject headings and geographic headings from *Music Index Online* are used by permission of Harmonie Park Press.

The *International Index to Music Periodicals* subject categories and subject terms are reproduced as follows: image published with permission of ProQuest-CSA LLC. ©2007, ProQuest-CSA LLC; all rights reserved. Further reproduction is prohibited without permission.

The RILM classification scheme and an example of RILM subject terms are used by permission of *RILM Abstracts of Music Literature.*

Citation index examples are used by permission of the *Arts and Humanities Citation Index* published by Thomson Scientific.

I am indebted to Margaret Kaus, original cataloger at Kansas State University Libraries, for checking and revising the Library of Congress information listed in Appendix 3, "Topical Guide to Music in the Library of Congress Classification."

Three music librarians were especially helpful to me in reviewing drafts of this text. Laurel Whisler, formerly at Furman University and now at Southern Wesleyan University, was most helpful with matters of organization and content. She gave much time to her review of the manuscript. Margaret Kaus, my close University of Tennessee colleague and now at Kansas State University, was an authority on matters of cataloging and classification. Chris Durman, now a music librarian at the University of Tennessee, provided a careful eye in the quest for relevance to students. I extend a heartfelt thanks to each.

Final words of appreciation go to my husband, Chuck, for his support throughout my sabbatical and the revision and publishing process. His confidence in me was a major factor in completion of this work.

Part 1

The Short Course:
Music Research and Writing

Part 1

The Short Course:
Music Research and Writing

Music research—what is it and why do it? Research is an endeavor to explore, learn, and contribute to the body of knowledge in a subject field. The process of scholarly writing becomes a continuous conversation between scholars because today's research is founded on the research findings and reporting of those who came before or who are still actively engaged in research. It is necessary to know the issues, concepts, and ideas about music —the body of knowledge that is accepted in the field—before it is possible to make new and original contributions. As a graduate student, at the master's or doctoral level, you are a participant in the research conversation. Perhaps you have only been a consumer so far, but to complete your degree you will need to become a contributor. "Research has become so much a part of graduate curricula in the arts that musicians are expected to be scholars as well as creators and performers." [1]

Whether your aspirations are for a performing career; for a professional post as a music teacher in the schools, as a private instructor, or at the college level; or in some aspect of the business of music, you need to become an independent learner. Doing real research will let you develop investigative techniques of value to your studies, your career, and even your everyday life. As consumers of research results and that daily overload of information, you need to understand how to evaluate claims and evidence and arguments. You need to know how to find information for yourself and draw appropriate conclusions from what you read. Think about your favorite performers. The best performers know a lot about music as well as knowing how to perform it well; they are informed and articulate about their art. They have developed a context for their musical expression. The more you learn to do research in music, the more you develop your own context for music and music making.

The focus of this book is on the aspects of music research done in libraries and using computer resources. Part 1 is called "The Short Course" because it treats the essentials of the research process, the most basic sources, addresses writing problems, and provides samples of the most typical outputs of the process. Chapter 1 provides an overview of the research process: its logical steps of investigation and evaluation as well as the recursive nature of the process. Chapters 2 through 4 introduce important resources used for initial information gathering and refinement of a research topic. Chapter 5 provides a case study as an illustration of the process of research. Chapter 6 deals with techniques of crediting the words and ideas of others through scholarly documentation, including style guides for writing about music in narrative text. It also covers basics of copyright, fair use, and the permissions process, all of importance to musicians. Music students report their research in course term papers, annotated bibliographies, or program notes for concerts and recitals. There are also a variety of extended research papers required for graduate degrees: the recital paper, master's thesis, doctoral essay, or doctoral dissertation. The literature review and bibliography are usually required components of a thesis or dissertation. Because examples are excellent learning resources, Chapter 7 supplies samples of research writing prepared by music students.

Note

1. Ruth Watanabe, *Introduction to Music Research* (Englewood Cliffs, NJ: Prentice Hall, 1967), v.

Chapter 1

The Research Process

Preview

The following are primary points in the research process that will be covered in this and subsequent chapters.

- Identifying and narrowing a research topic is the beginning. Start with an interest, ask questions, and learn more until you arrive at a single research question.
- Once you know of appropriate starting-point resources, exploration and evaluation of your topic can begin. Read for background knowledge and research leads. Read skeptically. What questions come to mind as you read about your topic? What kinds of reference books and other resources do you need to evaluate your topic?
- Discovery, selection, and evaluation of source materials occur several times in the process. First you will determine how much has been written on your topic and consider ways to revise it. Then you will try to locate useable sources, looking for evidence to support your thesis. Remember that you must evaluate the authority, currency, validity of the sources you discover.
- A thesis is a brief statement of the position or claim of your paper. In just one or two sentences, a thesis statement should present the main point of the research to be proved by argument and evidence.
- Sources provide information, but you can also learn how to build a case by studying an author's arguments and presentation. Intelligently make notes, always recording full citation details and distinguishing between quotation, paraphrase, and summary.
- The writing stage evolves from a fairly well-defined thesis statement to an outline for writing to a draft paper. As your thought processes sift and refine the evidence, your thesis will finalize. Be sure to plan enough time to revise the paper carefully, looking at its style, clarity of communication, persuasive argument, and matters of form and grammar.

This chapter provides a brief overview of the research process in three stages: topic development, gathering and evaluation of sources, and writing. However, many excellent books are available that give more in-depth coverage than is possible here. Especially useful are treatments of the process for creating a thesis statement and of argumentation. One of the most useful books with this emphasis is *The Craft of Research* by Wayne C. Booth, Gregory G. Colomb, and Joseph M. Williams.[1] Its authors, all university professors of research and writing, advocate planning as the essential ingredient of successful research. They provide practical actions and thought processes for writing to an audience, asking questions to move from an interest to a topic to a thesis statement, pulling together an argument, and drafting and revising the paper. This is a readable source full of clear and practical advice for students in all disciplines.

Another book, highly recommended as a classic on the subject, is *The Modern Researcher* by Jacques Barzun and Henry F. Graff,[2] historians at Columbia University. In its 6th edition (2004), this book is valued as a foundation study for the process of doing research.

The research process is not linear, nor is it entirely predictable. Still, it is possible to define components of the process and a logical order for them. As a researcher, you should expect to repeat some steps as you learn more about the topic, find authoritative authors, or see that certain types of data or information are required. You will need to repeat some parts of the process several times both for gathering information and for writing the research results. Let's explore some of the stages of a research process.

1.1 Preliminary Stage: Topic Development

This is the stage where you come up with a possible topic for your research. It is a good idea to find something that interests you and that you would like to learn more about. If you are going to spend a semester writing a seminar paper or perhaps a year or more writing a thesis, you do need to be interested in the topic. Start by asking yourself questions to gauge your own goals for learning. One of these areas may be appropriate for your research.

Probably you will identify a general topic; even a single composition is a general topic because there are many aspects of it that can be explored. Why was it written? How does it fit into the composer's works? Has this work influenced other composers? Was the composer strongly influenced by someone in the writing of the composition? Is it a landmark piece in some way? What does theoretical or stylistic analysis reveal about the work? Can you write the research in a twenty-page paper or will it take a book to do it justice? Has it been treated by so many authors that there is little left to add? You will need to narrow a topic so that you can make an original contribution by asking and answering a worthwhile question. Choose a specific aspect of a topic to narrow it.

Continue with the questioning process to move towards that narrower topic. Booth, Colomb, and Williams advocate this process in *The Craft of Research*: write your topic in a sentence, ask a question to focus on what you want to learn, and determine why it would be significant to a reader. Their formula is: "I am studying _____ (topic) because I want to find out what/why/how _____ (question) in order to help my reader understand _____ (significance)."[3]

The nature of your central research question will determine the kinds of information, or more properly the evidence, that you need to collect.

Telling questions lead us (like a smart bomb) right to the target. They are built with such precision that they provide a means of sorting and sifting during the gathering or discovery process. They focus the investigation so that we gather only the very specific evidence and information that we require, only those facts which illuminate the main question at hand.[4]

There are several types of resources that support the process of identifying and narrowing a research topic. Even if you have chosen a fairly narrow topic, use these sources to build your background knowledge of the topic and to supply research leads.

Use subject encyclopedias, dictionaries, and appropriate textbooks to obtain background information; ascertain the scope of a topic; or gather names, dates, relationships, and historical context. This kind of information provides a working knowledge of the topic and helps you decide whether it is too broad or too narrow. As you read this summary information ask yourself questions to gauge whether more research is needed. What aspect is unknown? What comparisons are unmade? What can be applied to new situations? Are there interdisciplinary aspects to investigate? Also look for referrals to other sources by checking the bibliography and footnotes. Look for authors who are cited repeatedly on the subject; they should be more authoritative sources and may be experts in the field. See Chapter 2 for a discussion of subject dictionaries for the general field of music and for its subfields.

Use subject bibliographies to provide referrals to books, journal articles, chapters in books or conference/symposia proceedings, and even web resources. There are specialized bibliographies, such as thematic catalogs and discographies, that you may need to use for verification of information: the original title of a composition, its opus or thematic catalog number, or its dedication. Discographies provide detailed information about sound recordings including outtakes, names of sidemen, or place and date of a recording session. Bibliographies are discussed at length in Chapter 4.

Use local experts—teaching faculty and librarians—to help you get started with a topic. Discussing a potential project with a faculty member is a good strategy because the faculty member may be able to give you some shortcuts. Perhaps she will suggest authors who have specialized in the area or published resources to use first. Librarians will help you with the techniques of library research and ways to identify starting-point resources or parts of the collection to browse. Chapter 14 explains the value of experts and ways to find them.

Before leaving these initial sources, determine whether you can handle the topic. Are there some special skills required that you don't have? It might be difficult to complete a project on Ukrainian folk song if you do not have a working knowledge of the language. Does it appear that enough information will be available or is your initial topic actually too narrow? Sometimes a contemporary composition will be hard to research because there has not been time for critical reviews or much discussion of the work in published literature.

Now is the time to prepare a draft thesis statement and to create a preliminary outline. What is a thesis statement? It is a brief statement of the position or claim of your paper. In just one or two sentences, a thesis statement should present the main point of the research to be proved by argument and evidence. You may wish to consider this initial statement as a hypothesis, what you believe at this point can be proven true or false. Hypotheses are meant to be broken so during the research process, you may need to change the statement of your point. In fact, you may wish to state it as a question to be answered in the paper. This focused statement can provide keywords, which will be the basis for Boolean searches of databases. You can use these terms to search catalogs and journal indexes as you move to the resource discovery phase of your project. Create a preliminary outline, at this stage, to organize component parts of your topic. The outlining process will help you decide what kinds of information to seek. Do you need facts, statistics, interviews, opinions, or historical information?

1.2 Gathering–Evaluation Stage

Plan for and implement search strategies or methods to acquire source materials in support of your initial hypothesis—your proposed explanation or main point. It will take time to discover and evaluate resources that will allow you to support or prove your main point. Take time now to build your understanding of the databases and reference books that facilitate the process. You need to assess your information needs to determine the type of materials that are likely to supply evidence. Do you need the latest research or current reports on musical events? Perhaps you need these kinds of sources to reflect contemporary views on historical topics. Then you will use journal or newspaper databases to search for periodical articles or newspaper reports from the appropriate time period. Do you need dissertations, specialized books, performances on sound or visual recordings, or printed music? Then the online library catalogs, including union catalogs such as *WorldCat*, will be vital. Bibliographies, discographies, and manuscript inventories will lead you to published materials, recordings, or music manuscripts. Chapters 2–4 of Part 1 offer guidance to starting-point resources. Part 3 provides guidance to more music resources according to type.

It takes time, practice, and often some guidance to be able to apply the various strategies or methods for identifying these materials. The order for information searching is not one set sequence. You may start with a Google search, but it is vital not to stop there. Part 2 is structured to introduce:

- Systematic browsing of a library's physical collection
- Use of online catalogs and music databases through:
  - Heading or field searches (author, title, subject heading) in library catalogs and journal indexes
  - Controlled-vocabulary searches, meaning use of subject headings or descriptors
  - Keyword searches based on Boolean logic
  - Related-record searches based on known items or as used in citation indexes
- Use of experts
- Internet searches

The best search strategy is never a matter of developing a single method of searching. Researchers must identify various ways of searching for source materials that are appropriate to the resource identification tools they use: library catalogs, journal indexes, browsing the collection, etc. But they also need to use multiple strategies within many of these tools. Searching for a composition (either the printed music or a sound recording) in a catalog might start with the most specific title information possible combined with the composer's name. If the results are not sufficient or not as expected, the searcher will need to think about the fact that such material may be part of collections. So the search strategy will need to change to a more general type of title, perhaps the form of the music, such as sonatas or symphonies, combined with the composer's name. At any rate, the basic approach should be to learn how to use a variety of search strategies and to be flexible in trying different approaches. Many details about database searching are covered in Chapters 9 through 13.

The central aspect of this phase of research, then, is to discover, select, acquire, and evaluate source materials whether they are books, journal articles and other current literature, theses and dissertations, criticism and reviews, scores, sound or visual recordings, web-based resources, or people who can provide expert advice.

Acquiring the sources you need may involve using the interlibrary loan service at your library. If your library does not own the item you need, look for an interlibrary loan request form; it will probably be an online form. Complete the information needed, submit it, and the staff for this service will acquire the material for you from another library. They will let you know when it is available. Interlibrary loan units have improved delivery speed significantly in the last few years, but be aware that it could take a week for material to be delivered. Articles may be delivered electronically to your computer, but the complete book or score requires physical delivery most of the time. Place your loan requests early in the process. Examine your library's website for information such as delivery processes, fees, or restrictions. Many libraries subsidize the service and may offer lending without cost to the user.

Evaluating resources and actually using them—reading the content and making notes—should happen in an incremental way. Points of evaluation should include authority and credibility of the authors, currency of information, accuracy or verification of data, objectivity, and documentation to sources of ideas and opinions. See pages 169–171 for specific evaluation guidelines for both print and online sources. As you discover and acquire a resource, use it. Intelligently make notes, including full citation information, and establish a system that will help you find specific information later at the writing stage. Use keyword identifiers at the top of the page or for paragraphs so that you can spot the specific nature of portions of your notes. Be sure to clearly distinguish in your notes whether you are writing down a quotation, or paraphrasing the words of an author, or summarizing in your own words. These notations will keep you from inadvertently plagiarizing the words of another author. Academic honesty requires great care in this matter. Chapter 6 provides information on the use of style manuals for notes and bibliographic citations as well as advice on how to handle music titles in narrative writing. Citation management software such as EndNote, RefWorks, or Zotero provides the key to managing your bibliographic information and automatically formatting in accord with a specific style manual.

Remember those telling questions you asked about your topic? Use them and your preliminary outline as you collect evidence. Many researchers give advice along these lines: (1) gather only the very specific evidence and information required, (2) gather sources which address the main question at hand, and (3) evaluate sources as you find them so you use only the most reputable, authoritative, and accurate sources.[5]

1.3 Writing Stage

The writing stage evolves from a clear thesis statement, to a detailed outline for writing, to a draft paper. Your thesis statement will have evolved over the course of gathering sources and reading them for specific points of evidence. If you haven't revised the thesis by now, stop and rethink it carefully. Hone your thesis statement until it expresses the main point of your research in clear terms that lay the basis for your argument and proof. The structure of an argument includes reasons to support your thesis (or claim) and evidence in support of each reason. Subpoints in your paper will be the reasons to accept your thesis, and you will need to present evidence to persuade your readers that these reasons and your thesis are legitimate.[6] Once satisfied with the final thesis statement, go on to revise your preliminary outline into one that covers all subpoints—the reasons and evidence—you want to address.

Perhaps the most important principle to remember while writing a first draft and then during revisions is this: every section, paragraph, and sentence should support your thesis. Do not add historical information because it might be interesting. Use it only if it is important to the case you are making. Do not describe the plot of an opera unless it is essential to your main idea. Don't pad, not even by including language that you think will sound more educated. Simplicity and clarity of communication are important goals when you need to make a convincing case. Be sure to plan enough time to revise the paper carefully, looking at its style, clarity of communication, persuasive argument, and overall form and grammar.

Review Questions

1. Explain several ways to narrow a research topic, including which types of resources might be useful.

2. How are subject encyclopedias and dictionaries of value at the start of a research project?

3. What is a thesis statement?

4. List and explain the nature of three primary stages of research.

Learning Exercises

1. Write a tentative research topic using the structure suggested in *The Craft of Research*: I am studying _____ (topic) because I want to find out what/why/how _____ (question) to help my reader understand _____ (significance).[7]

2. Begin to explore your topic in music dictionaries and encyclopedias. Create an online document to serve as a research journal where you list the sources consulted and take brief notes for people, dates, issues, and questions that you may need to investigate. Create a separate document as a working bibliography, and enter appropriate citations from the bibliography of each source you consult. Recommendation: Use EndNote or another software program to manage these citations.

3. Try a guided browsing approach to bibliographies. Many special bibliographies for topics in music are classed in ML128, usually in the music reference collection. Consult Appendix 4, "Bibliographies by Topic in ML128" in this textbook to check for your topic. If there is an appropriate one, use the classification number to browse at the shelf for subject bibliographies. For instance, band music bibliographies are

shelved in ML128.B23; jazz bibliographies are in ML128.J3; and bibliographies of operas are in ML128.O4.

    a.   Find an appropriate general topic in Appendix 4, and then examine books in the appropriate classification area in the library. Add these bibliographies to your working bibliography.

    b.   Now use the bibliographies to find specific books, journals, or other materials that relate to your topic. This activity is part of the process of discovering sources to use in support of your thesis.

Notes

1. Wayne C. Booth, Gregory G. Colomb, and Joseph M. Williams, *The Craft of Research*, 2d ed. (Chicago: University of Chicago Press, 2003).

2. Jacques Barzun and Henry F. Graff, *The Modern Researcher*, 6th ed. (Belmont, CA: Thomson Learning/Wadsworth, 2004).

3. Booth, *The Craft of Research*, 56.

4. Jamie McKenzie, "Telling Questions and the Search for Insight," *FNO* 7, no. 1 (September 1997), http://www.fno.org/sept97/telling.html (accessed 23 August 2007).

5. Bret Heim and Nancy Bolton, "Defining Your Research Topic & Starting Your Research, Lesson 3," *Information Literacy Tutorial*, http://camellia.shc.edu/literacy/tablesversion/lessons/lesson3/questioning.htm (accessed 23 August 2007).

6. Booth, *The Craft of Research*, 56.

7. Booth, *The Craft of Research*, 56.

Chapter 2

Starting-Point Resources:
Reference Books

Preview

- Most fields have a standard bibliography to identify types of materials and specific titles for information appropriate to the field. The index in such a bibliography is a critical aid in identifying whether books have been published for a specific topic. For music, the standard source is *Music Reference and Research Materials: An Annotated Bibliography* by Duckles and Reed.
- *WorldCat* is a union catalog, meaning it lists the holdings of many libraries. Use it to obtain a good view of the quantity of materials published on a topic, publishers for printed music, and a first step in the interlibrary loan borrowing process.
- Subject dictionaries and encyclopedias provide background information: people, dates, and ideas associated with a research topic. They also direct the researcher by summarizing information (composers' works lists) and leading to other accepted research (bibliographies).

As a first look at the literature of music, this chapter highlights starting-point resources. These are the basic research tools for topic development and initial investigations. They include standard bibliographies for the field of music, bibliographies of general reference books, union catalogs, music encyclopedias, and dictionaries.

At this point, it is important to reiterate some information about electronic or computer-based resources. Most databases mentioned in this book are available only by subscription; therefore, their use requires access to a subscribing library. College and university libraries provide access to their students, faculty, and staff on campus or from remote locations. Some will provide access to members of the public, but that will generally happen only within a library building.

2.1 Bibliographies of the Discipline

Bibliographies for Music Research

The following bibliographies are the most highly regarded (1) for information sources appropriate to music research or (2) as general research sources to address the interdisciplinary nature of music investigations today. **Music Reference and Research Materials: An Annotated Bibliography* is the standard bibliography of resources for music, presenting annotated citations for more than 3,800 titles. Originated by Vincent Duckles in 1964, its fifth edition (1997) was edited by Ida Reed with Michael Keller as advisory editor. This edition is strengthened in quality because of the direct contributions and reviewing done by almost two dozen music librarians. The bibliography is organized by type of literature and subarranged by topic. It provides detailed annotations and cites reviews of all works listed.

For guidance to non-music research sources, the standard is Keith Mixter's *General Bibliography for Music Research* (1996). Mixter provides cross-discipline guidance by describing subject bibliographies for the arts, education, humanities, religion, social sciences, computer science and data processing; indexes such as general literary and subject indexes, newspaper indexes, and book reviews; and of particular interest to singers, the bibliographies and indexes for vocal texts. This authoritative reference book was first published in 1962.

A recent selected bibliography, providing practical research guidance to music students, is Laurie Sampsel's **Music Research: A Handbook* (2008). Sampsel identifies tools and resources organized by type: encyclopedias, periodical indexes, discographies, historical sources, etc. A companion website includes supplemental information and a means of updating the handbook; it is available at www.oup.com/us/musresearch.

Bibliographies of General Reference Books

When it is time to identify sources of information in disciplines related to music, there are other bibliographies available to the music researcher either in the broad area of humanities or in a listing of reference books in all subject areas.

Start with Balay and Carrington's *Guide to Reference Books* (1996) when you expect a reference book to exist but do not know what it might be. This 11th edition contains citations and annotations for 15,875 titles; now it also has a separate section for the humanities. The majority of entries are for print sources. All titles are accessible through the book's classified organization or its extensive index. *The Humanities: A Selective Guide to Information Sources* by Blazek and Aversa identifies resources in music and in disciplines related to music especially dance, film, folklore, language and literature, mythology, philosophy, radio, religion, theater, video, and visual arts. The guide includes electronic and web-based sources in addition to those in print and provides in-depth annotations of all listings. While oriented towards librarians and library science students, it is a valuable resource for humanities scholars.

> HINT for discovering appropriate reference books: Go to standard bibliographies for a discipline or bibliographies of general reference books when you expect a reference book to exist but do not know what it might be.

2.2 *WorldCat*: A Union Catalog

You will certainly need to search your local library catalog to determine what materials are readily at hand, but union catalogs do some special things that are particularly helpful at the beginning of a research project. Union catalogs reflect the holdings of several to hundreds to thousands of libraries. Therefore, they are essential discovery sources for building a working bibliography. By searching a union catalog, you can discover the existence of resources even if your library does not own them. Searching *WorldCat*, for instance, gives you access to materials owned by 53,000 libraries today. Knowing that an item exists, you may then request it through your interlibrary loan service. If you are trying to determine if a composition has been recorded or which publishers have issued a specific musical work, *WorldCat* may help you answer these questions quickly. You may need to use other sources later, but it is an excellent starting point. Searching union catalogs that represent groups of libraries (a consortium) can help with expedited delivery of interlibrary loan requests or alert you to holdings in a nearby library where, due to a consortial agreement, you may be able to check out the materials.

WorldCat is a union catalog whose records are created and maintained by more than 60,000 member libraries, museums, and other institutions in 112 countries around the globe. It provides the opportunity to search both local and worldwide libraries all at once. The database is produced by OCLC and updated daily. As of April 2008, *WorldCat* contained records for more than 1.3 billion items. Each record contains information about libraries that own the item, thus facilitating interlibrary loan of materials. *WorldCat* provides a window to the manuscripts and published works in all aspects of human knowledge. In August 2006, it became possible to search *WorldCat* directly through a central web page at http://worldcat.org. You may even download a search box on your own computer. For information about *WorldCat* from the source, go to http://worldcat.org/whatis/default.jsp.

2.3 Music Dictionaries: ML100–109

General Dictionaries or Encyclopedias: ML100

Dictionaries provide information using an alphabetical arrangement of entries, whether the subject for the entry is a person, topic, or term. Music dictionaries are considered to be "general" when they include all three types of entry. Use a general music dictionary or encyclopedia to gain background information on a research topic, to identify dates or people or ideas associated with the topic, and to look for a bibliography for further reading. In multivolume music encyclopedias, there may be many well-qualified contributors who have authored the entries. Always look for names of specific contributors and credit them in your own notes and bibliographies.

When it comes to online encyclopedias, you have probably used the all-subject source called *Wikipedia*. Free, convenient, available at all hours and wherever you have computer access, it is a welcome starting point for summary information. However, when it comes to assessing authority, it is important to know that all of its content is contributed by users. There are editorial guidelines specified and requests for citation of sources, yet the information is accepted without standard editorial review. It is wise to verify information from *Wikipedia* before using it for scholarly research.

In music, there are three up-to-date multivolume general dictionaries in electronic or print form. As the standard English-language encyclopedia for music, ****Grove Music Online** is respected for its authority. It provides full-text searching of over 50,000 subject articles and bibliographies written by more than 6,000 worldwide experts. In 2008, it was relaunched as part of *Oxford Music Online*, a gateway that allows access to multiple resources. *Grove Music Online* now includes the full text of the print versions of several major reference sources:

- ***The New Grove Dictionary of Music and Musicians*, 2d ed. (Stanley Sadie and John Tyrrell, 2001)
- *The New Grove Dictionary of Opera* (Stanley Sadie, 1992 in print and 1999 online)
- *The New Grove Dictionary of Jazz*, 2d ed. (Barry Kernfeld, 2001)
- *The Oxford Companion to Music* (Alison Latham, 2002)
- *The Oxford Dictionary of Music,* 2d ed. revised (Michael Kennedy, 2006)

Planned additions of content:

- *Grove Dictionary of American Music,* 2d ed. (Charles Hiroshi Garrett, 2009–)
- *Grove Dictionary of Early Music* (beginning in 2009)
- *Grove Dictionary of Musical Instruments*, 2d ed. (date unknown)

Grove Music Online also has the advantage of regular updates occurring at least three times each year. Look for the date stamp on the screen to learn which articles have been updated since their first appearance in print. Bibliographies are detailed and frequently subarranged by format or topic. Composers' works lists provide essential information about compositions such as title, dates, dedication, instrumentation, publishers, opus or thematic catalog numbers, and references to location of the work in the composers' complete critical edition. Internal navigation provides access to illustrations, including some 3-D models of instruments and over 500 sound files associated with the articles. Links to related websites, chosen for quality, are listed in the articles under categories: general, literature, and organizations. The 2008 update also links to authoritative online resources (some requiring institutional subscriptions):

- *RILM Abstracts of Music Literature* for articles and other current literature (linked from bibliographies)
- *Oxford Dictionary of National Bibliography* (linked from biographies)
- Recordings in *Classical Music Library* and *Digital Recordings in American Music (DRAM)* (linked from the related content tab)

The second edition of *Die Musik in Geschichte und Gegenwart: Allgemeine Enzyklopadie der Musik (MGG)* is a monument of German and international scholarship by virtue of several thousand contributors who have authored subject and biographical entries. The set is under the editorial guidance of Ludwig Finscher. More than 1,500 subject entries in the 9-volume Sachteil (subjects) cover all topics from aesthetics, church music, popular music, instruments and genres to cities and countries. The biographical portion, Personenteil in 12 volumes to date, contains more than 18,000 entries on singers, instrumentalists, instrument makers, jazz and popular music figures, theorists, musicologists, librettists, publishers, and both Western and non-Western composers. Non-German readers can benefit from names and dates in entries, illustrations, lists of works for composers, and detailed bibliographies. Each multivolume segment has its own index on CD-

ROM. Volumes have been issued from 1994, and some of the biography volumes remain to be published.

**The Garland Encyclopedia of World Music* (1998–2002), in its print version, was the first encyclopedia devoted to world music. Edited by Bruno Nettl and Ruth Stone, the 10-volume resource has more in-depth coverage of music around the globe than is available in other music encyclopedias. It has been prepared by various scholars who are experts in these regions, is well illustrated, and contains extensive bibliographies and discographies. Geographically arranged by continent or subcontinent, each of the first nine volumes follows a similar pattern moving from general to more specific information. The organization is: (1) an introduction to music and culture of the region, (2) a discussion of issues and processes that link the music of the region, and (3) detailed accounts of individual music cultures. Most volumes include a set of study and research tools, glossary, lists of audio and visual resources, bibliographies, and an audio compact disc with musical examples. Volume 10 covers general perspectives and reference tools. For a complete listing of volumes, see the bibliography at the end of this book. In 2007, Alexander Street Press made this valued source available electronically as *The Garland Encyclopedia of World Music Online*. Initially the online content includes all of the articles of the print version. Future releases will contain more indexing as well as links to the associated audio examples for each volume.

There are also many useful one- and two-volume music dictionaries. Two among the recent authoritative dictionaries are *The Penguin Companion to Classical Music* (2004) by Paul Griffiths and Michael Kennedy's *The Concise Oxford Dictionary of Music* (2004). The smaller general music dictionaries are useful for the quick access of a desktop resource.

National Dictionaries: ML101

Dictionaries devoted to the music and musicians of a single country are classed in ML101. Some examples to illustrate this type include *The New Grove Dictionary of American Music* (4 volumes, 1986) edited by Hitchcock and Sadie; *Encyclopedia of Music in Canada* (1992) by Kallmann, Potvin, and Winters; *Enciclopédia da Música Brasileira: Popular, Erudita e Folklorica* (4 volumes, 1998) edited by Marcondes; and the 9-volume *Diccionario de la Música Española e Hispanoamericana* (1999–2002) by Rodicio, López-Calo, and Fernández de la Cuesta. Currently, none of these is available electronically.

Subject Dictionaries: ML102

There are a wealth of subject dictionaries for special areas of music, far too many to be listed effectively here. Some of the topics of these dictionaries include church music; opera; rock, country, jazz, or other areas of popular music; piano; percussion; and many more. As in other classifications where the books are arranged by topic, specific letter-number combinations put the topics in alphabetical order. If you know that ML102 is the primary classification for subject music dictionaries, you can just browse in that area for the topics.

Subject dictionaries may include biographical entries for people associated with the topic, term entries for its vocabulary, or descriptions of individual musical works. On the other hand, they may be restricted to only one type of entry. In any case, it is the subject that is most important here. Become familiar with the dictionaries in your subject area. For instance, there are many opera dictionaries, but they offer different kinds of information ranging from a comprehensive chronology of operas, *Annals of Opera, 1597–1940* by Loewenberg, to sources that identify major roles for each opera, *Guide to Operatic Roles & Arias* by Boldrey. An important multivolume dictionary for popular music, Colin Larkin's *Encyclopedia of Popular Music*, 4th edition (2006) is available in print and online through *Oxford Music Online* and is placed with other dictionaries on the subject in ML102.P66. The few examples of recently published subject dictionaries listed below serve only to give an idea of the wide range of these dictionaries. Their classification numbers have been added to illustrate how the topics are arranged alphabetically. Note, the full call number may vary from library to library, but the classification pattern will be very similar.

Blues:	ML102.**B6**S26 2001, *The Big Book of Blues: A Biographical Encyclopedia* by Santelli
Jazz:	ML102.**J3**V57 2004, *The Virgin Encyclopedia of Jazz* by Larkin
Opera:	ML102.**O6**O8 2001, *The Dictionary of the Opera* by Osborne
Piano:	ML102.**P5**E53 2003, *The Piano: An Encyclopedia* by Palmieri
Popular:	ML102.**P66**T38 2004, *The A to X of Alternative Music* by Taylor

Biographical Dictionaries: ML105–107

Biographical dictionaries provide information about people. Those covering people in music are classed as follows:
ML105 international
ML106 national, by country
ML106.3–ML106.4 United States
ML107 local

The standard work for music biographies is the 6-volume ***Baker's Biographical Dictionary of Musicians*, edited by Nicolas Slonimsky and Laura Kuhn. Now in its ninth edition, its origin was the groundbreaking dictionary by Theodor Baker published in 1900. The dictionary has expanded from coverage of classical musicians only to include significant numbers of jazz and popular performers. This edition was published after the death of Nicolas Slonimsky, who had been responsible for editions six through eight. Works lists and bibliographies are given in paragraph style; bibliographies omit journal articles, which were available in earlier editions.

Because biographical entries occur in dictionaries, subject encyclopedias, literary criticism, and other indexes, it is helpful to know about ***Biography and Genealogy Master Index*. This database identifies which reference books include biographical material on people from all time periods, regions, and subject fields. It indexes more than 15.7 million biographical sketches published in various sources. It does not index periodical articles or books of biography about a single individual. Search results include an individual's name, birth and death dates, and full citations to works that include information on the person. The print version was first published in 1980.

Two biographical dictionaries that are restricted to entries for living musicians are *International Who's Who in Classical Music* and *International Who's Who in Popular Music* (2007). The first contains over 8,000 entries for living classical musicians, composers, conductors, and others associated with art music. The second supplies biographical information on more than 5,000 popular names in pop, rock, folk, jazz, dance, world, and country music. Each includes a directory section for organizations worldwide.

Other biographical dictionaries in music are devoted to more discrete groups of people such as *Women and Music in America since 1900: An Encyclopedia*, edited by Burns (2002, classified with resources on women in ML82), *The Norton/Grove Dictionary of Women Composers* by J. Sadie and R. Samuel (1994), and *International Dictionary of Black Composers* by S. Floyd, Jr. (1999).

Term Dictionaries: ML108–109

These two classification areas are used for dictionaries of musical terms, for translations of foreign terms used in music, and for pronouncing dictionaries. Sometimes when limited to terminology of a specific subject area, a term dictionary will be classed along with other subject dictionaries. An example is *A Dictionary of Vocal Terminology: An Analysis* by Cornelius L. Reid, which is classed in ML102 along with other dictionaries for voice and opera.

As the standard terminology dictionary for music, Randel's *The Harvard Dictionary of Music* (2003) is now in its fourth edition. It is used frequently as a required text for music undergraduate students. Definitions are clear and precise; longer essays cover musical periods and concepts. The Library of Congress Classification number is ML100 because the entries cover terms, concepts, and historical styles or periods. Therefore, it is more "general" in nature than a term dictionary of brief definitions. Also available are very concise dictionaries of musical terms. For one that includes translations of foreign terms and definitions relating primarily to the elements of music, musical forms, and aesthetic terms, try *The Oxford Dictionary of Musical Terms* (2004) edited by Latham. Thomsett's *Musical Terms, Symbols and Theory: An Illustrated Dictionary* (1989) is especially helpful for secondary students and undergraduates. Its explanations are clear, and there are many illustrations of musical notation. It also includes a brief guide to instrument names in five languages. Popular in nature is *The NPR Classical Music Companion: Terms and Concepts from A to Z* by Miles Hoffman. Addressing music likely to be played on the radio or in concerts, this is a readable dictionary of basic musical terms plus background information presented in a conversational and sometimes humorous manner.

It can be difficult to find sources of pronunciation or translation of musical terms, but they do exist. They are classified as term dictionaries although they do not always include definitions. *The Well-Tempered Announcer: A Pronunciation Guide to Classical Music* (1996) by Fradkin was published to assist radio announcers. It is of assistance to anyone seeking the pronunciation of names of composers and performers as well as titles of musical works. For quick translation of musical terms between any of seven languages, consult the *Polyglot Dictionary of Musical Terms: English, German, French, Italian, Spanish, Hungarian, Russian (Terminorum musicae index septem linguis redactus*, 1978).

Review Questions

1. Name the standard bibliography for the discipline of music.

2. Identify three uses of union catalogs.

3. Explain the kinds of information that each of these dictionary types provide:
   a. General music dictionary or encyclopedia
   b. Subject dictionary
   c. Biographical dictionary
   d. Term dictionary

Learning Exercises

1. Compare these scholarly encyclopedias for music: *New Grove Dictionary of Music and Musicians* (print version) and *Die Music in Geschichte und Gegenwart* (*MGG*), addressing the following questions.
   a. How is the entire set organized?
   b. Are there indexes? Why are they useful?
   c. How are individual entries organized?
   d. How do you determine the author(s) of the entries?
   e. What special information is provided for composers?
   f. What kinds of information can you obtain from *MGG* even if you do not read German?
   g. Create a footnote you would use to cite one article from each encyclopedia.
   h. How might you use these works to determine the authorities in your field?

2. Examine *Grove Music Online*, and answer the questions listed below.
   a. Name the three dictionaries currently included in this database.
   b. Where do you find the names of the author(s) of specific entries, and what do the numbers mean when listed: author name (3), etc.?
   c. Try the various search methods and compare them: Advanced Search, Browse, Explore.
   d. Identify your chosen style manual, and create a footnote you would use to cite one article using that style.

Examine the subject dictionaries for music in your library's reference collection (ML102–103). Choose three that are especially helpful for your area of concentration as a graduate student, and prepare an annotated bibliography of these subject dictionaries. An annotated bibliography requires a citation and annotation for each and a decision on the order of works in the bibliography.

Chapter 3

Starting-Point Resources: Journals

Preview

- Journal literature and the databases that index articles in journals are critical to research in every field. Journals supply current information: research results, practical guidance, issues and events. Historically, they reflect the views and issues of the time. Remember that when evaluating journals, those that are peer-reviewed include articles that have been vetted by scholars in the field or passed through editorial review.
- Increasingly, the journal articles, themselves, exist in electronic form accessible through online databases.
- Journal indexes exist today primarily as online databases, and many provide direct links to the actual text of articles. They provide subject access to articles published in journals, magazines, newspapers, and sometimes other current literature such as books of essays, conference papers, symposium reports, and more.
- Google Scholar is a web search engine which provides access to full text of scholarly literature. It uses the openURL standard to link from an information resource (online index, catalog, or search engine) directly to the target that supplies the information needed (an article in full text).
- Consider whether you need to consult journal indexes in your subject or whether cross-disciplinary indexes may be of value to your research topic.

3.1 Journal Literature: ML1, ML5, and ML27 or Classed with Subject

Music journals, or periodicals, are a category of "current" information. To qualify as a journal or periodical, the issues of a title must be published on a repeating basis. The frequency may be quarterly, semiannually, three issues per year, monthly, or in some other pattern. Usually a library will receive paper issues and/or provide access to electronic issues. When checking a catalog to see if the library owns a periodical, be sure to make note of the call number (or whether they are shelved alphabetically in a special location), the holding library if there are branch libraries, which dates or volumes the library owns, and the format—electronic, current print issues, bound volumes, or microfilm. These holding details are important when it comes to obtaining the specific volume or issue you need. The historic value of periodicals from a particular time period or country cannot be overstated. They represent activities, opinions, and culture of their time recorded at that time. There are a variety of types of music periodicals that differ in style and audience.

Current News and Events in Music

Such journals may include articles of interest to concert audiences and serious musicians; interviews; reviews of books, recordings, and performances; calendar of concerts; advertisements for performances.

Examples: *Musical Times*
                    Tempo: A Quarterly Review of Modern Music

Practical Journals for Teaching

These deal with techniques of vocal or instrumental pedagogy or music education in the schools. Professional associations issue some of these titles. They may include articles on teaching; printed music, reviews of teaching materials, books, recordings; advertisements for instruments; music camps, teaching positions, competitions, schools, and festivals. Advertising can be quite helpful to the audience of teachers.

Examples: *The American Music Teacher*
                    Clavier
                    Music Educator's Journal
                    The Instrumentalist

Topical Journals

These periodicals treat topics such as church music, instruments, choral, band or orchestra ensembles, and opera. Some will be academic, scholarly journals; others will be more consumer oriented. They may include articles on performance, philosophy or technical matters for directing ensembles, or matters such as the business of music, auditions, and schools. Reviews and advertising are common.

Examples: *The Hymn*
                    Journal of Country Music
                    Opera Quarterly
                    Symphony Magazine

Scholarly Music Journals

Most subdisciplines have several scholarly journals in areas such as music education, conducting, musicology, ethnomusicology, music theory, and music technology. Generally they include lengthy research articles with notes and bibliographies as well as scholarly reviews of books, sound or video recordings, and scores.

Examples: *19th Century Music*
             Computer Music Journal
             Ethnomusicology
             Journal of the American Musicological Society
             Journal of Band Research
             Journal of Research in Music Education
             Music Theory Spectrum

Yearbooks

These annual publications tend to cover musicology; individual composers; special topics such as folk music, instruments, or opera. They may be publications of societies offering a collection of research papers, symposia papers, or bibliographies. Many offer significant research reports that may be longer than normal journal articles.

Examples: *Bach-Jahrbuch*
             Folk Music Journal from the English Folk Dance and Song Society
             Die Reihe: A Periodical Devoted to Developments in Contemporary Music

Classification Numbers for Music Periodicals

The Library of Congress Classification numbers assigned to music periodicals vary just a bit. Periodicals that treat music in a general way are classed according to their place of publication:

ML1 for those published in the United States
ML5 for those published in other countries

It is very easy to browse among the bound journals in book stack areas of ML1 and ML5. Just determine whether the journals are likely to be published in the United States or not, then look alphabetically, according to title, in the appropriate classification areas. For instance, the call number for *Opera Journal* is ML1.O74 and for *Opera Canada* is ML5.O664.

For those periodicals that treat specific subjects such as bands, or Gregorian chant, or music theory, it is likely they will be classed to match books on the same subject. *The Journal of Band Research* is classed in ML1300 with books about bands and band music. *The Journal of Music Theory Pedagogy* is classed in MT10 with other instructional materials. Journals, produced by professional societies, are classed in ML25–28 along with other publications they issue.

Remember to use the *Library of Congress Subject Headings* (*LCSH*) to find appropriate journals using a subject approach. Consult the catalog or *LCSH* volumes to determine the topical word or phrase for the subject heading and add "periodicals" as a form subdivision. "Bands–Periodicals" is an example of the controlled-vocabulary searching strategy.

3.2 Lists of Periodicals: ML128.P

Sometimes it is helpful to gain an overview of the periodicals that are available for an area of music, whether they are current journals or historical periodicals. At other times, it is a question of knowing whether a specific journal title is active, who publishes it, and at what price. Periodical lists or directories contain information to meet these needs.

The article **"Periodicals" written by Fellinger, Woodward, and others for *Grove Music Online* provides a history of music periodicals along with a comprehensive list of the periodicals from 1722 to 1999, arranged by continent and country. Coverage includes periodicals, yearbooks, and almanacs on music plus the annual reports of musical institutions. An alphabetical title index, bibliography, and list of periodical indexes are included. In the title index, look under the name of the sponsoring organization when the title is generic: bulletin, newsletter, or journal. Index references are national RISM *sigla* (abbreviations for the country and an entry number). Use a *siglum* to find the full entry in the geographically organized primary list.

While dated, *International Music Journals* (1990) by Fidler and James remains valuable for its descriptions and evaluations of 181 major music journals. Almost 50 contributors prepared the narratives, arranged alphabetically by journal title. For each item, there is a history, publication information, description, and evaluation. Separate lists provide access by year, country, and subject. Considered a bibliography of periodicals, it is classed in ML128.P.

Ulrich's Periodicals Directory is an international directory, available both as a bibliographic database and in print. It provides information on serials published throughout the world. *Ulrich's* covers academic and scholarly journals, consumer and trade magazines, newspapers, newsletters, monographic series, and electronic publications, whether they are active, ceased, or forthcoming. Use it to obtain publication information, cost, format, and details of where the title is indexed. *Ulrich's* was first published in 1932.

The Directory of Open Access Journals (*DOAJ*) fills a relatively new need for identification of journals. It is both a listing of journals and an index to articles in this new type of online journal and in 2008 included 29 scholarly music journals. Open access means the online journals are supplied free of charge for access, downloading, printing, etc. *DOAJ* lists only journals using this funding model that also exercise peer review or quality control based on editorial oversight.

3.3 Indexes to Journals and Other Current Literature

The following indexes are all electronic databases, and libraries provide access to them on the basis of paid subscriptions. So the list of databases will differ from library to library; some listed here may not be available at your university. Databases are changeable by nature; they change in content, appearance, and functionality. Some of the details listed below may not apply as the databases evolve.

For most research it is important to be comprehensive in a literature search; therefore, it is frequently necessary to use all three of the journal indexes for music. They cover different journals, and *RILM Abstracts* indexes more formats than journals alone. Their time period coverage varies as does the kinds of information they provide (citations, abstracts, or full text). These differences usually mean the researcher must search them all. A citation is the information that identifies the article and its source, while an abstract is a brief summary of the article. Full text, of course, is the full article online.

Databases for Music

Providing indexing and abstracts for more than 430 international music periodicals, the **International Index to Music Periodicals (IIMP* or *International Index to Music Periodicals Full Text*) also supplies full text for around 120 journals. Its current number of article records is over 530,000; about 38% are prior to 1996 and 62% from 1996 to the present. Because the index began in 1996, the current file dates from that year. The back file varies in start date journal by journal, but some journals are covered from their first issue. The earliest date of coverage is 1874. Besides providing its own full text resources, *IIMP* includes links to two full-text archives: *JSTOR* and *Project MUSE*. The links are openURL or durable URL, which may be copied and pasted into your own citations in reports or bibliographies for direct access to the full text. The updating frequency is monthly. You may limit a search to full-text articles only, peer-reviewed articles only, or to exclude reviews. It is possible to download or e-mail selections from a results list. Other offerings include: a Quick Search box on every page for easy keyword searching; Search or Browse Journals gets you to the journals by title or subject; Search or Browse Reference lets you look up glossary definitions of musical terms, find opera synopses, and pronunciation guides. For opera and music theater topics, a sister index provides citations, abstracts, and some full text: *International Index to the Performing Arts* (1998). *IIPA* covers over 240 performing arts journals for dance, film, drama, theater, stagecraft, musicals, storytelling, opera, pantomime, puppetry, and magic. The earliest journal is from 1864 and in *IIPA Full Text*, 84 full-text journals are indexed. Some libraries may provide combined access to both indexes under the title: *Music & Performing Arts Online*, 1998–.

**The Music Index Online: A Subject-Author Guide to Periodical Literature* (1975–present) is the oldest continuing index of music journals. The print version of *Music Index* began in 1949 and continues today; the online database covers journals from 1975 to the present and in 2008 included over 1.4 million records. It is updated quarterly. Covering more than 850 international music periodicals, its search results consist of citations only plus full-text links (openURL) to JSTOR participants. JSTOR is an archive of online journal articles in full text. Options exist to mark records and then print or e-mail them.

The third major journal index for music, **RILM Abstracts of Music Literature*, actually covers more than journals. *RILM Abstracts* is its short title with "RILM" being the acronym for *Répertoire international de littérature musicale*, or the *International Repertory of Music Literature,* in English. It was created as a joint project of the International Musicological Society and the International Association of Music Libraries, Archives, and Documentation Centers in 1966. Broader than a journal index, its mission is the indexing of current literature including journals (articles, reviews, etc.); essays in books and Festschriften (commemorative writing); papers published from symposia, conferences, and congresses; bibliographies; and dissertations. The database contains almost 500,000 records with coverage beginning in 1967. Approximately 30,000 new entries are added annually. Its citations and abstracts (summaries) cover all areas of music research plus studies of music in conjunction with other fields. While the database does not contain full text of documents, it provides links to full text for selected journals under the rubric "linked full text." It is enabled for linking to local catalog searches as well. Options exist to mark records and then print or e-mail them. Currently *RILM Abstracts* is available via five different vendors. The appearance and functionality of the search inter-face varies among these vendors.

RIPM Online: International Index to Nineteenth-Century Music Periodicals is an historical file published under the auspices of the International Musicological Society; International Association of Music Libraries, Archives, and Documentation Centers; and UNESCO's International Council for Philosophy and Humanistic Studies. Its acronym comes from the original project title: *Répertoire international de la presse musicale*. The online database currently consists of over 450,000 records that index the musical press of the 19th and early 20th centuries and is updated every six months. The index exists also on CD-ROM and in print. To make the literature itself (over 2,000 music periodicals from the 19th century and other sources) available, *RIPM* is in the process of publishing approximately 250 volumes, which likely will become a searchable database as well.

Databases for Music Education

Several specialized database resources exist for music education and related disci-plines. *Music Education Search System,* under the direction of Edward P. Asmus at the University of Miami, indexes 12 music education periodicals, provides 4,500 abstracts from pre-1965 publications, and indexes the journal *Boletín de invesigacio educative musical*. From the University of Texas Department of Music and Institute for Music Re-search comes *CAIRSS for Music (Computer-Assisted Information Retrieval Service System)*. It provides only citations to 27 periodicals related to the music side of education, psychology, medicine, and music therapy. *Music Education Resource Base* is an index covering about 35 periodicals normally indexed in *Canadian Music Index* since 1956.

Databases for Related Disciplines

For humanities and performing arts disciplines:

Providing cited references but not abstracts, *Arts & Humanities Citation Index* cov-ers about 1,100 arts and humanities journals, plus individually selected items from over 6,800 major science and social science journals. It may be searched as any journal index using the general search or to track citations of a known article or book. It is available online as part of the *Web of Science Citation Databases* as well as in print and on CD-ROM. *Humanities Abstracts* is an index of English-language periodicals in a wide range of humanities topics with index coverage beginning in 1984 and inclusion of abstracts from March 1994. It is updated weekly.

For education:

For topics in education, including music education, *Education Full Text* indexes and abstracts articles of at least one column in length, dating from 1983 to the present, from English-language periodicals and yearbooks; it also indexes English-language books re-lating to education published since 1995. Abstracts were added to the database in January 1994 while full-text coverage began in January 1996.

The ****ERIC** database (Educational Resources Information Center) is a complete bibliography of educational materials available since 1966. *ERIC* indexes published and unpublished sources on thousands of educational topics. Coverage includes research reports and journal articles from *Resources in Education Index* (*RIE*) and *Current Index to Journals in Education* (*CIJE*). Besides citations and abstracts, it offers several thousand full-text articles. The online database is available from various vendors on a subscription basis; access is free at http://www.eric.ed.gov. On the *ERIC* website, look for tabs marked "Eric Search" and "Thesaurus." The database originates in the Office of Educational Research and Improvement, U.S. Department of Education, Educational Resources Information Center.

For other disciplines:

The following databases are used primarily as journal indexes for a variety of subject disciplines related to:
   musicology (history, philosophy, religion)
   music performance (health, literature)
   music education (psychology, social sciences)
   technology and music (computer science)
Appropriate databases are listed here along with brief descriptions to raise your awareness of their existence. Check your library's database list to determine if you may access these databases or others that cover related fields.

Computer Science
IEEE Xplore, 1955–. Provides full text of most IEEE and IEE journals, proceedings, and
   active standards
INSPEC, 1969–. Indexes physics, computing, etc.

Cross-Disciplinary
Academic Search Premier, 1975–. Covers 3,900 scholarly publications
ArticleFirst, 1990–. Indexes 12,500 journals
Google Scholar, 2004–. Indexes full text of scholarly literature including websites, com-
   mercial journals, and open access repositories
Ingenta, 1988–. Covers 20,000 journals
PapersFirst, 1993–. and *ProceedingsFirst*, 1993–. Index conference and symposium
   proceedings

Health
Health Reference Center–Academic, 1995–. Gives full text for health-related consumer
   publications, nursing, etc.

History
America: History & Life, 1950s–. Indexes scholarly literature on U.S. and Canada
ArchivesUSA. For access to primary sources in 5,480 manuscript repositories
Historical Abstracts, 1950s–. Indexes scholarly literature on world history
International Medieval Bibliography Online. For scholarly articles on medieval Europe
Iter: Gateway to the Middle Ages and Renaissance. Covers 400–1700
LexisNexis Primary Sources in U.S. History. For U.S. history, African-American studies,
   women's studies

Literature
MLA International Bibliography, 1926–. For information on librettists and poets
Literature Online (LION), *1996–*. Covers poetry

Philosophy
Philosopher's Index, 1940–. Indexes and abstracts journal articles and books

Psychology
PsycARTICLES, 1985–. Provides full text of 53 APA journals
PsycINFO, 1887–. Gives access to journal articles, books, dissertations in all areas of
    psychology

Religion
ATLA Religion Database, 1949–. For articles and essays on world religions and social
    issues

Review Questions

1. Describe the nature of periodicals and journals and identify at least three categories
    of music journals.

2. Why are journal indexes critical to research?

3. Identify the three databases that concentrate on music journals or other current lit-
    erature in music.

4. Identify two databases for journals in other subject areas that could be helpful for
    researching an interdisciplinary music topic.

Learning Exercises

1. Use various searching techniques to create a list of five to seven journals for your
    music concentration area that are received currently in your library.

2. Which searching techniques are most helpful? Title keyword search? Subject-
    heading search? Browsing? Other?

3. What form subdivision can you add to a topical subject heading to find journals in
    your area?

4. Choose one journal from your list and describe it in detail. Use the following form as
    a guide to information for your description:

                        Journal Description Form
            Title:
            Frequency:
            Scope (purpose, audience):
            Regular features in each issue:

Types of articles:

Special features such as reviews, lists of new music, recital/concert calendars, artists, illustrations, musical examples:

Footnote or endnote citation for one article:

Information from your library catalog:

Subject heading as listed in the library catalog:

Call number:

Library holdings (dates, volumes, formats):

Information from *Ulrich's Periodicals Directory*:

Which periodical indexes provide indexing to the articles? (Look for tabs that let you access more information than the first screen.)

Subscription cost:

5. Find a research article in a journal covering your area of concentration. Examine it to determine the organization used in reporting research in your field. Then write a brief essay to describe the article and answer the following questions.
    a. What are the author and title of the article?
    b. Does it include an abstract?
    c. List the thesis statement. Where does it occur in the article?
    d. What headings and subheadings are used?
    e. Does it detail a methodology used for the research?
    f. What scholarly documentation is used: footnotes, endnotes, or author-date system? Does it provide a bibliography or sources cited? In what order are the bibliographic citations?

6. Compare the three journal/current literature indexes for music: *International Index to Music Periodicals* (or *Music & Performing Arts Online*), *Music Index Online*, and *RILM Abstracts of Music Literature*. Discuss the kinds of materials they index, time period coverage, types of information provided for each record, and output (saving, printing, etc.) possibilities.

7. For your research topic:
    a. Conduct searches for appropriate journal articles or dissertations in each of the music journal indexes available at your library:
        International Index to Music Periodicals (*IIMP*) or *IIMP Full Text* or
            Music & Performing Arts Online
        Music Index Online
        RILM Abstracts of Music Literature
    b. Find and print or e-mail the full records for two items from each journal index. Be sure to include your research topic and database search statement.

Chapter 4

Starting Point Resources: Bibliographies

Preview

- Scanning footnotes and bibliographies of newly discovered sources is a way to grow a working bibliography. Because scholarly documentation maps the trail of the research conversation, this method will aid in identification of authoritative writers and researchers of the topic. Add the most promising sources to your working bibliography. Find and read these sources; check their footnotes and bibliographies. Repeat the process as long as the sources are beneficial.
- Early discovery of subject bibliographies, whether as books or as journal articles, is important because they point to publications in the field or on the topic. A way to find book-length bibliographies is to attach the form subdivision "–Bibliography" to topical subject headings or to name subject headings in a library catalog search.
- Because bibliographies are so important, it is useful to know the major Library of Congress classifications for finding them in music collections: ML112, 120, 128, 132, 134, 136, 156. The types of bibliographies in each section are explained in this chapter.
- Music bibliographies list resources in two major categories: books about music and lists of the music itself as scores or recordings. Those for recordings are called discographies, and videographies list moving-image sources.

You are certainly familiar with bibliographies that occur at the end of journal articles, encyclopedia entries, books, or even chapters of books. You'll remember that one of the reasons to consult a subject encyclopedia or dictionary at the start of a research project is to make use of the bibliography appended to the entry. The list, essentially recommended by the scholar(s) who prepared the article, may suggest sources for further study whether they are musical editions, articles, books, or papers presented at scholarly conferences. Depending on the subject, there may also be a list of published sound recordings called a discography.

Almost by definition, scholarly books include bibliographies, but you can check on that aspect when searching in a library catalog. The full record usually indicates the presence of a bibliography with a special note. For instance, for *The Italian "Trio" Sonata*:

From Its Origins until Corelli by Peter Allsop, the following note is present: "Includes bibliographical references (p. [240]–252) and index."

Article-length bibliographies appear when the topic is narrow enough to be covered in a journal article or when the author has preliminary bibliographic findings to report. Sometimes such an article is termed "a checklist." The real gems, from an efficiency standpoint however, are the book-length bibliographies that document extensively the published research on a specific subject. Published subject bibliographies offer direction to existing resources; frequently they provide description or evaluation of the materials listed. Music library reference collections include many bibliographies, so an important step in the process of discovering sources is to identify and examine relevant bibliographies for your topic.

The single, most comprehensive bibliography for the study of music provides an organized survey of the literature for the field of music. Use it frequently at the start of a project.

> Duckles, Vincent H., and Ida Reed. *Music Reference and Research Materials: An Annotated Bibliography.* 5th ed. New York: Schirmer Books, 1997. [ML113]

While the latest edition was published in 1997, it is still a valuable source for identifying resources in all aspects of this field. Every music researcher should come repeatedly to this bibliography for guidance. The fifth edition had contributions by numerous music librarians, giving authority to its selective coverage, scholarly descriptions, and references to reviews of sources.

For more current but selected coverage of music resources, consult Laurie Sampsel's 2008 book. It provides annotated bibliographies of major resources for the music researcher. A companion website is available at http://www.oup.com/us/musresearch.

> Sampsel, Laurie J. *Music Research: A Handbook.* New York: Oxford University Press, 2008. [ML113]

4.1 Definitions and Types of Bibliographies

Bibliography. 1. A list of resources consulted in preparation of a paper, report, article, or book; may be termed "works cited." 2. A selective or exhaustive listing of sources published on a topic; may be published as a book or as a journal article. 3. The study of writing, publishing, or scholarship in a subject field.

Annotated bibliography. A list of bibliographic citations to which is added a paragraph or more of description or evaluation of each source.

Bibliography of bibliographies. A list of bibliographies published in a particular field or subject.

Discography. A list of sound recordings, which provides publication information including recording title, record company and manufacturer's number for the recording, contents, performers, and dates. It may include more detailed information as well: listing of sidemen (backup studio performers), matrix numbers for every track recorded, information on tracks recorded but not issued, and more.

Bibliographies and discographies provide full citation information for the resources they list. While generally organized alphabetically by author, they may be organized in a classified arrangement (by subject or topic) as well. The following figure identifies types of bibliographies and their Library of Congress Classification numbers. The bibliographies may cover music or works about music.

Figure 4.1 Bibliographies and Their Library of Congress Classification

Type of Bibliography	LC Classification
General bibliographies	ML113
Bibliographies, by period	ML114–119
Bibliographies, by geography, A–Z	ML120
Bibliographies, by topic, A–Z	ML128
Includes repertoire lists, guides to research, indexes to songs in collections, indexes for identifying compositions	
Graded lists of music for teaching	ML132
Bibliographies of works by and about	ML134
individual composers. Includes thematic catalogs.	
Bibliographies of works by and about	ML134.5
individual performers and groups	
Catalogs: libraries, art, exhibitions, publishers, and	ML136–152
dealers	
Discographies, by source (record company),	ML156–158.8
topic, individual composers, individual performers, reviews	
Bibliographies of video recordings, films	ML158.4
Bibliographies of computer software	ML158.8

4.2 How to Find Bibliographies

Use the browsing method, in the stacks or reference collection, to find bibliographies published as separate books. It is easy when you use the table above to determine which kind of bibliography you need: for 17th-century (Baroque) music (ML116); for music in Algeria (ML120.A); for a specific topic such as choral music (ML128.C), opera (ML128.O) or piano (ML128.P); for Ravel (ML134.R) or the Beatles (ML134.5.B); or for recordings published by Sun Records (ML156.4.S). Notice from these examples that the second part of each call number starts with a letter relating to the subject of the bibliography. Most music libraries will shelve these bibliographies in the music reference collection. For a complete list of the A–Z topics in the ML128 topical bibliographies and their classification numbers, see Appendix 4.

Without the classification chart at hand, the way to locate bibliographies is to search a library catalog using controlled vocabulary. Determine an appropriate topical subject heading in the *Library of Congress Subject Headings* (*LCSH*), and add the form subdivision "Bibliography" to the topical word(s). Then input the complete subject heading in an online catalog subject-heading search. Alternatively, if you know or can try an initial subject-heading word, you may wish to search directly in the catalog. Then browse the results list looking for a heading with the subdivision "Bibliography," for instance:

> Choral music–Bibliography
> Clarinet–Bibliography
> Ethnomusicology–Bibliography
> Musical analysis–Bibliography
> Opera–Bibliography
> Performance practice–Bibliography
> Women musicians–Bibliography

For bibliographies of individuals, remember that their birth and death dates are part of the subject heading:

> Ravel, Maurice, 1875–1937–Bibliography.

If you don't know the exact dates, just enter a surname in a subject-heading search and browse the results for the subdivision, " –Bibliography." Otherwise you could do a keyword search in the subject field using the composer's surname and the term, "bibliography."

To find published lists of bibliographies, use this subject heading:

> Bibliography of bibliographies–Music

A useful book in this category, *General Bibliography for Music Research*, points to listings of sources for cross-disciplinary research. A singer may need to find books about poetry or poets. The church organist may require resources about liturgy or religion. For a study on popular music in the 1950s, it might be valuable to learn about research techniques in sociology.

Mixter, Keith E. *General Bibliography for Music Research*, 3d ed. Detroit Studies in Music Bibliography, no. 75. Warren, MI: Harmonie Park Press, 1996.

Journal articles may be bibliographic in nature: as a review of the literature on a topic, a checklist of sources to consult, a preliminary listing of a collection of materials or resources on a topic, or an annotated bibliography of sources recommended for a specific purpose. Below are examples of search strategies in the three journal (or current literature) indexes devoted to music and in two general-coverage indexes. The "women in music" example illustrates functional differences among these indexes and possible strategies to consider—controlled vocabulary, field-searching choices, and keyword searching.

4.3 Bibliographies in Databases for Music

Music Index Online

Check the Music Index Subject List in the database to find these valid headings: women, women in management, women in music, bibliographies. Because the word "women" appears in all of the first three headings, it makes sense simply to enter "women and bibliographies" in the subject field. The result of this subject search is 12 articles.

Entering the same terms in the full citation search box results in 44 documents. However, this set includes multiple book reviews of some bibliographies instead of article-length bibliographies on women in music. It is your decision on whether it will be helpful to find a combination of document types—both articles and reviews. To eliminate reviews, it is possible to set the document type to "article." With this limit, the results set is reduced to 16 articles.

International Index to Music Periodicals

The most common search strategy is to enter simply "women and bibliographies" in the keyword search box. The result for this search is a retrieval set of 117 records. By choosing the limit "Exclude reviews," the set is reduced to 67 records. However, a more targeted approach would involve controlled-vocabulary searching. *IIMP* provides a "subject terms" field with the option to "select from a list." Searching the list for "bibliography" indicates that the controlled word is "bibliographies," and selecting it puts the exact phrase in the subject terms field. Now enter the word "women" in the keyword field. The system will combine the keyword and subject term with the Boolean operator AND giving a retrieval result of 33 records. Finally, a choice to limit by selecting "Exclude reviews" reduces the retrieval to 14 items. This latter combination gives useable results.

Any time you "select from a list" multiple times, the various words or phrases will be connected with the Boolean OR. That means the results will be broadened. If you had chosen both terms as subject terms connected with OR the results set would have been 3,086! If you were to change the automatically inserted OR operator to AND, the results drop to 12; adding the exclusion of reviews drops it further to 5.

RILM Abstracts of Musical Literature

Starting with a keyword search of "women and bibliography" to be searched in the default fields, the results list includes retrieval of 355 records. That is a lot of records to examine, and it happens because many default fields could contain these words: Author, Title, Subject, Abstract, RILM Classification, Document Type, Physical Description, Affiliation Information, or Collection Name. It seems reasonable to try some other strategy to obtain a small retrieval set. Simply limiting the document type to "all articles" instead of "all" reduces the retrieval to 145 records.

Note, however, that *RILM Abstracts* offers classification groups, and because bibliographies are a form of reference material, an appropriate subject classification would be:

01-12 Reference & research materials

Adding this classification limit to the default field search of "women and bibliography" brings a result of 41 records. Further limiting this search to the document type "all articles" results in 3 records. Now the limiting may have gone too far, but you see how various search strategies produce different results. It is up to the researcher to make informed choices and then evaluate results. Note that *RILM Abstracts* searches singular and plural forms of words automatically.

4.4 Bibliographies in Multidiscipline Databases

When searching multidiscipline databases, remember that you may need to add the word "music" to your search for clarification purposes. The other search terms you use may have different meanings in other subject areas. Here are two examples using *Academic Search Premier* and *Web of Science*.

Academic Search Premier

This multidisciplinary database covers over 3,900 journals in many subject fields. Keyword searching in the default fields means that all authors, all subjects, all keywords, all title information (including source title), and all abstracts are searched. So an initial try using the keywords "women and bibliography" retrieves 1,035 records! One of the reasons for such a large retrieval set is that these bibliographies relating to women occur in almost every subject. When searching in a multidiscipline database, many times it is essential to include the word "music." The keyword search "women and music and bibliography" in default fields retrieves 23 records. Further, this database permits post-retrieval limiting by providing the option to see results from academic journals, magazines, or books/monographs.

Web of Science (ISI Citation Indexes)

Under general search, inputting "women and music and bibliography" returns 14 results, some of which are book reviews. It is possible to use a document type limit, but it may not always help. Using either the document type "bibliography" or "article" to eliminate book reviews and retrieve only articles that are substantially bibliographies may reduce the results too much. Choosing either of these document types in a search for "women and music" returns only 1 citation. Evaluate whether the discovery of book reviews might help you become aware of books of interest. If you seek only bibliographic articles, then consider adding appropriate document type limits to your search.

4.5 Bibliographies in the Reference Collection: ML112.8–158.8

Subject bibliographies are a cornerstone of research, prepared by experts on fairly broad to extremely narrow aspects of a discipline. In the field of music, there are bibliographies that list writings about music and those that list compositions themselves. We have bibliographies about individual composers (sometimes titled as guides to research) as well as bibliographies of their compositions (called descriptive catalogs, *catalogues raisonnés*, and thematic catalogs). The category of bibliographies called catalogs lists the holdings of libraries or private collections. And, finally, there are listings of sound and visual recordings termed, respectively, discographies and videographies. At a minimum, bibliographies include the facts of publication so that other readers or scholars may find the same item in a library collection or available for purchase. Annotated bibliographies include a brief description and, possibly, an evaluation of each work. Bibliographies are ordered on the shelves this way:

ML112.8	Theory, practice and history of bibliography
ML113	General works
ML114–119	By period
ML120	By region or country, A–Z
ML125	Local, A–Z
ML128	By topic, A–Z. See Appendix 4 for the full alphabetical list.
ML132	Graded lists
ML134	Individuals; includes thematic catalogs
ML136–152	Catalogs
ML156–158.8	Discographies, Videographies, Reviews, Computer software

Bibliographies in Series

Three important series of music bibliographies may be found shelved together in ML111 or ML113. The College Music Society sponsors a series, *Bibliographies in American Music*, consisting of fourteen volumes to date. Titles include *George Gershwin: A Selective Bibliography and Discography*, by Charles Schwartz, no. 1; *American Piano Concertos: A Bibliography* by William Phemister, no. 9; and *The Charles Ives Tunebook* by Clayton W. Henderson, no. 14. A much larger series is that of the *Detroit Studies in Music Bibliography*. Now comprised of 84 volumes, this series is also a wide-ranging one. It includes titles such as *Anthologies of Music: An Annotated Index* by Sterling E. Murray, no. 68; *American Operas: A Checklist* by Edith Borroff, no. 69; *American Organ Music of the Twentieth Century: An Annotated Bibliography of Composers* by Sharon L. Hettinger, no. 77; and *The Solo Cantata in Eighteenth-Century Britain: A Thematic Catalog* by Paul F. Rice, no. 84. *The MLA Index and Bibliography Series*, sponsored by the Music Library Association and currently distributed by Scarecrow Press, consists of 31 volumes. It provides indexes, bibliographies, and thematic catalogs on a wide range of topics. One volume of particular interest to researchers is volume 34: Arthur Wenk's *Analyses of Nineteenth- and Twentieth-Century Music, 1940–2000*. This volume indexes music analyses published in periodicals, monographs, Festschriften, and dissertations.

Series where each volume covers a different topic are usually classed in ML128 and separated so each falls within the appropriate topic. *Music Research and Information Guides, 1987–2001*, addresses such topics as: *The Art Song, Baroque Music, The Blues, Ethnomusicology Research, Music and War, Music in Canada, Opera, Performance Practice: Medieval to Contemporary, Piano Information Guide, Polish Music, The Symphony, The Traditional Music of Britain and Ireland*, and *Tudor Music*. Some volumes of the *Routledge Music Bibliographies* series also treat music by topic. Some of the titles published since 2000 are: *Chamber Music, Choral Music, Ethnomusicology, The Musical,* and *The Recorder*. Series offering bibliographies of individuals include the *Garland*

Composer Resource Manuals and some volumes of *Routledge Music Bibliographies*; both are classed in ML134 according to the subject of the biography.

Musical Sources: ML113

An important discussion of the nature and value of manuscript sources to modern music research is found in *Grove Music Online*, entitled "Sources, MS." Written by Stanley Boorman and others, it includes sections on various repertories before 1600 arranged by subject and date. Other relevant articles in *Grove Music Online* include "Sources of instrumental ensemble music to 1630," "Sources of keyboard music to 1660," and "Sources of lute music."

The *International Inventory of Musical Sources* (*RISM*) is an international publishing project providing catalogs of manuscript and printed music and writings about music. An essential aspect of the inventory is that library locations are provided for each entry. Abbreviations for the libraries, called *sigla* (meaning signs), are provided in the list of holding libraries. The project is a joint endeavor of the International Musicological Society and the International Association of Music Libraries, and its acronym comes from its French title, *Répertoire Internationale des sources musicales*. Series A concentrates on works by individual composers and is subdivided into printed sources (A/I) and manuscript sources (A/II).

RISM Series A/I. Einzeldrucke vor 1800 (1971–81; corrections, 1986–99).

The printed works are restricted to compositions published between 1500 and 1800. It includes composers whose careers were largely in the 18th century, even though they lived into the 19th century: for example, including Haydn but excluding Beethoven. This part is published in nine volumes plus supplements and lists about 200,000 works by about 8,000 composers in over 1,100 libraries in 29 countries.

RISM Online. RISM A/II exists only as a database containing bibliographic records for music manuscripts written between 1600 and 1800. It provides bibliographic data, library locations (sigla), and graphical images of music incipits. Over 510,000 music incipits are searchable and can be viewed as musical scores. The manuscripts cataloged in this database are found in over 6,050 libraries in 31 countries. Contributions to the database are continuing through the RISM Office at Harvard University. The database is available on a subscription basis. Also available as a CD-ROM: *Manuscrits musicaux après 1600 = Music Manuscripts after 1600 = Musikhandschriften nach 1600*.

RISM Series B consists of independently published volumes that serve as catalogs of groups of source material. Fourteen separate topics are represented such as Arabic music, Hebrew writings concerning music, printed writings about music up to 1800, and lute and guitar tablatures. Some of these volumes are still in preparation.

RISM Series C, in five volumes, is the directory of libraries owning materials in the inventory.

Dissertations and Theses: Online or ML128

While *Music Index Online* and the *International Index to Music Periodicals* provide access to music dissertations, there are also specialized indexes devoted to dissertations and theses that would, of course, include those written on music topics. Prime among these is *Dissertation Abstracts Online*. Its coverage includes almost all dissertations accepted at accredited institutions in the United States since 1861. Master's theses have been selectively indexed since 1962. In addition, it includes increasing numbers of dissertations from Canada and other countries. Abstracts are included for doctoral dissertation records from July 1980 to the present. This online version of the print index is updated monthly and provides subject, title, and author access.

Many colleges and universities now require submission of theses and dissertations as computer files that are made available online. Known as an ETD, electronic thesis or dissertation, these scholarly works are accessible through the *Networked Digital Library of Theses and Dissertations (NDLTD), ETD Union Catalog.* The most comprehensive source for dissertations or theses in full text is **ProQuest Dissertations and Theses—Full Text (PQDT).* It includes more than 2 million dissertation and master's theses citations, produced internationally from 1861 to the present. Of these, 1 million are available in full text and downloadable in pdf format (for a fee or free if from your university). There is full text for most dissertations since 1977 and many older ones as well. An RSS feed is available to keep up with new additions to the database.

Online dissertation indexes exclusively covering music include *Dissertations in Progress (DIP)* for music education, and *Doctoral Dissertations in Musicology Online: DDM-Online. DIP* began in 1999 and is available at no cost on the Internet. The Council for Research in Music Education produces it as a continuation of its print publication, *International Directory of Dissertations in Progress (DIP). DDM-Online* is sponsored by the American Musicological Society and produced at Indiana University. *DDM* was a print resource from 1952 to 1995. The online version is free and provides both in-progress dissertations and those completed since mid-1995. The database is being updated to include records of dissertations previously published in the earlier print editions.

Song and Analysis Indexes: ML128

The primary classification for songs is ML128.S3, where both the bibliographies and indexes to song collections are found. There is a distinction to be made between bibliographies of songs and song indexes. Song bibliographies are lists or annotated lists of songs while song indexes point to the location of specific songs in published collections or anthologies. Remember that an index always points to the location of information. Because libraries frequently purchase songs in collections rather than as separately published sheet music and because the contents of these collections are rarely listed in library catalog records, song indexes are essential to efficiently locate individual songs. The indexes provide access by title, composer, and sometimes librettist or topic of the song. A print song index will always include a list or bibliography of the collections it indexes; an online song index will provide the same collection information within the records for individual songs.

An example of a song bibliography is *Art Song in the United States, 1759–1999: An Annotated Bibliography* by Judith Carmen and others. Its purpose is to identify and describe American art songs, not to indicate in which collections the songs may have been published. Some examples of song indexes in print versions are *Song Finder: A Title Index to 32,000 Popular Songs in Collections, 1854–1992* by Ferguson, *Literature for Voice: An Index of Songs in Collections and Source Book for Teachers of Singing* by Goleeke, and Goodfellow's *Where's That Tune? An Index to Songs in Fakebooks.* Both types of bibliographies are found together in ML128.S3.

Online song indexes are particularly helpful because you can search several of them from any computer. Once you know the titles of published collections that include the song you need, search for that book's title in your local catalog. There is a mix of coverage—popular songs and art songs—in these databases. The California Library Systems' *Cooperative Song Index,* http://www.sjvls.org/songs/, provides indexing to about 180,000 song titles (mostly popular music) from 2,000 sheet music collections published in various songbooks and scores held by libraries in California. *Popular Song Database,* http://db.lib.washington.edu/popsong/, is a keyword index to song titles in the collections held by University of Washington and not included in *Where's That Tune? An Index to Songs in Fakebooks* by William D. Goodfellow. For popular, folk, and art songs found in collections of songs owned by the Arizona State University Music Library, consult http://www.asu.edu/lib/resources/db/songindex.htm for *Song Index.* It supplies song title, composer, lyricist, first line, and the collection in which it is found. The *UT Song Index,* http://www.lib.utk.edu/music/songdb/, gives access to about 50,000 songs of all types in more than 1,500 published song anthologies owned by the George F. DeVine Music Library at the University of Tennessee. This database provides ten access points including composer, song title, author of text, subject, large work title, language of text, accompaniment type, geographic or ethnic source, first line, and chorus first line.

Similarly, finding analyses or descriptions of individual musical works is also problematic. The following indexes will help to solve this access problem. In book form, Harold Diamond has compiled *Music Analyses: An Annotated Guide to the Literature.* He provides indexing to analyses of music in books and dissertations commonly owned by libraries. Access is by composer and title. Another database from The University of Tennessee Music Library is the *UT Analysis Index,* http://www.lib.utk.edu/music/analysis/. It indexes program notes and descriptions or analyses of musical compositions in books owned by the UT Music Library and located primarily in LC classifications MT90–MT145. The database does not duplicate the indexing available in Harold Diamond's book. Arthur Wenk's index *Analyses of Nineteenth- and Twentieth-Century Music, 1940–2000* primarily covers journal articles plus monographs, Festschriften, and dissertations when the emphasis is on analysis of musical compositions.

Music in Print: Online or ML128

The *Music-in-Print Series,* like *Books-in-Print,* is a database that serves to identify which scores (printed music) are currently available, the publisher, and sometimes the price. Separate listings are provided for music in these categories: band, brass, chamber music, choral (sacred), choral (secular), guitar, handbell, miscellaneous, orchestral, organ, percussion, piano, popular music, recorder, string, vocal (classical), and woodwind. The "Master Index" provides a single search interface for all categories. Under the "New Search" listing is a publisher directory, abbreviations list, and search tips. Separately published indexes for most of these categories exist in print and are updated every few years. One of the recent titles is *Orchestral Music in Print* (2002) by Margaret Farish. Several music vendors also provide free online databases offering up-to-date and accurate information though perhaps not as comprehensive as the *Music-in-Print Series.* Examples include: Theodore Front, http://www.tfront.com; J. W. Pepper, http://www.jwpepper.com/sheet-music/welcome.jsp; and Hal Leonard, http://www.halleonard.com/.

Bibliographies of Music—Repertoire Lists: ML128 and Graded Lists: ML132

Bibliographies of music, for ensembles or for solo instruments, give performers a source to find a variety of music for study or performance. When level of difficulty is added to such a list of music it is called a graded list. These bibliographies are shelved together but arranged in a very sensible way. Both the bibliographies of music in ML128 and graded lists in ML132 are subarranged alphabetically by topic. There is one caveat about the classification of repertoire lists. Sometimes they will be classed by specific subject rather than with bibliographies for that topic. An example is: Cohn's *The Literature of Chamber Music*, which is classed in ML1100 with books about chamber music. The following chart illustrates the arrangement system and gives examples of such bibliographies.

Figure 4.2 Examples of Repertoire Lists in ML128 and Graded Lists in ML132, Illustrating Their Subarrangement by Topic

Ensemble/ Instrument	Classification	Title
Repertoire Lists:		
Band	ML128.B3	*Instructional Literature for Middle-Level Band* by Kvet
Chamber music	ML128.C4	*A Conductor's Repertory of Chamber Music: Compositions for Nine to Fifteen Solo Instruments* by Scott
Choruses	ML128.C5	*Catalogue of Choral Music Arranged in Biblical Order; Supplement* by Laster
Orchestra	ML128.O5	*American Orchestral Music: A Performance Catalog* by Koshgarian
Piano	ML128.P3	*A Guide to the Pianist's Repertoire* by Hinson
Wind instruments	ML128.W5	*The Wind Ensemble Catalog* by Gillaspie and others
Song	ML128.S3	*A Singer's Guide to the American Art Song, 1870–1980* by Villamil
Wedding music	ML128.W4	*Wedding Music: An Index to Collections* by Goodfellow
Graded Lists:		
Band	ML132.B3	*Best Music for Beginning Band: A Selective Repertoire Guide to Music and Methods for Beginning Band* by Dvorak and Floyd
Song	ML132.S6	*Songs for Young Singers: An Annotated List for Developing Voices* by Hopkin

Bibliographies of Individuals: ML134, Including Thematic Catalogs

Bibliographies of composers are classed in ML134, and those of performers are nearby in ML134.5. In these areas we find two resource categories. First, there are guides to research for individuals in music, many of which have been published in two publisher's series.

Garland Composer Resource Manuals were published between 1981 and 2000. The latest volume in this series is William Smialek, *Frédéric Chopin: A Guide to Research* (New York: Garland Publishing, 2000). Other volumes in the series treat Adolph Adam and Léo Delibes, Albéniz, Bartók, Berg, Berlioz, Bloch, Brittten, Byrd, Carter, Chávez, Chopin, Debussy, Donizetti, Elgar, Falla, Fauré, Foster, Frescobaldi, Gluck, Handel, Haydn, Isaac, Joplin, Josquin des Prez, Kodály, Lasso, Liszt, Machaut, Gustav and Alma Mahler, Monteverdi, Mozart, Nielsen, Ockeghem and Obrecht, Pergolesi, Puccini, Purcell, Rachmaninoff, Rameau, Rimsky-Korsakov, Alessandro and Domenico Scarlatti, Schütz, Sibelius, Vaughan Williams, Verdi, Victoria, Weber, and Wolf.

Routledge Music Bibliographies. The composer, performer, and teacher research guides began in 2001 and continue to be published. Many are available as electronic books from NetLibrary. One example is: *Samuel Barber: A Guide to Research* by Wentzel. Other volumes on individuals include: C.P.E. Bach, Bellini, Bernstein, Brahms, Delius, Gluck, Handel, Hindemith, Ives, Liszt, Ravel, Rossini, Saint-Saëns, Schenker, and one on a category of performers: Pianists.

The second category includes catalogs of the works of individual composers, which are vital to the research process in music. Descriptive catalogs or *catalogues raisonnés* list a composer's works and provide essential information about each but do not include musical incipits for identification. Thematic catalogs do provide musical incipits, that is, the opening notation and text for each movement or section of a composition. Providing much information about each work and a composer's entire output, they are unique music research resources. Chapter 15 of this text is designed to help you learn to use them.

Discographies and Reviews: ML156–ML158.8

Bibliographies of audio and visual materials as well as computer software for music are classed in ML156 through ML158. Common terms for these specific types of bibliographies are: discographies for sound recordings, videographies for video recordings, webliographies for web-based resources, and mediagraphies for lists of mixed format materials.

Discographers generally provide more than publication information in their listings because they wish to trace the formative history of recordings. They may include information pertinent to each recording session whether the "takes" were issued in the final product or not. Such data often include place and date of each session and all performers. The most critical publishing information for sound recordings is the label name (the manufacturer), manufacturer's number that appears on the physical case, and the format of the recordings. Other numbers, called matrix numbers, may be included for individual takes as a way of documenting them.

ML156–ML158   Discographies

ML156–156.2	By source, collection (includes general trade catalogs)
ML156.4	By topic, A–Z (same as ML102 and ML128)
ML156.5	Individual composers, A–Z
ML156.7	Individual performers, A–Z
ML156.9	Reviews, indexes, etc.
ML158	Other, not A–Z
ML158.4–6	Video recordings, films, etc.
ML158.4	General works
ML158.6	By topic, A–Z: African American music, Conductors, Operas, Piano music, Swing
ML158.8	Computer software

While the LC Classification system provides an excellent system for organizing discographies—by source, topic, composers, and performers, plus an area for works that review sound recordings or index such reviews—there are other ways to think about the kinds of discographies that have been produced. The majority of discographies are located within the topical framework of ML156.4. Some of their functional purposes include documentation of individual record companies or labels, listings by instruments or voice or ensembles, type of music (country, rock, classical), ratings of recordings (by *Billboard* and other record charts), and evaluative or critical discographies that seek to make recommendations. The following examples of discographies illustrate the variety of content for this type of reference book.

Topical Discographies [ML156.4 A–Z]

Like topical bibliographies in ML128, topical discographies are subarranged in alphabetical order of topic, J for jazz, O for opera, etc. The examples should make this arrangement clear.

Topic: **Jazz**   ML156.42J3   Type: Genre
The Blue Note Label: A Discography by Cuscuna and Ruppli

Topic: **Opera**   ML156.4.O46   Type: Genre, Evaluative
Opera: A Critic's Guide to the 100 Most Important Works and the Best Recordings by Tommasini

Topic: **Popular Music**   ML156.4.P6
Joel Whitburn's Top Pop Singles, 1955–2002   Type: Commercial ratings
The Green Book of Songs by Subject by Green   Type: Genre

Topic: **Trumpet**   ML156.4.T8L68   Type: Instrument/Ensemble
Lowrey's International Trumpet Discography

Topic: **Vocal Music**   ML156.4.V7   Type: Instrument/Ensemble
Choral Music on Record by Blyth

Composer or Performer Discographies [ML156.5–56.7]

Discographies of both composers and performers are subarranged simply by last name of the subject, but they have separate classification numbers: ML156.5 for composers and ML156.7 for performers. For example, *Gustav Mahler's Symphonies: Critical Commentary on Recordings since 1986* by Smoley is classed as ML156.5.M33, while *A Glenn Gould Catalog* by Canning is classed as ML156.7.G68.

Indexes to Record Reviews [ML156.9]

These indexes are helpful for studying the performance history of compositions or performers. For current reviews of recordings, use music journal indexes to search for specific reviews. For historical reviews, try the series of three books edited by Kurtz Myers. These large compilations of record review indexes were published originally in the journal, *Notes*. They cover reviews in 1949–1977, 1978–1983, and 1984–1987. The last volume, compiled by Palkovic and Cauthen, indexes reviews of CDs and records in 1987–1997. Taken together, these volumes provide access to record reviews for historical investigations.

Review Questions

1. Browsing for subject bibliographies in music is aided by learning where they are classed. Identify the classification numbers (Library of Congress system) used for these types of bibliographies:
    a. Topical bibliographies
    b. Bibliographies of composers
    c. Discographies

2. When you need to cross disciplines to investigate a topic adequately, it is advisable to consult bibliographies. What single-letter LC classification is used for bibliographies in a number of subjects? How might you learn the full classification for a non-music subject (class letters and numbers)?

3. Define these terms: bibliography of bibliographies, annotated bibliography, thematic catalog. There are terms used for bibliographies of special format materials. What words are used for bibliographies of sound recordings, films, visual recordings, and web-based resources?

4. Identify the major bibliography that provides a survey of the field of music.

5. Identify a bibliography of bibliographies that provides the music researcher with leads to resources in related disciplines.

6. Describe several strategies for finding article-length bibliographies in journal indexes.

7. Name a database that lists and describes dissertations. Besides these dissertation databases, what other kinds of databases also list dissertations?

8. What is the difference between a song index and a song bibliography? Why do we need song indexes?

9. The ML128 classification is used for subject bibliographies for various topics in music. How are the books organized to help you find specific topics in this bibliography area?

10. What classification number is used for bibliographies of individuals in music? Describe some of the kinds of books found in this area.

Learning Exercises

1. Look for bibliographies to support an information search on your research topic.
    a. Browse in the ML128 subject bibliographies. If your research topic relates to a single composer, also browse in ML134.
    b. If you don't find any by browsing, do a subject-heading search in the catalog. Remember that the form subdivision, "–Bibliography" may be added to a topical or name subject heading. It may be that you will identify some bibliographies that are part of a series or classed in other bibliography areas.
    c. Prepare an annotated bibliography for at least four bibliographies that will be helpful for your research project.

2. Look for bibliographies that are repertoire lists and graded lists for your instrument, voice, or ensemble.
    a. Identify the classification number used for repertoire lists and that used for graded lists.
    b. Prepare annotated bibliography entries for four of these bibliographies of music. If there are no graded lists appropriate, all may be repertoire lists.

3. Identify discographies that support your area of study (jazz, performance area, conducting, musicology or ethnomusicology, sacred music, etc.). Prepare annotated bibliography entries for four such discographies.

Chapter 5

A Case Study

This case study provides an opportunity to review your understanding of the research process and basic information-searching strategies. It covers the first two stages of research from topic development to gathering and evaluating sources as applied to a potential topic. Note that extensive explanations of search methods are provided later in this textbook in Part 2, "How To." Also refer to Chapter 2, "Starting-Point Resources," for an introduction to key bibliographies, union catalogs, dictionaries, journals, and journal indexes used in this case study.

The case: Elizabeth Rose, a graduate student in piano performance, wants to do research on some aspect of Chopin's piano music.

5.1 Narrowing the Topic

Elizabeth starts to get more information about her topic and begin her explorations using some of the "starting-point" resources discussed in Chapter 2.

Dictionaries and Encyclopedias

At first Elizabeth tries to assemble background information to narrow her topic and to make sure she has at least a working knowledge of it. She finds the article on Chopin in *Grove Music Online*, the electronic version of *The New Grove Dictionary of Music and Musicians*. In reading about Chopin's piano music, she becomes intrigued with the idea of genre and Chopin's development or treatment of several Romantic genres. Kornel Michalowski and Jim Samson are co-authors of the Chopin entry, and their statements about scherzos, ballades, and Chopin's contributions to stability of these genres seem of interest.

Scherzos

Thus at the heart of all four Chopin scherzos lies a reinterpretation of the element of contrast essential to the conventional genre, such that the central formal contrast is built into the detailed substance of the work.

Ballades

Likewise all four ballades transform the sonata-form archetype in such a way that the resolution of tonal tension is delayed until the latest possible moment. This in turn helps to condition the larger "plots" of these works, which may well have been inspired by the tradition of the literary ballad. ... the ballades take on the character of a story by invoking and then modifying conventional schemata, and by focusing the events through a distinctive (generic) characterization of themes, the "personae" of the drama. And in most cases the story culminates in that "whirlwind of musical reckoning" so characteristic of the poetic ballad.

Chopin's achievement was to give generic authority to the free-ranging devices of an emergent, early 19th-century piano repertory, ... when titles were used casually and interchangeably, and often emanated from the publisher rather than the composer. Where such stability exists, genre can take on a powerfully communicative role....[1]

So Elizabeth checks out the bibliography that is a part of this encyclopedia entry. She finds:

- An article on genre: J. Samson : 'Chopin and Genre,' *Music Analysis*, viii (1989), 213–31
- 11 listings under "Ballades," six of them in English
- A chapter on both ballades and scherzos: J. Samson : 'Extended Forms: the Ballades, Scherzos and Fantasies,' *The Cambridge Companion to Chopin* (Cambridge, 1992), 101–23
- A number of collected essays, *Chopin Studies* (1988), *The Cambridge Companion to Chopin* (1992), and *Chopin Studies 2* (1994)
- Because she is curious about Chopin's own explanations of his genres, she notices references to nine collections of letters, although only two are in English.

At this point, Elizabeth has an interest that might develop into a research topic: Chopin and genre as illustrated by either his ballades or scherzos. She makes a note in her research journal of the citation for this Chopin article in *Grove Music Online*, and adds a reminder to return to the encyclopedia to look up "scherzo," "ballade," and "genre." Elizabeth knows that all of Chopin's works are also listed with the article; she will need some of the identifying information for these works later.

Using Controlled-Vocabulary Searching, Bibliographies, and Browsing

For details of these search techniques, see Part 2, "How To: Discover and Use Resources."

To focus her research idea and assess the amount of information available, Elizabeth starts with her own university library catalog. Using the controlled-vocabulary approach, she inputs "piano music" as a heading search in the subject field and then selects a number of specific subject headings to use in this or other library catalogs.

     9   Piano music–19th century
     7   Piano music–19th century–History and criticism
    16   Piano music–Analysis, appreciation
    21   Piano music–Bibliography
    24   Piano music–History and criticism

Using "Chopin" as a subject heading, she finds the following pertinent headings:

36   Chopin, Frédéric, 1810–1849
2   Chopin, Frédéric, 1810–1849–Bibliography
1   Chopin, Frédéric, 1810–1849–Congresses
5   Chopin, Frédéric, 1810–1849–Criticism and interpretation

3   Chopin, Frédéric, 1810–1849–Thematic catalogs
3   Chopin, Frédéric, 1810–1849. Works

These two searches let Elizabeth know that there are plenty of books that may treat her idea in some way. She also sees the value of browsing through relevant subject headings because she has learned of some very specific sources: seven books on history and criticism of 19th-century piano music and a number of bibliographies on piano music. She sees that the biographies of Chopin are listed under just the heading for his name and all have ML410 as the classification number. Now she knows where to browse in the book collection for books about his life and works. She also sees a thematic catalog, which will list all of his works, and that the library has a scholarly edition of Chopin's complete works when she needs to look at quality versions of the scores. Elizabeth may want to follow the links of these subject headings to select books for her working bibliography. Otherwise, she may wish to go into the book stacks to browse the biography section, ML410.C.

Examining the list of brief records from the subject-heading searches, Piano music–Bibliography" and "Chopin, Frédéric, 1810–1849–Bibliography," Elizabeth finds two excellent bibliographies to help her obtain targeted leads on her research topic:

Frédéric Chopin: A Guide to Research by William Smialek, 2000. [ML134.C54...]

Bibliografia chopinowska, 1849–1969 by Kornel Michalowski, 1970. [ML410. C54...]

Because there seem to be a fair number of books available, Elizabeth wonders whether the topic might be too broad. She could choose to trace the history of either the scherzo or ballade, and identify significant examples of compositions over time. That topic might culminate in Chopin's treatment of the genre. Or she could choose one of the two genres and investigate Chopin's influence on subsequent composers. As she examines the bibliographies and moves on to other information sources, it will be essential to continue to ask questions of the sources and of herself until she can lay claim to a narrow topic with one central question for her research project. She has listed the following information needs and online sources to search:

Information needed:
- Books, scores, sound or visual recordings, dissertations, manuscript collections

Resources to search:
- University library catalog because these materials will be available quickly
- Regional consortium catalog because of quick delivery of interlibrary loans
- *WorldCat* because it covers holdings of thousands of libraries

Information needed:
- Journal articles, conference or symposium papers, dissertations, reviews

Resources to search:
- *Music Index Online, IIMP Full Text,* and *RILM Abstracts*
- *Humanities Abstracts*
- *Arts & Humanities Citation Index*
- *Dissertation Abstracts* (possibly)

Note: Is it possible to do a metasearch of all of these catalogs or all of these indexes at the same time?

5.2 Preliminary Thesis Statement

The heart of Stage 1 of a research project is moving from a topic idea to development of a thesis. Once Elizabeth read some background information and sketched out possible directions, she asked questions about what she read and then searched library catalogs and union catalogs to determine what has been written on these topic possibilities. Now she must choose a narrowed topic and state a single question she will answer in her research project. This question along with reasons her audience will want it answered will become the framework for gathering evidence and writing the report.

Having read *The Craft of Research,*[2] Elizabeth takes the advice of its authors, Booth, Colomb, and Williams, on formulating a research problem. Her preliminary statement reads, "I am studying Chopin's four ballades (topic) because I want to find out, compositionally, how he defined this poetic and dramatic genre (question) to help my reader understand that Chopin's ballades exemplify a pinnacle of piano music genre development (significance)."

If Elizabeth pursues this topic, she will need to decide on one central question that she can answer by assembling evidence and make a case based on that evidence in her research report. She will probably make progress towards a thesis as she prepares for searching a variety of databases that cover journal articles, dissertations, and other current literature. The database search form will come in handy to prepare Boolean search statements for keyword searching.

Keyword Searching

Examine the Database Search Planning Form that Elizabeth used to clarify the concepts and terminology related to her topic. She used this form as a preliminary step before searching for journal articles, dissertations, and other current literature that will inform her research. She will need to determine which databases are most relevant and check for specific instructions on searching in each. The more Elizabeth learns about her subject, the more she needs to refine her searching. That means going back again to a database to search for more specific concepts. For instance, after Elizabeth analyzes the scores to Chopin's ballades, she will know about specific compositional devices and concepts of formal development he used. This knowledge will need to be applied to compositions in the genre by other composers. It requires new searches for their scores and for writings that might help identify Chopin's influence. The research process always includes repetitions as more knowledge informs the researcher of new directions to pursue.

Database Search Planning Form

NOTE: Combine synonyms for a concept with OR. Combine concepts with AND.

Write your Research Topic in a full sentence:

What aspects of Chopin's Ballades had an influence on other Romantic composers of this genre?

Identify the different concepts in this topic:

Concept 1:	Concept 2:	Concept 3:	Concept 4:
Ballade or Ballad	**Chopin**	**Genre or Form**	**Influence**

         AND   AND   AND

Other concepts: **development, history of the ballad* in poetry and music**

Write a complete search statement. Use appropriate Boolean operators, proximity operators, truncation symbols, and parentheses for nesting.
Example: *computer* and (teaching or instruction) and (music and theory)*

Ballad* and Chopin and (genre or form or influence or composition)

Ballad* and (music or poetry) and (development or history)

Identify helpful restrictions or limits: **articles not reviews; English; dissertations**

5.3 Working Thesis Statement

Keyword and controlled-vocabulary searches in library catalogs and journal databases provide Elizabeth with information sources to add to her working bibliography. After reading, and making notes, she is able to refine her thesis statement as follows:

Chopin's narrative ballades for piano, based on thematic metamorphosis, influenced other 19th-century composers of the genre: Franck, Liszt, and Brahms. This paper investigates Chopin's compositional techniques in his *Four Ballades* for piano and demonstrates how he influenced three Romantic composers who followed.

Notes

1. Kornel Michalowski and Jim Samson, "Chopin," in *Grove Music Online*, ed. by L. Macy, http://www.grovemusic.com (accessed 30 August 2007).

2. Wayne C. Booth, Gregory G. Colomb, and Joseph M. Williams, *The Craft of Research*, 2d ed. (Chicago: University of Chicago Press, 2003), 56.

Chapter 6

Scholarly Writing

Preview

- The documentation system of notes (footnotes, endnotes, or in-text citations) and bibliographies (references or works cited) is required of scholarly writing. It provides a way to give credit to the ideas and arguments of other writers.
- To format citations correctly for a final paper, it is vital to choose an appropriate style manual early and consult it often. Consider using software to help manage your references on such major projects as theses or dissertations.
- Consider using citation management software such as EndNote or RefWorks to organize your resources and format your references (in-text citations or endnotes and lists of references or bibliography).
- The U.S. Copyright Law of 1976 and subsequent additions provide a set of rights to the holders of copyright on creative works. These exclusive rights are limited in some ways by a series of exemptions, among them the fair use exemption in Section 107. Musicians and educators need to learn as much as possible about copyright.
- Style guidelines are available to address problems of formatting musical notation and titles of compositions in your narrative writing. Suggestions are given in this chapter.

The writing stage of the research process brings you to your ultimate goal: communicating results and conclusions to your readers. Scholarly writing demands attribution of the ideas of others, so you need to be prepared to use footnotes, endnotes, or text references plus a bibliography of works cited in your paper to provide appropriate credit. Careful note taking is the way to achieve accuracy in terms of representing ideas of other scholars. Make it a habit to let yourself know whether your notes are a summary, a paraphrase, or a direct quote. Always take down all of the facts of publication relating to your source. Recording complete bibliographic citations from the start will save hours of frustration later. Many books and websites discuss effective note taking and how to avoid plagiarism. Brief but practical advice is available in *The Craft of Research*.[1] This chapter provides information on the system of scholarly documentation (bibliographic citations). It continues by addressing sources of information for questions of style when using titles of music compositions and musical notation in narrative writing. The final segment highlights the basics of copyright, which is another aspect of scholarly work whether in publishing, teaching, or performing.

6.1 Scholarly Documentation: Bibliographies and Notes

Learning to cite the words and ideas of other scholars is absolutely essential for those writing in the scholarly arena. Using notes and citations in bibliographies is the way to acknowledge the work of others that you wish to mention in your own writing. The system of scholarly documentation aids in the conversation between researchers over time, allowing us to retrace the development of ideas and positions.

Definitions

Bibliography. Also called references or works cited. A list of books, journal articles, or any other materials used in preparation of the work at hand. Normally it will include every reference cited; it may also include those items consulted but not cited. The bibliography normally occurs in a separate section following the main text.

Note. Also known as footnote or endnote. Generally a note occurs as a reference number in the text, following the quotation, paraphrase, or idea of another writer, with the text of the note appearing at the foot of the same page or at the end of the chapter or end of the entire work. The note may be informational but more often is a citation to the work referenced. Depending on the style manual used, an in-text citation may replace a note.

In-text citation. A method of citation within the text, used in place of footnotes or endnotes. In APA and Chicago style, it combines a reference in parentheses in the narrative text with a reference list where the author is followed immediately by the year of publication. The Chicago style manual refers to this method as parenthetical text citation in author-date style. The MLA style for in-text citations uses parenthetical references with the author's name and page number; the works-cited list remains in alphabetical order by author.

Style Manuals

Find out early which style manual is appropriate for your research project. Does the music school or department require a specific style? Does the faculty member require or recommend one? If you are preparing research for publication, check the journal or publisher for a specification. If there is no required use of a specific manual, make a choice based on your experience or the most common style for publications in your field. Probably the most common style manual used for music writing is the *Chicago Manual of Style*. It is an accepted standard for history and many fields in the humanities and arts. However, for music education, music therapy, and ethnomusicology, the commonly accepted style is that of the American Psychological Association (APA). This choice can be traced to the strong relationships of these music fields with disciplines in the social sciences, where the APA style is the norm. The MLA style is used for English and many fields in the humanities.

When it comes to choosing one handy style guide, consider Diana Hacker's *A Pocket Style Manual*. It is inexpensive, portable, and inclusive of three standard style manuals

(Chicago, APA, and MLA), thus being extremely useful for students. Use it to check forms for notes and bibliographies and also for guidance on writing: clarity, grammar, punctuation, and mechanics. Do be cautious, however, because more complex style questions may require you to consult the style manual of choice in full.

For the APA style, there are two choices, both from The American Psychological Association. Its *Publication Manual of the American Psychological Association* (2001) is the standard in social sciences and education. Because of the strong relationships between ethnomusicology and various social sciences, this style is recommended for students in ethnomusicology. Besides the APA editorial style and reference list, the book includes information on reducing bias in language, preparing manuscripts for publication, and checklists for submitting manuscripts in print or electronically. Many journals require the APA style for articles being submitted. A briefer version is available in print and online: *Concise Rules of APA Style* (2005).

Holding primary importance for writers and researchers in the humanities is *The Chicago Manual of Style* (2003). The majority of people who use this book use it as a style guide for notes (footnotes or endnotes) and bibliographies in scholarly writing and publishing. Chapter 16 provides the basic patterns of documentation while Chapter 17 gives specific examples for different types of publications. The book as a whole does more than this, however. It provides guidance for every step of publication from manuscript preparation and editing, to rights and permissions, to indexing. The 6th edition of *A Manual for Writers of Term Papers, Theses, and Dissertations* (1996) by Turabian, Grossman, and Bennett is based on the Chicago style. Frequently, this condensed manual is recommended for student use. However, at this time it does not conform to the latest patterns of the Chicago style (15th ed.), especially for citing electronic documents.

The other manual recommended for graduate students, scholars, and professional writers in the humanities is that of the Modern Language Association of America: *MLA Style Manual and Guide to Scholarly Publishing* (1998).

6.2 Citation Basics

Citations, both for notes and bibliographies, have standard elements:
- Author (or some other responsible individual such as editor, compiler, or translator). Composers are listed as authors of musical works. Performers may be considered authors in jazz or popular music.
- Title and subtitle
- Date of publication
- Publication information

Publication information varies according to the format. For books, the imprint includes place of publication, publisher, and year. For journal articles, citations require the journal name, volume number, issue number, year of publication, and page number(s). For other sources that are not printed—audiovisual or electronic works—the medium is added such as compact disc or DVD. Electronic works are those accessed via computer; it is customary to add the Internet address at the end of the citation (URL, or universal resource locator such as http://www.lib.utk.edu/music/).

A writer must determine the exact arrangement of these citation elements, the exact punctuation, and format on the page. How do you find out? You use a style manual regularly, consistently, always. Remember that for the citations you see, the layout of publication information varies depending on where you find them. Library catalogs have a peculiar style that puts extra spaces around some punctuation marks, and they never capitalize words of a title except the first word of the title, first word of a subtitle, and proper nouns. The style in catalogs, then, is far different from that of any of the three primary style manuals.

So you cannot just copy a catalog citation and leave it as it comes in your paper. For published bibliographies, it is the editor or the publishing house that decides exactly what form citations will take. They may use bold or italic fonts where they are not normally expected or routinely leave out certain pieces of information. When a source provides you with a format for citing that work (as in *Grove Music Online*), it may not be a format you can use. You must check with your style manual and follow those instructions instead. Even the title page of a book will not provide publication information in exactly the form you need. Book titles and subtitles are rarely separated by any punctuation, but you will need to use a colon between them according to all three style manuals. There may be a variety of dates to sort out: copyright and printing dates.

Compare the following examples of bibliographic information from a variety of sources and observe how that data get translated into citations following rules of three major style manuals used today.

Examples of Publication Information in Sources versus Scholarly Citations

1. From the book's title page:

Classical Music in America
A History of Its Rise and Fall

By Joseph Horowitz

W. W. Norton & Company, Inc.
New York

2. In a library catalog:

> Classical music in America: a history of its rise and fall / Joseph Horowitz. New York : W.W. Norton & Co., c2005.

3. Following the pattern of a published bibliography, *Music Reference and Research Materials:*

> Horowitz, Joseph. Classical Music in America: A History of Its Rise and Fall. New York: W. W. Norton, 2005.

4. Reformatted according to Chicago style.
    For a bibliography:
    Horowitz, Joseph. *Classical Music in America: A History of Its Rise and Fall*. New York: Norton, 2005.

    For a note (first use with full information):

Joseph Horowitz, *Classical Music in America: A History of Its Rise and Fall* (New York: Norton, 2005), 193–94.

For a subsequent note:
Horowitz, *Classical Music in America*, 216.

5. Reformatted according to APA style.
    For references:
    Horowitz, J. (2005). Classical music in America: A history of its rise and fall. New York: Norton.

    For in-text citation:
    (Horowitz, J., 2005, p. 193–94).

6. Reformatted according to MLA style.
    For works cited:
    Horowitz, Joseph. Classical Music in America: A History of Its Rise and Fall. New York: Norton, 2005.

    For in-text citation:
    (Horowitz 193)

It is up to you to make the appropriate transformation of information and to format it according to the style you are using. The example above was a simple one: a book having a single author, but there are many more complicated situations. To use a style manual effectively, you must ask a number of questions as you look at the source information.

- Is there one author, two or more, five?
- Is there an editor, compiler, or translator instead of an author?
- Is there an author and an editor, compiler or translator?

Then seek out the rule and example for the specific case you have. There are many other questions to ask about books:

- Is this an edition other than the first? Find out how to list a specific edition.
- How do you indicate the number of volumes for a set of books? What if you want to cite only a specific volume of a multivolume set?
- Is this book published in a numbered series? Find out how to list a series title and number.
- Is this a chapter in a book? Find out how to list a component part if all parts are by one author or if each part is by a different author.
- How much of a publisher's name should be used? Do you include "Inc." or "Co."?
- What if several cities are listed for the publisher? Do you have to include all of them? Which one should you choose if they are not all required?

And often, you'll need to put multiple rules together:

- What if it is a multivolume work with a translator in a reprint edition by a different publisher?

Slightly different kinds of information are required to cite different formats of information: books, journal articles, dissertations, scores, sound recordings, visual recordings, unpublished materials, interviews, web-based resources. Usually style manuals organize the instructions and examples first by format and then provide information for the specific cases for that format. Consult your style manual for various publication formats.

And, of course, you know that notes or in-text citations are quite different in appearance from citations for bibliographies, references, or works cited. For the Chicago style, there are striking differences in indention (a hanging indention for bibliography citations but a paragraph style indention for notes) and in punctuation (elements separated mainly by periods for bibliography citations but by commas for notes).

Today, researchers also have the option of using software to help organize references as they collect them and to format them for notes and bibliographies in manuscripts. Perhaps this is the time to consider the use of packages such as EndNote, ProCite, Reference Manager, RefWorks, or other brands of bibliographic management software.

6.3 Style Guides for Writing about Music

There are several aspects of writing about music that seem difficult. Usually they relate to titles of works and musical notation. How do you capitalize titles of compositions or parts of them, and do you use italics or quotation marks? How do you refer to musical pitches and key names in terms of capitalization and punctuation? The books listed here are available to help answer these questions.

Kern Holoman's *Writing about Music: A Style Sheet from the Editors of 19th-Century Music* (1988) is a small gem. While intended for authors submitting to the journal *19th-Century Music*, this concise guide can be very helpful to anyone writing about music. Holoman provides explanations and examples of special problems in music narrative writing: form of titles of musical compositions, key signatures, musical examples, etc.

Because *The Chicago Manual of Style* (2003) is a guide for editors and publishers as well as writers, it includes chapters on the full range of instructions for publishing in many fields. Chapter 7, "Spelling, Treatment of Words, and Compounds," includes recommendations for typographical conventions for music in paragraphs 7.71–7.75: musical pitches, octaves, chords, major and minor keys, and dynamics. Chapter 8, "Names and Terms," explains usage patterns for names of musical works in paragraphs 8.202 through 8.205: operas and songs, instrumental works, opus [numbers], and recordings. It is noteworthy that the editors also refer those needing detailed guidelines to Holoman's work.

How to Write about Music: The RILM Manual of Style is the newest source of guidance for the writer on music topics. Editor James R. Cowdery seeks to guide writers from the experience and international view of writing about music that comes from the editing rules of *RILM* itself. Students need to be aware, however, that this style manual is international and may not offer advice that coincides with style manual recommendations in the United States.

6.4 Copyright

Very much related to the matter of scholarly documentation is a more fundamental issue of whether you can use materials created by others at all. That is what the copyright law and subsequent judicial decisions are about: the rights and permissions associated with intellectual property.

- What exclusive rights do creators have?
- What is the fair use right for the benefit of society?
- How is permission to use, copy, arrange, etc. requested and granted?

Georgia Harper provides a telling preamble to her excellent "Crash Course in Copyright," http://www.utsystem.edu/ogc/IntellectualProperty/cprtindx.htm. "Someone owns just about everything. Fair use lets you use their things, but not as much as you'd like to. Sometimes you have to ask for permission. Sometimes you are the owner—think about that!"[2] Use the tutorial for an excellent introduction to copyright issues.

Copyright Law

In the United States, the copyright law as revised in 1976 is our guide. An easy way to find the law itself, and explanations of it, is to look for information on the website of the U.S. Copyright Office at the Library of Congress, http://lcweb.loc.gov/copyright/. Circular 1 provides a definition of copyright: http://www.copyright.gov/circs/circ1. html#wci.

What Is Copyright?

Copyright is a form of protection provided by the laws of the United States (title 17, U.S. Code) to the authors of "original works of authorship," including literary, dramatic, musical, artistic, and certain other intellectual works. This protection is available to both published and unpublished works. Section 106 of the 1976 Copyright Act generally gives the owner of copyright the exclusive right to do and to authorize others to do the following:

- To reproduce the work in copies or phonorecords;
- To prepare derivative works based upon the work;
- To distribute copies or phonorecords of the work to the public by sale or other transfer of ownership, or by rental, lease, or lending;
- To perform the work publicly, in the case of literary, musical, dramatic, and choreographic works, pantomimes, and motion pictures and other audiovisual works;
- To display the copyrighted work publicly, in the case of literary, musical, dramatic, and choreographic works, pantomimes, and pictorial, graphic, or sculptural works, including the individual images of a motion picture or other audiovisual work; and
- In the case of sound recordings, to perform the work publicly by means of a digital audio transmission....

It is illegal for anyone to violate any of the rights provided by the copyright law to the owner of copyright. These rights, however, are not unlimited in scope. Sections 107 through 121 of the 1976 Copyright Act establish limitations on these rights. In some cases, these limitations are specified exemptions from copyright liability. One major limitation is the doctrine of "fair use," which is given a statutory basis in Section 107 of the 1976 Copyright Act. In other instances, the limitation takes the form of a "compulsory license" under which certain limited uses of copyrighted works are permitted upon payment of specified royalties and compliance with statutory conditions. For further information about the limitations of any of these rights, consult the copyright law or write to the Copyright Office.[3]

When Does Copyright Start?

Legal copyright protection vests immediately and automatically upon the creation of an 'original work of authorship' that is 'fixed in any tangible medium of expression.' An 'original work' needs to have a minimal amount of creativity. For example, alphabetical listings in the phone book are not original, but advertising layouts, photographs, software, and many other works are likely 'original.' To be 'fixed in a tangible medium of expression' is defined as the work being sufficiently permanent or stable to allow it to be perceived, reproduced, or otherwise communicated. For example, scribbles on paper or documents saved to disk are clearly 'fixed.'[4]

Best practice is to use the copyright symbol © followed by the name of the owner and date on the work. Registration of copyright further ensures that the copyright holder will be identifiable to those who might wish to use the work in some way. The U.S. Copyright Office at the Library of Congress handles registration, deposit of materials for copyright, and copyright records. See http://lcweb.loc.gov/copyright/ for information on registration, forms, and fees.

Today copyright duration is defined as the life of the author plus 70 years, whether the work was published or not. Works published before 1923 are in the public domain. They do not have copyright protection, meaning that they may be used freely. Those created or published between 1923 and 1978 have copyright duration of varying lengths. For a handy chart detailing the duration of copyright, see Lolly Gassaway's guide, "When U.S. Works Pass into the Public Domain.," http://www.unc.edu/unclng/public-d.htm.

The federal copyright law did not cover sound recordings until 1972. It is important to remember that there are usually two copyright owners for works on sound recordings: the copyright holder for the recording itself (the performance) and the copyright holder for the original work (the composer and/or author of text of the composition). To seek permission for use, you would need to track down these individuals or companies at least. However, Tim Brooks states that, "although other copyright works routinely entered the public domain, this is not the case for recorded sound."[5] There are many complexities to tracking down copyright owners for sound recordings.

Fair Use

It is beneficial to have a balance of rights between creators and users of works. For the benefit of society's advancement of knowledge, it would not be good if all books, journal articles, and other creative works required payment or permission for every type of use. Congress added fifteen sections to the law giving specific exemptions to the exclusive rights of copyright holders. Section 107, on fair use, is extremely important when it comes to research and educational uses. Find this section of the Copyright Law at http://www.copyright.gov/title17/92chap1.html#107.

§ 107. Limitations on exclusive rights: Fair use.

Notwithstanding the provisions of sections 106 and 106A, the fair use of a copyrighted work, including such use by reproduction in copies or phonorecords or by any other means specified by that section, for purposes such as criticism, comment, news reporting, teaching (including multiple copies for classroom use), scholarship, or research, is not an infringement of copyright. In determining whether the use made of a work in any particular case is a fair use the factors to be considered shall include:

(1) the purpose and character of the use, including whether such use is of a commercial nature or is for nonprofit educational purposes;

(2) the nature of the copyrighted work;

(3) the amount and substantiality of the portion used in relation to the copyrighted work as a whole; and

(4) the effect of the use upon the potential market for or value of the copyrighted work.

The fact that a work is unpublished shall not itself bar a finding of fair use if such finding is made upon consideration of all the above factors.[6]

Understanding applications of the copyright law and its exemptions is difficult because legislation often is not totally clear until a body of judicial case law provides sufficient interpretation. The four factors of fair use must be weighed and evaluated on a case-by-case basis. One recommendation is to learn to use the "Fair Use Checklist" from the Copyright Advisory Office of Columbia University, http://www.copyright.colum bia.edu/fair-use-checklist.htm. Be sure to read the explanation of how to use the checklist. It is a good idea to complete the form whenever you are trying to decide if the use of copyrighted material that you wish to make is permissible under the fair use section. Keep a copy of the form as a record of your good faith effort.

Teach Act

New legislation, called "Technology, Education and Copyright Harmonization Act" and known as the "TEACH Act," was enacted on October 4, 2002. It addresses the use of new technologies in distance education by completely revising another exemption, Section 110 on certain performances and displays. Previously, materials such as sound and video recordings could not be sent via computer to remote site classrooms. The new provisions, while allowing certain uses of copyrighted works without permission or royalties, require educational institutions to meet rigorous requirements. The Copyright Center at IUPUI provides a "Checklist for Compliance with the TEACH Act" at http://www.copyright.iupui.edu/teachlist.htm.

Copyright Information Sources

Recommendations here include books and chapters of books that provide information on copyright legislation for music practitioners. Internet websites provide up-to-date information, access to copyright forms, tutorials covering copyright basics, and more. For detailed information on these resources, see the bibliography at the end of this book.

Two relatively recent books on copyright deal exclusively with music. First is *The Public Domain: How to Find & Use Copyright-Free Writings, Music, Art & More* (2006), prepared by attorney Stephen Fishman, who is also the author of *The Copyright Handbook*. The book is organized to define the public domain and then assist users in determining whether individual works are public domain or copyrighted works. Separate chapters deal with various formats such as music (sheet music, arrangements, derivative works, sound recordings), and most begin with a checklist to determine public domain status. Chapter 21 provides guidance on researching copyright records. Two notable appendixes are "Popular Songs in the Public Domain," which lists 450 titles and "Public Domain Documentation Worksheet," which gives a simple form to track your uses of public domain works. Second is *Music and Copyright* (2004), edited by Frith and Marshall. A dozen authors supplied essays for this book on the conceptual bases of copyright and every day aspects of it. Chapters elucidate copyright from the perspective of composers, musicians, and media; they also deal with copyright and power in the music industry, the relationships with technology, and piracy.

The 10th edition of *This Business of Music: The Definitive Guide to the Music Industry* (2007) by Krasilovsky, Shemel, Gross, and Feinstein is a valued source. It is organized primarily to address the record industry, music publishing and writing, and other aspects such as names and trademarks, agents and managers, taxation, and more. The chapters that focus on the United States Copyright laws are an excellent source of information including definitions and explanations, registration procedures, and fair use; international copyright; and other legal matters such as contracts and licensing arrangements. The approach is informative and practical. If you are already a user of *The Chicago Manual of Style*, consult its chapter, "Rights and Permissions," which provides a basic survey of copyright legislation and issues.

Use Internet copyright websites for up-to-date information, copyright registration forms, fair-use test forms, and even tutorials. The following five sites are among hundreds available, but these hold especially valuable information. See the Bibliography at the end of this book for their Internet addresses.

The official site of the U.S. Copyright Office, at the Library of Congress, provides essential information from the government office in charge of copyright including:

- About Copyright: Copyright Basics, Frequently Asked Questions (FAQ), Current Fees, and Top Searches
- Search Copyright Records: Registrations and Documents, Notices of Restored Copyrights, Online Service Providers
- Publications: Circulars and Brochures, Forms, Factsheets, Reports and Studies
- Licensing Information
- How to Register a Work: Literary Works, Visual Arts, Performing Arts, Sound Recordings, Serials/Periodicals
- How to Record a Document: Record a Document
- Law and Policy: Copyright Law, Federal Register Notices, Current Legislation, Regulations, Mandatory Deposit

Columbia University operates its Copyright Advisory Center and website to serve higher education. The information is aimed particularly at faculty and students with major sections covering:

- Copyright Quickguide! For quick access to copyright information
- Fair-Use Issues for teaching, research, and more. Includes the "Fair Use Checklist" at http://www.copyright.columbia.edu/fair-use-checklist.htm. It is useful for evaluating whether the use you plan is likely to be a fair use. Keep the form as documentation of your good faith effort to establish a fair use.
- Permissions Information, including how to identify the copyright owner

Offered from the standpoint of music librarians and advocating fair use in higher education is the Music Library Association site: "Copyright for Music Librarians." The information provided is useful for anyone dealing with music copyright issues.

- FAQs provide scenarios and guidance about general copyright provisions and specific situations for musicians
- Current Issues on news, pending legislation, and court cases

- Guidelines gives full text of various guidelines relevant to music and education as adopted by professional organizations

The Music Publishers Association offers the "Copyright Resource Center." Its Copyright Search Center gives guidance for researching the copyright holder or publisher of a composition, forms for obtaining permission to arrange a work or make copies of out-of-print music, plus links for more information on copyright.

If you know little about copyright, try Georgia Harper's "Crash Course in Copyright." Harper is a well-regarded copyright expert at the University of Texas System's Intellectual Property Section. Two sections of the tutorial are particularly helpful: "Fair Use" and "Who Owns What?"

Permissions and Licensing

Obtaining permission to use a creative work may occur by directly communicating with the copyright holder, for instance, when you wish to reproduce a page of music in your thesis. The Music Publishers Association offers to facilitate the permissions process through its Copyright Resource Center, available online at http://www. mpa.org/crc.html. It provides an online form to obtain permission for arranging a work or for making copies of out-of-print music.

In the realm of performing and broadcasting musical works, there are some agencies that exist primarily to protect the rights of their members. Such commercial firms include ASCAP, BMI, and SESAC in the United States, although they function internationally. ASCAP, the American Society of Composers, Authors, and Publishers, was founded in 1914. Broadcast Music, Inc. (BMI) has a similar mission, as does SESAC (originally named Society of European Stage Authors and Composers in 1930, now known as SESAC). These performance rights organizations collect royalties from radio stations, TV stations, Internet marketers, etc. and then pay the various publishers, songwriters, or authors associated with specific works or recordings.

Review Questions

1. Define the appropriate word for each of the following, depending on your choice of style manual. What is the purpose of each?
   a. Note, footnote, endnote, or in-text citation
   b. Bibliography, references, or works-cited

2. Identify some of the exclusive rights of a copyright holder.

3. For what reasons might the fair use exemption be used?

4. Explain the four factors to be evaluated when determining if fair use applies in a given situation.

5. Where might you look for guidance when you wonder whether to use italics or quotation marks for the name of a composition or part of it?

Learning Exercises

1. Which style manual is most suitable for your area of study in music? What is your conclusion based on the following investigations?
    a. Find a research journal in your area and examine it for the style of notes and bibliographic citations. Can you discern which style the journal uses: APA, Chicago style, or MLA? Are there any directions for authors in the journal? If the editor directs authors to a website for guidance, take a look at the site.
    b. If the following book is available in your library, check it to find research journals in your area of study.

        Basart, Ann P. *Writing about Music: A Guide to Publishing Opportunities for Authors and Reviewers.* Berkeley, CA: Fallen Leaf Press, 1989.

    c. Find one or two titles and verify that they are still being published. Then see what style manual Ann Basart has listed for them. Note that this bibliography about publishing in music journals is a helpful guide even though some of its information may not be current.

2. Prepare one page of endnotes to include:
    a. Journal article
    b. Dissertation
    c. Compact disc
    d. Chapter in a book with an editor and author
    e. Book having three authors
    f. Article from an online encyclopedia or dictionary

3. Go to Georgia Harper's website and take her "Crash Course in Copyright": http://www.utsystem.edu/ogc/IntellectualProperty/cprtindx.htm.
    a. What does copyright protect?
    b. When does it begin and end?
    c. What is fair use?
    d. What is public domain?

4. Write a brief description of a situation where you will need to decide if a use of a composition will be fair use (in study, teaching, other professional work). Then from the website, http://www.copyright.columbia.edu/fair-use-checklist.htm, complete the "Fair Use Checklist." An analysis of all four factors is important in assessing fair use in each specific case. Is your planned use a "fair use" or should you seek permission from the copyright holder?

Notes

1. Wayne C. Booth, Gregory G. Colomb, and Joseph M. Williams, *The Craft of Research*, 2nd ed. (Chicago: University of Chicago Press, 2003), 201–207.

2. Georgia Harper, "Crash Course in Copyright," University of Texas System, Intellectual Property Section, 2001, http://www.utsystem.edu/ogc/IntellectualProperty/cprt indx.htm (accessed 22 August 2007).

3. U.S. Copyright Office, "Circular 1. Copyright Office Basics," Rev. July 2006, http://www.copyright.gov/circs/circ1.html#wci (accessed 22 August 2007).

4. Kenneth D. Crews, "You and Your Copyrights: Securing, Managing, and Sharing the Legal Rights," Rev. December 26, 2002, http://www.copyright.iupui.edu/youright .htm#Register (accessed 22 August 2007).

5. Tim Brooks, *Survey of Reissues of U.S. Recordings* (Washington, DC: Council on Library and Information Resources and Library of Congress, 2005), v.

6. U.S. Copyright Office, "Circular 92. Copyright Law of the United States of America and Related Laws Contained in Title 17 of the United States Code, Chapter 1. Subject Matter and Scope of Copyright, Section 107. Limitations on Exclusive Rights: Fair Use," http://www. copyright.gov/title17/92chap1.html#107 (accessed 22 August 2007).

Chapter 7

Writing Samples

Preview

- Successful program notes rest on knowing the music well, writing to the level of your audience, and being succinct. It should be worthwhile for your audience to read the notes.
- An annotated bibliography adds value to a standard list of works (the citations) by providing a paragraph or more describing the contents of each source and often evaluating it as well. Usually the focus of the annotations is on specific contributions of a source to the topic rather than a description of its overall organization, although that may be included.
- A literature review is an important part of a thesis or dissertation because it provides a comparative overview of the published works related to a research topic. Through literature reviews, degree candidates demonstrate their knowledge of research that has been done in their area of study. They also make a case for the need for further research, thereby introducing the research work that they plan to complete. When the purpose is to identify seminal works and provide a review for an audience outside the realm of dissertation or thesis writing, it may be called a bibliographic essay.
- The review, whether of books, recordings, scores, or performances, may vary from one or two paragraphs to several pages in length. Reviews require critical assessment of quality of the publication or performance and perhaps discussion of its historical context. Usually published in magazines, journals, and newspapers, of course, many are written by professional music and media critics.
- The research paper or research report is created to document an investigation into some aspect of music. Seminar and course papers exhibit mastery of concepts or methodologies studied and should answer a research question through scholarly arguments, evidence, and documentation. The recital paper is usually a culminating scholarly work covering one, several, or all of the compositions to be performed in a recital. It will make use of historical, analytical, and stylistic investigative methods.

- A thesis is a major research paper that serves as the culminating requirement for a master's degree, while a dissertation serves the same purpose for a doctorate. A dissertation should be completely original research so it is important at the proposal stage to verify that other dissertations are not in progress on the same topic.

Based on the precept that we learn from examples, this chapter presents a brief introduction to several types of writing in the music discipline, from brief program notes to the extensive doctoral dissertation. Examples from student writing projects are given to illustrate outcomes of research and to clarify the purpose and style of such projects. The authors have given permission for the use of their work in this textbook.

7.1 Recommended Readings for Music Research Reports

In addition to *The Craft of Research*, which was recommended in Chapter 1, consult the following books for more guidance in planning research projects and writing your music research results. Boyle, Fiese, and Zavac have created *A Handbook for Preparing Graduate Papers in Music*, which provides guidelines for graduate writing projects in music: recital papers, theses, essays, and dissertations. Useful chapters cover the proposal process for doctoral degrees, master of music recital papers, sample citations for music materials, and use of music notation in text. A standard source by Demar Irvine has been revised by Mark Radice and issued as *Irvine's Writing about Music*. While primarily a style manual, its consistent citation and sampling of music writings makes it relevant to the music student. Its three sections include "Style in the Manuscript," "Writing Skills," and "Combining Words and Music." Use Part 3 to check on the form of expression for musical matters such as composition titles, scales, tempo markings, or octave designations. Its authors address fundamentals of music notation and provide a glossary of terms for types of scores and musical sources. An older guide, *Words & Music: Form and Procedure in Theses, Dissertations, Research Papers, Book Reports, Programs, Theses in Composition*, by Helm and Luper remains useful for quick and concise answers to music writing questions.

A helpful source for planning research in many subject areas is *Practical Research: Planning and Design* by Leedy and Ormrod. The eighth edition was published in 2005. Part 2 supplies particularly helpful advice on developing a research problem, doing a literature review, designing research, and writing the research proposal.

7.2 Program Notes

Program notes can be an effective part of the whole communications package of a recital or ensemble concert. While a performer or director spends time and thought to plan a meaningful program, it is possible to further enhance the concert experience for an audience by engaging the audience in thinking about the compositions they will hear.

Critical factors in writing effective program notes are: (1) knowing your audience and (2) brevity. Before the concert there is not much time available for reading program notes, and neither is there much space available to print them in a program booklet. For these reasons, the commentary should concentrate on just one or a few points that will enhance the listening experience. What can you describe that a listener will be able to discern? How much background information on the composer or the work is really relevant to a live musical presentation? Will the audience consist of children, the general public, or music students and faculty? Write and revise carefully to make an impact and to engage the listeners in noteworthy facets of the music.

Program notes may be written for some or all of the works involved. The length is generally from a paragraph to just over a page in the program booklet. Frequently for vocal works the text is printed as well, with a translation, if necessary. More guidance is available in a recent article in *College Music Symposium*: "Musicians as Authors: Teaching the Art of Writing Program Notes," by Michele Henry and Laurel Zeiss. While focusing on teaching future choral directors to write program notes, their experimental program provides a guide to anyone with such an assignment. Writing suggestions include use of similes or metaphors to make points, using active verbs and interesting adjectives, and choosing from aspects such as text and music relationships, historical or biographical content, or musical patterns. The process of learning about the works programmed and a team approach to creating notes could be replicated as a learning experience for secondary school ensembles.

The layout of a recital or concert program itself varies according to patterns established by the performing organization or the department/school of music. Typical inclusions are the sponsor, place, program name or type, date, and performer(s). For each composition to be performed, the title, composer, and usually the composer's birth and death dates will be listed. Possibly, the date of composition will be included. Always gather information and follow style instructions of the sponsoring body.

Program notes, written as class assignments by Elizabeth Gaile Stephens and Sean McCollough, are included here to illustrate attention to audience and commentaries that are suitable for different types of music. Stephens' paired set of notes for adults and children, for Debussy's *La Cathédrale Engloutie*, provide an interesting contrast. The first set for adults consists of four paragraphs, each with a separate purpose: (1) giving historical context and an evaluative comment phrased to give credit without requiring a footnote, (2) telling the program of the piece, (3) explaining some of the compositional techniques to a general audience, and (4) expressing the value of the composition as felt by the writer. For the children's set of notes, the explanations are briefer, and the language is intentionally simplified. The children are addressed directly and told that they will hear the same composition twice. They are given questions to think about and instructions about listening and drawing conclusions. The tone for both sets of notes by Stephens is informal. Notice that while there is one brief direct quotation in the first paragraph, she gives credit within the text instead of in a footnote. Footnotes would be too scholarly for the communication intended in program notes.

THE UNIVERSITY OF TENNESSEE

Presents

DEBUSSY FOR CHILDREN

Performed by
JENNIFER QUAMMEN
and
THE UNIVERSITY OF TENNESSEE
SYMPHONY ORCHESTRA
Under the direction of
ELIZABETH GAILE STEPHENS

Saturday, April 2, 2004
2:00 p.m.
James R. Cox Auditorium

PROGRAM

La Cathédrale Engloutie   Claude Debussy
Jennifer Quammen, piano   (1862–1918)

La Cathédrale Engloutie   Claude Debussy
                                                                    (1862–1918)
                                                           Arr. by Henri Busser

University of Tennessee Symphony Orchestra
Oboe soloist: Charlotte Smith Cook

PROGRAM NOTES

La Cathédrale Engloutie was composed by Claude Debussy as a part of his first book of preludes and arranged for orchestra by Henri Busser. First performed in 1910 by Debussy himself, *La Cathédrale Engloutie* "is (now) considered to be one of the most extraordinary piano compositions written during this century," according to Reginald Hache in his article from the June 1986 issue of The Journal of the American Liszt Society. As such, *La Cathédrale Engloutie* is an important part of the repertoire of many modern pianists, and the orchestral arrangement, while not as well known as the piano piece, is noted for its beautiful oboe solo.

Debussy wrote *La Cathédrale Engloutie* to tell the legendary story of the fated French village of Y's, located on the coast of Brittany in the fifth century. There are conflicting legends about the village; however, most agree that because of the foolish and evil deeds of the people in the village, the ocean rose up to engulf the entire town including the cathedral. No building remains of the village of Y's, but according to legend every one hundred years the sunken cathedral of the village rises to the surface of the sea as a warning to all people of the consequences of evil deeds. Then almost as suddenly as it appears, it sinks back into the ocean's depths.

As the piece begins, Debussy creates the aura of chimes heard through the mist by using parallel chords. With the progression of the music the cathedral's chimes increase in volume and the sound of monks' chants, represented by the use of the church modes, can be heard. The fog lifts and the cathedral comes into full view over a developmental area in the music which transitions into a resonating chorale representing the cathedral as it majestically rises out of the sea. Within the cathedral chorus there are touches of modal chords in the treble and bass voices to represent the singing of the monks. Then, just as the cathedral has appeared, the bass changes to new chords representing submerging waves. Increasing in volume, the bass chords began to drown the chorale melody. Slowly, as the chorale fades, the grand cathedral sinks beneath the waves of the new chords to wait for another hundred years to emerge again.

La Cathédrale Engloutie is a wonderful exploration into the world of Debussy's unique and innovative composing. The orchestral arrangement also lends itself wonderfully to the telling of this legend through a wide use of color and a wonderful display of the beauty of the oboe. No matter what the medium, *La Cathédrale Engloutie* is a moving piece, which is a true work of genius by one of the most famous composers of the twentieth century.

!Kids Notes!

La Cathédrale Engloutie is a piece of music that tells a wonderful story about a mysterious French cathedral that rises from the ocean. The man who composed this piece was named Claude Debussy. He was a famous composer and pianist. He wrote this piece to tell one of his favorite legends or stories.

The legend says that over five hundred years ago evil villagers caused a whole town, including its church, to be swallowed by the sea. As a reminder to people not to do evil, the church or cathedral is supposed to rise from the sea every one hundred years.

You will hear the piece twice today. The pianist will play the piece once and then the orchestra. After the performance see if you can tell your parent or guardian how these two performances are different.

Also, in both performances, listen carefully to hear the sound of the cathedral's chimes. That will be the signal that the cathedral is going to rise from the sea. What do you think happens to the cathedral as the music becomes louder? What about when the music is softer, can you hear the cathedral sink into the ocean?

McCollough's program notes, below, illustrate an appropriate content and description level for popular music for a general audience. With admirable brevity, he explains historical significance, musical style, first occurrence of the song, and how it was disseminated and rose to its current stature.

Jubilee Folk Music Series
June 18, 1999

Sean McCollough, voice and guitar

We Shall Overcome   Traditional
                                                                        Date Unknown

Program Notes

Most likely born out of an old slave song, "We Shall Overcome" has been transformed through an amazing history into an international song of struggle. It can still be heard in the South Sea Islands sung in an old "shout" style with syncopated clapping and stomping. Its roots can be traced to two different but similar songs in the African American Church—"I'll Be Alright" and "I Will Overcome." The contemporary version uses melodies and words from both.

The first time the song was sung, as part of a social movement, was in 1945 by members of the Food, Tobacco and Agricultural Workers Union in Charleston, South Carolina. The workers slowed the tempo down, changed "I" to "We" and added words about their strike. Union members took the song to the Highlander Folk School (New Market, Tennessee), then a training school for union organizers. The school's music director, Zylphia Horton, changed the melody to make it more singable and taught it at workshops to other union leaders who took it back to their communities.

Pete Seeger learned it from Horton, changed the rhythm some and spread it through the North. A "California Hillbilly" named Guy Carawan learned it from Seeger and others and spread it through the South during the Civil Rights Movement. They helped to make it the anthem of that movement. African Americans, who were Civil Rights activists, made it their own by adding new melodic phrasing and inflections. Since the 1960s it has spread around the world and can be heard sung from South Africa to Ireland to China. "We Shall Overcome" is a song that stands apart as an almost universal statement of the struggle for peace, justice and equality.

7.3   Literature Review or Bibliographic Essay

A comparative overview of published works related to a research topic, especially for a graduate thesis or dissertation, is called a review of the literature. Through such reviews, degree candidates demonstrate their knowledge of research that has been done in their specific area of study. You will demonstrate your ability to locate appropriate research, to evaluate it, and to use it to plan your own research. It is important to establish the value of the research you plan to carry out by putting your project into the context of accepted, published research. A similar example of writing may be called a bibliographic essay when the purpose is to identify or recommend important works on a topic to readers outside the thesis or dissertation realm.

Consider these guidelines, by Mildred Patten, for writing a literature review:

- Introduce the purpose of your research—the broad problem and any definitions needed to clarify it.
- Describe the importance of the problem by showing that others have investigated it. Provide names and dates of appropriate research.
- Describe relevant research for each topic associated with your problem. Descriptions should cover both methodologies and results. It might be helpful to trace the history of a problem from its first article to show how theories have changed about the problem.
- When similar studies exist, it is possible to group these citations together.
- To conclude, summarize the review and relate existing research to your own study.

The following excerpt from a literature review is taken from a dissertation by Kathy Forester Adkins, accepted by the University of Tennessee for the Doctor of Education degree in 2003. This dissertation is entitled, "The Singing Schools of New Salem, Georgia." The abstract is included here to provide its research context.

Abstract

The purpose of this study was to document the singing schools held in the community of New Salem, Georgia, and their use of the shape-note teaching method. This method was compared to those of earlier singing school teachers to see if these methods have a place in the modern day choral classroom. Thirteen singing school students and teachers were interviewed and historical documents collected. The study was conducted primarily as a historical research project....

The interviews revealed that the singing schools had been held in the community since 1911 and possibly before that time. Several students attended normal schools held by the Stamps-Baxter Publishing Company and one student became a professional singing school teacher. The interviews also revealed that the students greatly valued the music education they received at the singing schools and it has instilled in them a love of gospel music. The teaching methods derived from the interviews were compared to others found in the research process and recommendations were made including the need for additional research.

What does a literature review look like? How do you organize it? Frequently the review of literature chapter is divided into sections paralleling various aspects of the research problem. In the second chapter of her dissertation, Adkins provides an historic overview of "The Community," "The Early Singing School Tradition," "The Instructional Method," "The Post-Revolutionary War Singing School," "The Shape-Note Method," and "The Twentieth Century." She then provides a review of the literature covering each of these aspects followed by relevant historical material—documents, numerical records, oral statements, and relics—that she examined or collected. This latter section is similar to an annotated bibliography because she lists each item, its owner, and provides a description of it.

As you read the following excerpt from her literature review, note that Adkins summarizes and compares published literature, this being the primary objective of a review of the literature. She weaves the authors, titles, and dates into her summary in a way that still allows her thoughts to flow easily. Your focus, like hers, should be on communicating the amount and content of known research while avoiding awkward insertions of bibliographic information. It is best to limit the amount of quotation to maintain a smooth presentation, but quotations may be important when the way a researcher made the statement is important. Adkins uses an in-text citation method following the APA style manual for her dissertation.

Review of Literature

The early American singing schools came to be in order to aid parishioners in the singing of the hymns. The roots of these classes have their origins in the English countryside and systems for such instruction of vocalists can be found as far back as the 11th century in the Guidonian monks. Willard (2000) illustrated this early history in chart form, which can be found in Appendix C.

The subject of early American hymnody has been dealt with extensively in *The new Grove dictionary of music and musicians* by several key authorities in the field. Crawford (1980, 2000) examined psalmody, Protestant vocal music, from the time of the settlement of Massachusetts through the next two centuries. Eskew (1980) described the unorthodox notational system which started in New England, which was made popular by singing school teachers, and was eventually forced out of the North by orthodox European musical notation. These shaped-notes, described by Eskew (1980), evolved into two distinct areas—the first, the older folk hymn tradition where "singing schools and group singings use the *Sacred Harp* (four-note) and *Christian Harmony, New Harmonica Sacra*, and *New Harp of Columbia* (seven-note)," and the second, where the "gospel music tradition using Aiken's seven shapes, singing and singing schools, use the paperback convention books published each year by Stamps-Baxter and others" (p. 228). Eskew and Downey (2000) surveyed rural American music which used note heads designated by shapes which are "intended to help singers with little musical expertise to sing at sight without having to recognize pitches on the staff or understand the key system" (p. 208). They defined the "new Southern rural shape-note hymnody" as a synthesis of the "four-shape hymn repertory" and the Northern gospel hymnody (p. 211).

...The itinerant teachers of early America taught this solmization method in singing schools using the tune-books as their textbooks. Each of these tune-books contained an introductory section containing basic music terminology and the hymns to be sung. The introductory section, or the "rudiments" as it was called, was thoroughly examined by Britton (1950) in his dissertation entitled "Theoretical Introductions in American Tune-books to 1800." Britton stated:

> In general, tune-book compilers had little to say concerning solmization beyond defining the order of the syllables and stating the rules to find mi. Use of a solmization system was taken for granted—indeed, the fasola syllables were always referred to as "the names of the notes," letter names being applied only to the lines and spaces of the staff. The phrase "to sing by note," as used by 18th century writers, meant to sing in fasola syllables (p. 191).

Britton (1989) also acknowledged that these singing schools with teachers, students, and textbooks provided the beginnings of American music education. The teachers had one goal—to teach their students or "scholars" to read music.

The work of Britton was extended in a similar study by Perrin involving the tune-book repertoire from 1801–1860. Perrin (1970a) stated that the introductory or rudiment sections "were written for adults who studied music formally for only two weeks each year" (p. 65). The rudiments section was a "precise presentation of facts necessary to read simple music" (p. 65).

...Mention must be made at this time about how the history of American music has been perceived. Crawford (1983) stated that "American musical histography [sic] has been dominated by two different perspectives" (p. 1). The first of these found writers tracing the history of American music as it extended from its European predecessors. The second perspective "rejected the assumption that European music-making is the worthy and inevitable model for American music-making" (Crawford, 1983, p. 1).

The shape-note method of instruction, which used the European solmization syllables, originated in America and therefore must be perceived through Crawford's second perspective—it is truly an American idiom. This American idiom has also been dealt with from two perspectives—the historic view and the cultural view of the subject. An objective historical perspective of the singing school and its unique shape-note instructional method was provided by Crawford and Steel (1986) in *The new Grove dictionary of American music* which also contained types of singing schools still being held in the 20th century. Also in this book can be found an examination of rural American sacred music written in shape-notes and its outgrowth into white gospel music (Eskew and Downey, 1986).

...Scholarly studies involving shape-notes have tended to be more qualitative than quantitative in nature. Kyme (1960) found that children who were taught to sight-read using the seven-shapes found in Jesse B. Aiken's *The Christian Minstrel* (1846) were better sight-readers than those instructed in regular orthodox notation. Another interesting observation by Kyme was that 67% of the students who had participated in the study groups who learned using shape-notes signed up for the choral class for the next year as opposed to 20% of students from other elementary schools who had not participated in the study.

...Graham (1971) documented the singing schools found in Kentucky Appalachia stating that "It is known that a singing school existed in Lexington in 1797, contemporaneous with the singing school movement in the Northeast" (p. 77). Because relatively little documentation existed about these singing schools, Graham collected primary information from seven teachers who had given instruction in that geographic region. He asserted that "It is reasonable to assume . . . that singing school practices of the early 20th century reflected, to some degree, practices of earlier years" (p. 78).

Although the history of early American psalmody, singing schools, and shape-note hymnody has been well documented by scholars in the field, the work of Jackson in the 1930s opened the door to a tradition practiced only in America—that of shape-note singing. The importance of this is great because this was a form of music instruction, which existed outside the realm of public school music education and well-trained music instructors. Music learning was taking place by students with little other music instruction and teachers who often learned their trade through the oral tradition. As stated by Lee (1999), "For the purpose of historical research, music education is defined as all deliberate efforts to pass music of any style from one generation to another" (p. 115). The music education method maintained in the singing school tradition and generally passed from generation to generation through the oral tradition exemplifies a process unique to rural America. The topic certainly warrants further examination.

Relevant excerpts from Adkins' bibliography are provided below to demonstrate the linkages between these imbedded references in the APA style (updated to match the 5th ed., 2001) and the bibliography to which they refer.

List of References

Britton, A. P. (1949). *Theoretical introductions in American tune-books to 1800*. Ph.D. Dissertation, University of Michigan.

Britton, A. P. (1989). The how and why of teaching singing schools in 18th century America. *Council for Research in Music Education*, 99, 23-41.

Crawford, R. (1980). Psalmody II: North America. In S. Sadie (Ed.), *The new Grove dictionary of music and musicians* (Vol.15, pp. 345-347). London: Macmillan.

Crawford, R. (1983). Music learning in 19th century America. *American Music* 1 (1), 1-11.

Crawford, R., & Steel, D. W. (1986). Singing School. In H. W. Hitchcock & S. Sadie (Eds.), *The new Grove dictionary of American music* (Vol. 4, pp. 233-234). London: Macmillan.

Eskew, H. (1980). Shape-note hymnody. In S. Sadie (Ed.), *The new Grove dictionary of music and musicians* (Vol. 17, pp. 223-228). London: Macmillan.

Eskew, H., & Downey, J. C. (1986). White gospel music. In H. W. Hitchcock & S. Sadie (Eds.), *The new Grove dictionary of American music* (Vol. 2, pp. 248-261). London: Macmillan.

Graham, J. R. (1971). Early twentieth century singing schools in Kentucky Appalachia. *Journal of Research in Music Education*, 19 (1), 77-84.

Kyme, G. H. (1960). An experiment in teaching children to read music with shape notes. *Journal of Research in Music Education*, 8 (1), 3-8.

Perrin, P. D. (1970a). Systems of scale notation in 19th century American tunebooks. *Journal of Research in Music Education*, 18 (3), 257-264.

Willard, K. (July 16, 2000). *Sacred Harp Time Line* [On-line]. Available: http://www.fasola.org/timeline.html

Literature Review and Bibliography in the Chicago Style

For comparison, here is a small excerpt from Adkins' review of the literature and relevant bibliographic citations formatted using the author-date system of *The Chicago Manual of Style*, 15th edition. In this case the two requirements are a complete list of sources cited, called a reference list, and very brief citations in parentheses within the text. For an overview of the author-date system, see rule 16.4 of *The Chicago Manual of Style*, 15th edition. The excerpt is also repeated to illustrate regular note reference numbers in the text, endnotes, and bibliography using the standard Chicago style.

LITERATURE REVIEW [1] Adapted to match the author-date system of the Chicago style

Mention must be made at this time about how the history of American music has been perceived. Ruth Crawford stated that "American musical histography [sic] has been dominated by two different perspectives." The first of these found writers tracing the history of American music as it extended from its European predecessors. The second perspective "rejected the assumption that European music-making is the worthy and inevitable model for American music-making" (Crawford, 1983, 1).

The shape-note method of instruction, which used the European solmization syllables, originated in America and therefore must be perceived through Crawford's second perspective—it is truly an American idiom. This American idiom has also been dealt with from two perspectives—the historic view and the cultural view of the subject. *The New Grove Dictionary of American Music* provides an objective historical perspective of the singing school and its unique shape-note instructional method along with types of singing schools still being held in the 20th century (Crawford and Steel). Also in this book can be found an examination of rural American sacred music written in shape-notes and its outgrowth into white gospel music (Eskew and Downey).

References

Crawford, Ruth. 1983. Music learning in 19th century America. *American Music* 1 (1): 1–11.

Crawford, Ruth, and D. W. Steel. 1986. Singing school. In *The New Grove Dictionary of American Music*, ed. H. Wiley Hitchcock and Stanley Sadie, 4:233–234. London: Macmillan.

Eskew, Harry, and J. C. Downey. 1986. White gospel music. In *The New Grove Dictionary of American Music*, ed. H. Wiley Hitchcock and Stanley Sadie. 2:248–261. London: Macmillan.

LITERATURE REVIEW [2] Adapted to match the traditional Chicago style

Mention must be made at this time about how the history of American music has been perceived. Ruth Crawford stated that "American musical histography [sic] has been dominated by two different perspectives."[1] The first of these found writers tracing the history of American music as it extended from its European predecessors. The second perspective "rejected the assumption that European music-making is the worthy and inevitable model for American music-making."[2]

The shape-note method of instruction, which used the European solmization syllables, originated in America and therefore must be perceived through Crawford's second perspective—it is truly an American idiom. This American idiom has also been dealt with from two perspectives—the historic view and the cultural view of the subject. Crawford and Steel's article on singing schools in *The New Grove Dictionary of American Music* provides an objective historical perspective of the singing school and its unique shape-note instructional method along with types of singing schools still being held in the 20th century.[3] Also in this book can be found an examination, by Eskew and Downey, of rural American sacred music written in shape-notes and its outgrowth into white gospel music.[4]

Notes (shown in shortened form)

1. Crawford, "Music Learning in 19th Century America," 10.
2. Ibid.
3. Crawford and Steel, "Singing School," 233–234.
4. Eskew and Downey, "White Gospel Music," 248–261.

Bibliography

Crawford, Ruth. "Music Learning in 19th Century America." *American Music* 1, no. 1 (1983): 1-11.

Crawford, Ruth, and D. W. Steel. "Singing School." In *The New Grove Dictionary of American Music*, ed. H. Wiley Hitchcock and Stanley Sadie, 4:233–234. London: Macmillan, 1986.

Eskew, Harry, and J. C. Downey. "White Gospel Music." In *The New Grove Dictionary of American Music*, ed. H. Wiley Hitchcock and Stanley Sadie, 2:248–261. London: Macmillan, 1986.

Literature Review and Bibliography in MLA Style

LITERATURE REVIEW [3] Adapted to match the text reference system of MLA

Mention must be made at this time about how the history of American music has been perceived. Ruth Crawford stated that "American musical histography has been dominated by two different perspectives." The first of these found writers tracing the history of American music as it extended from its European predecessors. The second perspective "rejected the assumption that European music-making is the worthy and inevitable model for American music-making" (Crawford, 1983, 1).

The shape-note method of instruction, which used the European solmization syllables, originated in America and therefore must be perceived through Crawford's second perspective—it is truly an American idiom. This American idiom has also been dealt with from two perspectives—the historic view and the cultural view of the subject. *The New Grove Dictionary of American Music* provides an objective historical perspective of the singing school and its unique shape-note instructional method along with types of singing schools still being held in the 20th century (Crawford and Steel). Also in this book can be found an examination of rural American sacred music written in shape-notes and its outgrowth into white gospel music (Eskew and Downey).

Works Cited

Crawford, Ruth, 1983. "Music Learning in 19th Century America." *American Music*, 1, 1: 1-11.

Crawford, Ruth, & Steel, D. W., 1986. "Singing school." <u>The New Grove Dictionary of American Music.</u> Vol. 4. Ed. H. Wiley Hitchcock & Stanley Sadie. London: Macmillan. 233-234.

Eskew, Harry, & Downey, J. C., 1986. "White gospel music." <u>The New Grove Dictionary of American Music.</u> Vol. 2. Ed. H. W. Hitchcock & S. Sadie. London: Macmillan. 248-261.

7.4 Annotated Bibliography

Sometimes an annotated bibliography is assigned as a course project to allow you to identify important sources of information on a topic and to describe them briefly for an audience of other students or researchers. An annotated bibliography can be very useful to readers because it offers a summary and perhaps critical assessment of the materials listed. Usually the focus of annotations is on specific contributions to the topic rather than a description of the overall organization of the source. Follow scholarly writing patterns avoiding first and second person; just state an opinion or evaluation as part of the annotation.

The format of annotated bibliographies differs from one to another. Of course, the citation format is quite regular based on a specific style manual or the style of a publishing house. The exact placement of the annotation is what varies. It may begin immediately after the citation information on the same line, may start on a new line with or without indention, or there may be a line between the citation and annotation. It may be permissible to use some phrases rather than full sentences in an annotation. Try to vary the wording to keep your reader interested.

The following excerpt is from an annotated bibliography on a research topic, which was written as a class assignment by Nathalie Hristov and used with her permission. Its audience is other researchers, at least at the graduate level, who would have interest in the topic. Notice that the annotations address the content of each work and its value to her topic rather than summarizing the book or journal generally. By reading all of the annotations, you obtain a view of the information and evidence she will be able to use as she writes her paper. Hristov has examined the *Chicago Manual of Style* with care. Compare her Siepmann entry to that of Leikin. For Siepmann, the entire book is of interest, but she directs the citation to one part using "see esp. chap. 8." The Leikin entry is for a component part of a book, one single chapter whose title is given in the citation.

Misunderstood Romanticism: Exploring the Controversy
Surrounding Frédéric Chopin's Chamber Music
An Annotated Bibliography

by Nathalie Hristov
December 2004

Frédéric Chopin left behind five chamber works, four of which prominently feature the violoncello. Considering how prolific Chopin was when it came to composing for the piano, the chamber works are often considered to be somewhat of an anomaly. As a result, music scholars have paid little attention to these gems of the romantic period, and some have even described these pieces as Chopin's inept attempt at expanding his compositional horizons. In response to the harsh criticism, this article will demonstrate the immense value these pieces bring to nineteenth century string literature by placing these pieces in their historical context and exposing some innovative, compositional elements. Ultimately, it is hoped that the arguments presented in this paper will prompt greater acceptance of these chamber works among musicologists and performers.

Chodkowski, Andrzej. "Notes on Chopin's Piano Trio." *Chopin Studies* 2 (1987): 55-62.
Saturated with compelling arguments, this article addresses the findings from a thorough dissection of Chopin's Piano Trio. In response to some of the harsh criticism this chamber work has received, Chodkowski methodically debunks each point presented by skeptical critics. By examining Chopin's letters to his colleagues and tracing the compositional process Chopin used, the author gives readers a profound understanding of the Trio's role in the Romantic chamber literature. Chodkowski argues that by experimenting with an unfamiliar medium, Chopin introduced new compositional conventions that expand the possibilities for the usage of stringed instruments in chamber music. Addition-

ally, Chodkowski examines specific passages of the Piano Trio that may have been influenced by the chamber works of Haydn, Mozart and Beethoven.

Delgado, Imelda. "The Chamber Music of Chopin." D.Mus. diss., Indiana
   University, 1975.
   Through painstaking examination of each of Chopin's chamber works, Imelda Delgado offers the most comprehensive and thorough analyses of these pieces in existence. Not only does she offer a complete analysis of the form and structure of each work, but she summarizes the criticism and controversy that surround these pieces, most of which address their relative worth. The author herself offers an argument relevant to these discussions by pointing out how the unconventional use of rhythm and dynamics in particular sections of the different pieces offers a distinctive musical effect. In the final chapter of this monograph, Delgado outlines Chopin's progressive development from one chamber work to the next, emphasizing the contribution each piece makes to the chamber music literature.

Goldberg, Halina. "Chamber Arrangements of Chopin's Concert Works." *The
   Journal of Musicology* 19, no. 1 (2002): 39-84.
   In this article, Goldberg demonstrates the adaptability of many of Chopin's concert works to mediums not commonly associated with Chopin, particularly string chamber ensembles. Although never addressing the works Chopin originally composed for chamber ensembles, through numerous examples, Goldberg explains how the stylistic structure of Chopin's music is suitable, often ideal for chamber arrangements. This would further support an argument that Chopin's distinct musical style can be expressed and highlighted in a chamber setting.

Leikin, Anatole. "The Sonatas." In *The Cambridge Companion to Chopin*, edited by
   David Fanning, 184-187. Cambridge: Cambridge University Press, 1992.
   In this chapter, Anatole Leikin discusses the influence two noteworthy cellists and friends of Chopin, Josef Merk and Auguste Franchomme, had on Chopin's compositions for the cello, particularly the Sonata in G Minor, Op. 65. Leikin briefly describes the painstaking process Chopin endured while writing this sonata, mentioning the many revisions and drafts produced prior to completion. Leikin clearly asserts that Chopin had already established a signature pattern for his sonatas that can be identified clearly in the cello sonata. According to Leikin, Chopin's cello sonata is among the three most mature sonatas of Chopin's repertoire. Finally, Leikin concludes this chapter by stating that, "the traditional underestimation and misconstruction of these works [is] gradually giving way to an understanding of their true structural and aesthetic power."

Siepmann, Jeremy. *Chopin: The Reluctant Romantic*. London: Victor Gollancz, 1995.
   See esp. chap. 8, "Interlude: Chopin and the Sonata."
   Siepmann acknowledges that Chopin's Sonata in G Minor may have some interesting moments, but goes on to criticize the work for lacking the conviction of the two piano sonatas composed around the same time period. He also contends that the outer movements of the cello sonata are characteristically "anti-Romantic," but he fails to offer any justification for that assertion. The most beneficial element of this resource is the summary Siepmann provides of the criticism/controversy surrounding the cello sonata, particularly addressing the first movement and some of its unique compositional devices.

Sutcliffe, W. Dean. "Chopin's Counterpoint: The Largo from the Cello Sonata, Opus 65."
   The Musical Quarterly 83, no. 1 (1999): 114–33.
   Using the Largo from Chopin's Cello Sonata, Sutcliffe demonstrates how Chopin's innovative use of counterpoint created a distinctive texture to the sound. He contends that

Chopin would exchange the contrapuntal lines according to the register of each instrument (cello or piano), in order to balance the sound so that neither instrument would assume dominance over the other. Ultimately, Chopin was more interested in the effect created using the timbre of each instrument than in conforming to the accepted voice-leading rules of harmony and counterpoint. This style of composition is unique to Chopin, and the attention given to sound texture is characteristically "romantic."

Zielinski, Tadeusz Andrzej. "The Many Shades of Genius." Chopin Foundation: Publications. http://www.chopin.org/pages/publication/pages/tadeuszAndrzej.htm (accessed October 24, 2004)
   While this article does not specifically address Chopin's chamber works, it is essential reading when studying any of the composer's musical works. Zielinski, a respected Polish musicologist, examines Chopin's perception of harmony, melodic and thematic development, and concepts of musical form. He demonstrates how Chopin's unique and imaginative style provides audiences with a musical experience that is both intelligent and aesthetically pleasing. According to Zielinski, few composers have been able to successfully infuse the same level of elegance to their works. Scholars studying Chopin's chamber works can easily apply the information presented in this article to specific examples found in his chamber music. By making those connections between Chopin's compositional style and the application of that style in his chamber works, the argument lending value to these works can be more strongly supported.

7.5 Research Paper or Recital Paper

The research paper or report is created to document an investigation into some aspect of music. Seminar and course research papers exhibit mastery of concepts or methodologies studied and should answer a research question through scholarly arguments, evidence, and documentation. The recital paper is usually a culminating scholarly work covering one, several, or all of the compositions to be performed in a recital. Writers will make use of historical, analytical, and stylistic investigative methods, and may address performance problems or challenges of the works to be performed as well. Preparation of a recital paper is an opportunity to communicate your understanding of the music you perform.

The most critical point about research is that you must have a question to investigate, and you must answer that question with an argument supported by evidence. So the primary activity of the research process is collection of evidence. State the research question clearly as you write your report. Librarian William Badke gives good advice about research questions: (1) Your readers will look for a question to give purpose to your paper. It should not be a question that has already been answered in an encyclopedia entry. (2) Focus your question so that it is really answerable in a research paper. (3) Limit yourself to a single question rather than many of them. (4) Be sure that the question can be answered by data that you can obtain. Plan for the kind of data required to answer the question. The conclusion of the process is to draft the research paper with as much care and planning as possible. Organization and clarity are essential as is setting aside enough time to revise your work.[1]

No sample paper is included here due to the length of most research or recital papers. For further clarification, seek samples of recital papers submitted to your institution. For research papers, check the nature of articles submitted to research journals in your area of interest. In fact, the most valuable preparation for writing research papers is to read as many as possible in the research journals of your field. Read the work of researchers in your field to learn how they organize their findings and present their results. Frequently the introduction serves as a literature review to set the context for the problem to be addressed.

7.6 Reviews

If and when the opportunity comes to write for publication, writing reviews is an excellent way to begin. New books, recordings, educational films, software, scores, and performances are reviewed in many music journals. Such reviews are important current-awareness articles for scholars, teachers, and performers. Of course, reviews provide evaluative information for students as they assess the quality of resources in their research as well. Depending on the journal or its review editor, the length of reviews may vary from a paragraph to several pages. Normally, review editors ask specialists to write reviews, but the review process takes time. It may be months to a year or more from the time of publication of the book or CD to the time of its first published review. If sufficient space is allowed, reviewers often try to place the work in its historical context, compare it to similar works, and especially to provide a critical assessment of the value of the work. *Notes: Quarterly Journal of the Music Library Association* is an excellent journal to consult for examples of reviews of music materials.

While Bonna Boettcher's review of the 2001 edition of *Baker's Biographical Dictionary of Musicians* is a lengthy book review, it stands as an excellent example of one that addresses the historical reception of a long-standing reference book, and one that offers valuable critical evaluation. Notice the writing strategy for her review.

Because Boettcher is reviewing the 9th edition of this reference work, her introduction centers on points made by reviewers of the earlier editions of the dictionary. She moves on to discuss the authority of the editors and their work with Slonimsky, editor of editions 7–8. Next she discusses the current editors' process of selection and editorial practice and the resulting content of the work. She comments on their problematic use of the label "discographies" in most articles, identifies new indexes, and touches on reception of this edition by music librarians. Her logical presentation concludes by addressing how earlier critical comments have been remedied or ignored in this edition. A reviewer's task is twofold: to let her readers know about the content of a book and to evaluate that content. Notice that the evidence to support her criticisms comes from a comparison of earlier critical commentary with the editors' stated decisions in the preface and with actual content of the dictionary.

Baker's Biographical Dictionary of Musicians

Centennial edition. Editor emeritus, Nicolas Slonimsky; Series advisory editor, Laura Kuhn. New York: Schirmer Books, 2001. [6 vols. ISBN 0-02-865525-7. $595.]

Almost as interesting as new editions of *Baker's Biographical Dictionary of Musicians* are the reviews that accompany each new offering. As reviewers articulate their comments, praise, and criticism, they make clear the respect given to this long-standing icon of music reference. In reviewing the ninth edition—the first edition comprising multiple volumes, and with substantially expanded contents and significant attention to jazz and popular music performers—I turn first to several reviews of past editions. In

1979, Stanley Sadie reviewed the sixth edition of Baker's (*Notes* 36, no. 1 [September 1979]: 81-83). Sadie acknowledged the expanded size of the work and welcomed the new edition, noting "an aggregate increase of nearly 30 percent in wordage" (p. 81). In addition to comments about the format of entries and the usual selected errata, Sadie raised the question of Baker's continuing as a cumulative dictionary and suggested that selected biographies of those whose influence had waned could be removed to include those of more current musicians: to use Sadie's words, "revision" versus "full reassessment." Editorial policy did not appear to concern Michael Tilmouth in writing his review of the seventh edition of Baker's (*Music & Letters* 67 [1986]: 408-9). Tilmouth commented on Nicolas Slonimsky's writing style and also on "his talent for following the sometimes indistinct trails left by musicians in their earthly existence" (p. 408).

The review that should be read by all interested in the past and future of Baker's is that of the eighth edition, written by Susan T. (Suki) Sommer (*Notes* 49, no. 1 [September 1992]: 67-70). Sommer devoted a good portion of her review to a historiography of Baker's, beginning with the first edition, prepared by Theodore Baker and published in 1900. In addressing the eighth edition, Sommer raised questions both cosmetic and intellectual. The sheer physical size of the dictionary, combined with a change in font size and spacing conventions, made the volume slightly unwieldy. The more important questions articulated were those of audience and the editorial policy of the publisher. Should Baker's be allowed to grow, unchecked? Had the publisher allowed the dictionary to take on a life of its own, relying "on Baker's reputation and Slonimsky's as well, failing to recognize the growing divergence between product and audience?" (p. 70).

Given reviewers' comments on past editions, I turn to the one at hand: the ninth and so-called "Centennial" edition. Both the classical editor, Laura Kuhn, and the associate classical editor, Dennis McIntire, have a long-standing association with Baker's, having worked with Slonimsky on both the seventh and eighth editions of the dictionary. Lewis Porter, jazz editor, and William Ruhlmann, pop editor, have made significant contributions to the literature in their areas of expertise. But how has Baker's fared without the continued leadership of Nicolas Slonimsky?

In her Preface (pp. vii-viii), far shorter than Slonimsky's unique and witty essays that preceded the sixth, seventh, and eighth editions, Kuhn reflects on the changes in editorial process and practice in producing the ninth edition. Ruhlmann adds his own essay describing the decisions resulting in the additions of jazz and popular music figures to Baker's (pp. viii-x). In his introduction, Ruhlmann states: "It remains to be noted that, no doubt, this first attempt at describing the lives of popular and jazz musicians is not perfect" (p. ix). Since this represents neither the first attempt at documenting popular and jazz musicians in music reference works nor the first such attempt in Baker's, this is a curious statement. The changes in leadership have not removed Slonimsky from Baker's. Those who have enjoyed Slonimsky's style will be pleased, while those who have found his style elitist and overly acerbic will wish for more significant revisions. The editors have chosen to reprint Slonimsky's Prefaces to the sixth, seventh, and eighth editions, ensuring that those who know Baker's only by the ninth edition are able to read these essays on the joys of lexicography. And the adjectives remain. Although the entry on John Browning in the ninth edition is several lines shorter than the previous one, he remains a "brilliant American pianist," while Dawn Upshaw moves from being an "American soprano" to the status of "greatly admired American soprano." According to the Preface (p. viii), one thousand new classical entries have been added to the dictionary. While I did not attempt to locate even a small percentage of the new names, several which I did locate, such as Pedro Antonio Avondano and Veljo Tormis, have only brief entries, although that for the "promising pianist and composer" Jake Heggie is more substantial.

The larger changes in content are for the popular and jazz musicians. Hoagy Carmichael's single-paragraph entry in the eighth edition has been completely rewritten and expanded to two and one-half pages, and he has moved from being an "American pianist

and composer of popular music" to a "rustic American composer, singer, and actor."
Carole King, described as all "American pop singer and songwriter" in the eighth edition
and whose entry occupies only a short paragraph, is now described as a "prolific songwriter in the 1960s," and then "one of the first and most popular female singer-
songwriters of the 1970s," with a biography expanded to a full page. In addition to greater
coverage of popular and jazz musicians included in the eighth edition, numerous new biographies have been added in the ninth.

The decision to label as "discographies" the partial lists of major songs and albums
included with many popular and jazz musicians' entries is unfortunate. A discographer
traces the history of the recording, from recording sessions to release, documenting when
possible the place and date of each session, the personnel involved, other takes from the
session, and release information. While Ruhlmann and Porter obviously could not under-
take full discographical research for this project—nor could Baker's have devoted the
necessary space to include even selected discographies—the lists of major hits should be
labeled as such and include at least a modicum of useful information such as the manufacturer's name and number, and the format.

Several indexes have been added to this edition, including genre, nationality, and
women. The genre index includes as major subdivisions classical, jazz, and popular; the
nationality index is subdivided by country or by a hyphenated combination (e.g., Argen-
tine-German); the women's index is simply alphabetical. It does appear that all these
entries are included in indexes. I am amused at finding in the nationality index Dolly Par-
ton and the Partridge Family sandwiched between Harry Partch and Thomas Pasatieri,
and Styx between Jule Styne and Morton Subotnick.

Perhaps due to its appearance on the heels of the online version of the second edition
of *The New Grove Dictionary of Music and Musicians* (*GroveMusic*, www.grovemusic.
com), Baker's ninth did not generate much discussion on MLA-L, the music librarian's
online discussion group (the archives are available at list-serv.indiana.edu/archive/mla-
l.html). Primary questions raised revolved around whether any of the errors from the
eighth edition had been corrected, which musicians were excluded, how indexing decisions were made, and the dramatic increase in the size of the dictionary. It was also
questioned whether another multi-volume biographical dictionary was needed when we
have a wide variety of recent, reputable sources for jazz, popular, and classical music.

Did the ninth edition of Baker's address questions raised in the reviews cited earlier
in the present review? The move from a single-volume, relatively affordable reference resource to an expensive ($595), six-volume dictionary does raise concerns, particularly
concerns of audience (which Sommer raised in her review of the eighth edition) and
scope (which Sadie raised). To be sure, some of the cosmetic issues have been addressed.
With no additional spacing between paragraphs, and minimal margins, the publisher has
returned to a more readable font size, reasonable spacing, and generous margins. Users
still must face the paragraph-style works lists and bibliographies, which, in the case of a
composer such as Johann Sebastian Bach and his nearly six-page list, can drive readers to
other, more user-friendly sources. The bibliographies appear to have received the greatest
editorial attention: in scrutinizing a handful of entries, I find them to be arranged in
chronological order rather than alphabetically by author. While books and dissertations
are cited, I find no references to journal articles, a staple in earlier bibliographies.

From the Publisher's Note (p. vi), it would appear that Schirmer Books has no inten-
tion of considering a careful review of the scope of this publication: "its caretakers
continue to strive toward that elusive goal of comprehensiveness." In 2001, is comprehensiveness an achievable goal? And even if it is, is comprehensiveness a laudable goal?
Librarians with substantial budgets will continue to purchase Baker's; others may need to
choose between this and several other resources. The price of the ninth edition places it
out of reach of most individuals wanting a reliable home or office reference.

Sommer concludes with a call to the publisher to "redesign this potentially elegant vehicle in a format energy efficient enough to last another century" (p. 70). The stated goal of comprehensiveness makes it clear that future editions of Baker's will only increase in size. In addition, I have not been able to find any statement of intent to move Baker's out of a print-only format and into the online arena. I trust that those who are the caretakers of this resource are involved in discussions of cost, scope, format, and audience so that Baker's will continue to thrive well past the ninth edition.[2]

7.7 Thesis or Dissertation

Not all graduate degrees in music require a thesis or dissertation; however, they are usually required for musicology, ethnomusicology, theory, composition, and often in music education or music therapy. Non-thesis programs, such as performance or conducting, may require a recital paper or a doctoral essay related to the works to be performed in recitals required for a degree.

The thesis or dissertation proposal lays an important foundation for the final research product. Frequently a proposal will include an introduction to provide background and context for the proposed investigation, description of the problem, the purpose and significance of the research, a review of literature related to the problem or methodology, methods of investigation, and references. The advanced graduate student will work closely with a thesis/dissertation advisor. The advisor and the rest of her graduate committee will review her proposal before giving final approval to do the research. The committee will read the completed thesis or dissertation. A defense is a session when the candidate answers questions from her committee to explain her research methodology, findings, and conclusions as presented in her written document. The defense is required before the thesis/dissertation is accepted for the degree.

The outline for Kathy Forester Adkins' dissertation, "The Singing Schools of New Salem, Georgia," is a good example of the contents of a dissertation on a music topic. It is detailed and contains typical chapters. Her introduction includes a statement of the problem, purpose and significance of the research, definitions, scope of the research—its delimitations and limitations, assumptions, methodology, organization and validity. Depending on the nature of the research, these subsections could be separate chapters. Adkins combines her literature review with historical context and types of documents she collected. Notice that she had many different areas to address in her review of the literature to cover writings on singing schools in different time periods, instructional methods, use of shape-notes in instruction, etc. The summaries include her actual findings, from which she gathers conclusions and recommendations. The long list of appendices is typical because dissertations frequently result in examination of primary sources or need to show the exact methodology used by including surveys, data-gathering instruments, or the data collected.

TABLE OF CONTENTS

One thing that this table of contents conveys is the exhaustive nature of a dissertation. The topic will be narrow, but the coverage will be extensive. It is essential to be thorough when researching a dissertation. A thesis will be much less extensive because the student is early in the process of learning to become a researcher. Still, the strategies for information searching covered in Part 2 of this textbook, are important to all researchers. Learn how various searching strategies work, and then use them as appropriate to effectively and efficiently identify resources for your research.

Review Questions

1. What are some similarities and differences between an annotated bibliography and a literature review?
2. How might you write program notes to account for different audiences?
3. What differences are there between theses, dissertations, and research papers for a seminar or other course?

Learning Exercises

1. Program Notes
   Choose a musical work (or small group of works by one composer) appropriate for performance. Investigate this work; then prepare program notes and a bibliography of

sources consulted. Remember to consider your audience and the appropriate length for program notes. These are not to be liner notes for a recording or a review of a recording. Suggestion: List the work as you would for a recital program, then type the notes below. See the samples in this chapter. Example topics for this project:

- J. S. Bach. Unaccompanied Sonatas for Violin
- Frédéric Chopin. Ballade, op. 38, no. 2, F Minor
- Robert Schumann. Dichterliebe
- Giuseppe Verdi. Selected arias from *La Traviata*
- George Gershwin. 3 Preludes, piano
- A jazz set by Miles Davis

2. Annotated Bibliography for a Research Topic

Choose a research topic to investigate. Use the annotated bibliography excerpt in this chapter or annotated citations throughout the book as examples. Consult other annotated bibliographies as models.

    a.   On a cover page, list the title of the research paper and a synopsis of the research problem. Provide a brief description of its focus or scope, the thesis, problems you have discovered that would need to be addressed if you were to write a paper on this topic, etc. State which style manual you are using.

    b.   Prepare a typed, annotated bibliography of materials in support of your topic. Bibliographic items should be as varied as possible given the nature of your research topic. Include books and journal articles. As appropriate, include dissertations, scores, sound recordings, videos, liner notes to sound recordings, articles in dictionaries or encyclopedias, interviews, etc. Prepare citations in standard form following the style manual most appropriate to your area of study and follow each citation with an annotation. An annotation consists of a brief comment on the content, quality, or usefulness of each item cited. Cite and annotate the work as a whole or only those portions that are relevant to the topic. Each description should indicate quite specifically what kind of information the source provides for the topic at hand. Be evaluative.

    c.   You may be asked to turn in parts of this project at specified deadlines throughout the semester or to meet with the professor to discuss your progress.

3. Literature Review for a Research Topic

Choose a research topic to investigate. Use the literature review excerpt in this chapter as an example or examine literature reviews in other theses or dissertations.

    a.   Include a title page.

    b.   Begin your review of the literature with an introduction of the research problem. Define the focus or scope of the research and clearly state your thesis. As you compare various sources, use appropriate text references or notes according to your chosen style manual.

    c.   Prepare a bibliography of all materials reviewed. Bibliographic items should be as varied as possible given the nature of your research topic. Include books and journal articles. As appropriate, include dissertations, scores, sound recordings, videos, liner notes to sound recordings, articles in dictionaries or encyclopedias, interviews, etc. Citations should be in standard form; identify the style manual at the end of the bibliography or in a note.

d.   You may be asked to turn in parts of this project at specified deadlines throughout the semester or to meet with the professor to discuss your progress.

4.   Review of a Book or Score

Choose a relatively new book or score, and write a review of it. Examine a variety of other published reviews to observe the writing techniques appropriate to various audiences. Identify a journal for which this would be an appropriate review.

5.   Research Journal and Guide to Resources

For your area of study or for a specific research topic, identify print and online resources of use to you in your professional career.

a.   Keep a journal to track your information searching strategies. Note sources, their scope and coverage, search statements, and results.

b.   Prepare an annotated bibliography of reference sources you use or create a worksheet to complete for each reference source including type of source, bibliographic citation, call number, and evaluation of the source.

Notes

1. William B. Badke, *Research Strategies: Finding Your Way Through the Information Fog* (New York: IUniverse, 2004), 9-11.

2. Bonna Boettcher, review of *Baker's Biographical Dictionary of Musicians*, edited by Nicolas Slonimsky and Laura Kuhn, *Notes: Quarterly Journal of the Music Library Association* 58 no. 3 (March 2002): 544–547.

Part 2

How To: Discover and Use Resources

Part 2

How To: Discover and Use Resources

The essential function of a library . . . is to discover books of whose existence the reader had no idea, and which turn out to be of prime importance to him.[1] — Umberto Eco

It is a process of discovery that is the foundation of research. The purpose of this section is to present a range of discovery strategies and to provide skill-building instruction in using them effectively. You do not start out by knowing who has written on a topic, what kind of data are available, or what facts and theories have already been discussed. These are things you need to learn. Discovering where to look for information may be termed resource discovery, step 1 of the process. Learning about "where" involves getting to know library catalog databases, journal article indexes, citation indexes, the Internet, and other online resources. Learning about "where" also means understanding the systems that enable informed browsing directly in library collections, becoming familiar with the literature of your field, and understanding how and when to identify people, experts, as sources of information. Comprehensive investigation of a research problem frequently requires searching of multiple sources in multiple formats, both online and in print. And, it takes a variety of strategies to discover quality information sources among the millions of publications and electronic documents available today. It requires repetition of discovery strategies as your topic and your understanding of it evolve.

Once you discover resources, add them to your working bibliography. Step 2 of the process may be termed information discovery; at this stage evaluation becomes critical. Some evaluation takes place as you winnow an online results list to the information sources that "look" appropriate. Of course, you must obtain the sources to proceed. Then you must evaluate them for authority and credibility, currency, accuracy and verifiability, and documentation. Finally, you read the information sources for content, argument, and evidence that could support your thesis.

Note

1. Umberto Eco, "De Bibliotheca," *Bostonia* (Spring 1993): 59.

Chapter 8

Browsing as a Discovery Strategy

Preview

- Library collections arrange books by subject so browsing is possible. There are two advantages: (1) you can make an in-depth inspection of books, and (2) you may find useful, related works without having to identify each one through the catalog.
- The Library of Congress Classification (LCC) system helps us to find related materials on the bookshelves. A subject-heading search in the catalog enables you to identify a classification area to browse. It is also easy to search for a known book or score, note its call number, and then browse in that classification area. It is also possible to browse through catalog records, reading descriptions or even tables of contents to assess the value of resources.
- *The Library of Congress Subject Headings* (*LCSH*) in print serves as an index to the subject-organized physical collection. Many subject headings list a related LC classification number for that subject.
- Scanning books in a subject area lets you assess their contents directly by examining the table of contents, index, chapter subheadings, etc. In suitable chapters, the footnotes and bibliography will provide more potential sources to add to your working bibliography.

8.1 Why Browse?

Why would a seemingly unsophisticated technique such as browsing be suitable for research? It is because subject access in a catalog is not always sufficiently in depth. Due to time and financial constraints, catalogers usually assign one to three subject headings, while the actual number of subjects or facets of subjects treated in a book may be much higher. Inspection of the books themselves will reveal aspects of their subject and specific information not retrievable remotely through a database. Furthermore, you, the researcher, will be able to recognize suitable materials when you see them instead of trying to predict how they will be described and accessed in a database. You will find them as you are examining other works on the same subject.

By examining related books in a systematic way, you may also expand your working knowledge of the research topic and find other resources to consider. Looking at the footnotes and bibliography of relevant items is a way to add to your working bibliography.

There are two clear advantages to browsing in classified collections. First, you are able to find books that are related to one another without having to identify each title through a database search. And second, in the collection itself, you can examine and assess the books firsthand. Because browsing in a collection rests on a subject arrangement, or classification, it is important to remember that a book can occupy just one place on the shelf and have a single shelf address, its call number.

Limitations of the browsing method include the fact that some books may be checked out or kept in a remote storage facility, and related materials may be shelved in another classification area. While a book may treat a number of subjects, catalogers must choose just one shelf location. To overcome this limitation, consult the *Library of Congress Subject Headings* (*LCSH*) to help identify various classification areas to browse. Look up a subject term in *LCSH*, and frequently you will find a classification area assigned to that subject. Thus, you have a pointer to a part of the collection where you might browse.

8.2 The *Library of Congress Classification* System

Browsing in the library collection, in "the stacks," is a valid method to search for information. It does not need to be a process of walking up and down the aisles trying to find relevant materials at random, either. If items are placed on the shelves using an organized system, then you may already know generally where to look for something. In a grocery store, cereals are shelved together as are fresh fruits and vegetables in the produce area or dairy products in their own special section. There are complications in the grocery, too. Condiments might not be shelved together by their form (condiments), but by another category, i.e., jellies are not generally next to mustard.

Similarly, books and other library materials are assigned classification numbers (part of the call number on each item) precisely to put them near other books on the same subject. The *Library of Congress Classification* system (*LCC*) provides subject organization on the shelves of most academic libraries in the United States. The *Dewey Decimal Classification* is used in public libraries and in a relatively small number of college and university libraries. The use of a classification system puts many like materials together, but when several subjects are treated in a source only one will determine the classification assignment.

How does the LC Classification system work? In the M-Class, for the subject of music, it provides three major classification areas:

M for music (M = the music itself), the scores and sometimes recordings of musical works

ML for literature on music (ML = music literature) which includes magazines and journals, books on music history, biographies, the history and construction of instruments, ensembles, vocal music, national and popular music, and more

MT for musical instruction and study (MT = music teaching), which covers professional music education in the schools, music theory and composition, analysis and listener's guides, pedagogy guides and instructional or juvenile editions of music for individual instruments, voice, and ensembles

Most materials in a library collection are both cataloged and classified, that is, a cataloger prepares the bibliographic record describing the item and assigns a call number to it. The call number is its unique identification using an LC Classification letter and number plus a sequence of letters and numbers (the author or Cutter number) to place it alphabetically within that class. The call number provides a shelf address, which puts the item in proximity to others like it. For instance, here is a call number sequence for some opera full scores:

M1500.**P423**S4 1970	Pergolesi's *La Serva Padrona*
M1500.**P83**B6 1953	Puccini's *La Bohème*
M1500.**P83**M3 1990	Puccini's *Madama Butterfly*

With just a little information, it becomes easy to see that the letter-number sequence in the call numbers puts Pergolesi operas before those of Puccini and organizes Puccini operas alphabetically by title. Here's how it works. They are all full scores, classed together in M1500. The letters and numbers after the decimal point are the "author number." P423 for Pergolesi puts that opera alphabetically before those of Puccini (P83), and the next letters, B for the title word Bohème and M for Madama, put the Puccini operas in order.

Vocal scores for the same operas have a slightly different LC class number: M1503. So we can observe immediately that opera full scores are classed together in M1500, and opera vocal scores are classed together in M1503. Here is the call number sequence for the same opera titles in the vocal score format:

M1503.**P4**S3	Pergolesi's *La Serva Padrona*
M1503.**P977**B72 2000	Puccini's *La Bohème*
M1503.**P977**M3 2002	Puccini's *Madama Butterfly*

On the shelf in either classification area, specific operas are arranged alphabetically first by composer and then by title.

In the music literature area, biographies are placed together on the shelves in a similar way: ML390–406 for collective biographies, ML410 for biographies of individual composers, ML416–423 for biographies of individual performers (instrumentalists, vocalists, conductors). Within each classification number, the individual books are assigned letters and numbers to organize them alphabetically:

ML410.**B1**W71 2004	*The Life of Bach*
ML410.**B4**D29 2002	*The Character of Genius: Beethoven in Perspective*
ML410.**B8**M113 2001	*Brahms*

Books on various aspects of musical instruments and instrumental music range from ML459 to 1093. That is a large area, but it is organized as one might expect, in families of instruments and then single instruments within each group:

ML749.5–750	Stringed instruments (History)
ML755	Stringed instruments–Construction
ML800–897	Violin (History)

ML850–892	Violin–Performance
ML900–905	Viola (History)
ML910–915	Violoncello (History)
ML915	Violoncello music–History and criticism
ML920–925	Double bass (History)

Similarly organized are books about wind instruments:

ML929–990	Wind instruments
ML930–931	Woodwind instruments, collectively
ML933	Brass instruments, collectively
ML935–990	Individual wind instruments

The classification sequences given above illustrate some overall principles of the M–Class: (1) general topics come before specific ones, (2) collections come before separate works, and (3) instrumental music occurs sequentially before vocal music in all three subclasses: M, ML, and MT.

Subclass M (scores and recordings)

Instrumental music:	M5–1490
Vocal music:	M1495–2199

Subclass ML (books about)

Instruments, instrumental music:	ML459–1380
Vocal music:	M1400–ML3275

Subclass MT (instruction and study)

Instrumental techniques:	MT170–810
Singing and vocal technique:	MT820–949

For further information on the LCC for music, see Appendix 2, "Outline of the Library of Congress M–Class," and Appendix 3, "Topical Guide to Music in the Library of Congress Classification."

HINT for browsing: As you use the library catalog and the library's books, scores, and other materials, observe the LC Classification numbers that you use most frequently. Soon you will be able to go directly to some sections of the stacks to browse in areas important to your studies.

8.3 Where to Browse

There are several good ways to find a starting point for browsing the collection. You might find the call number for a known item in the catalog and start in that classification area. For instance, if you know *The Music of Africa* as a book title, you can find its record using a title-heading search in the catalog. The book's call number begins with ML350. You may expect to find other books like it in ML350 and books about music in specific African nations following that class. You could also do a subject-heading search and examine the list of headings that result. The catalog display, with all cross-references, often will list the LC Classification numbers used for a particular subject heading.

An alternative to searching the catalog for an appropriate starting point is to use the print version of the *Library of Congress Subject Headings* (*LCSH*) as an index to the classified layout of materials on the shelves. Here are some examples to illustrate how *LCSH* indexes the physical collection. For a research topic investigating performance practices for piano music of a particular time period, you might start by searching "performance practice" in the print version of *LCSH*.

Performance practice (Music) (May Subd Geog) [ML457]
Here are entered works on the conventions or styles of performance characteristic of particular periods, places, or groups. General works on musical performance are entered under Music–Performance.

Music–Performance
UF Musical performance practice
    Performing practice (Music)
BT Music–Performance
SA subdivision Performance under individual musical instruments and families of
    instruments, e.g., Piano–Performance
NT Embellishment (Music)
    Musica ficta

You see chronological subdivisions by century and for earlier time periods:
    Performance practice (Music)–15th century [*ML457*]
    Performance practice (Music)–20th century [*ML457*]
    Performance practice (Music)–500–1400 [*ML457*]
    Performance practice (Music)–To 500 [*ML457*]
Note that all of the subject headings for "performance practice" in music refer to LC Classification, ML457. That is one area of the collection where you will want to browse.

If you are interested in a more focused aspect of performance practice relating to ornamentation, you will see that the valid heading is "Embellishment" and the LC Classification is MT80:

Embellishment (Music) (May Subd Geog) [MT80]
UF Diminution (Music)
    Ornamentation (Music)
    Ornaments (Music)
BT Music–Performance
    Performance practice (Music)
NT Embellishment (Vocal music)

You may also notice the see also (SA) listing:
    SA subdivision Performance under individual musical instruments and families of
    instruments, e.g., Piano–Performance

Following that lead gives you two more areas to consult: ML700–742 and MT235.

Piano–Performance (May Subd Geog) [ML700–742]
UF Piano playing
BT Piano music–Interpretation (Phrasing, dynamics, etc.)

Piano music–Interpretation (Phrasing, dynamics, etc.) [ML700] [MT235]
NT Piano–Performance

By looking up relevant subject headings in *LCSH* and checking for their related LC Classification numbers, you now have a list of call number areas for browsing: ML457 for performance practice in general, MT80 for ornamentation or embellishment, ML700–742 for piano performance matters, and perhaps ML700 or MT235 for interpretation of piano music.

8.4 How to Browse Effectively

When you have found an LC classification relevant to your research topic, browsing needs to turn into more than reading the titles of the books. This is your chance to make an assessment of the appropriateness of each book to your research as well as a preliminary evaluation of the quality of its content. As in all evaluations of content, you need to examine parts of the book and consider a number of questions.

Examine both sides of the title page for the full title and subtitle of the book, names of the author(s) or editor(s), publisher, and date.
- Is this a well-known publisher?
- Have you ever heard of the author/editor(s)?
- Is the book recent enough to be appropriate? Or is date of publication not a factor for your research?

You may have to investigate these matters later by seeking further information to evaluate your sources. Here is a simple evaluative process to follow:
- Scan the table of contents and index to see how much of the book relates to your topic and whether there are particular sections that focus on it.
- Scan the preface and introduction to learn the author's intent, limitations, and approach to the subject.
- Determine which sections correspond to your specific focus by reading introductions, section headings, and conclusions of appropriate chapters.
- Is this a scholarly or popular treatment of the topic? If footnotes, bibliography, and one or more indexes are present, it is probably a scholarly book.
- Examine the footnotes and bibliography for leads to other scholars who have contributed to this area of research. Note appropriate citations for your working bibliography.

Review Questions

1. Name three ways to identify Library of Congress classifications in which to browse.

2. What parts of a book need to be examined in systematic browsing?

3. What do the M-class subdivisions M, ML, and MT stand for? Remember they sound like what they mean.

4. What general organizational patterns occur in all the subclasses?

Learning Exercises

1. Using your research topic, determine several specific classification areas in the book stacks where you will browse for suitable materials.
    a. Write down the classification numbers. How did you identify them?
    b. Record complete bibliographic citations for at least two books that you discovered.
    c. Check the bibliographies and footnotes in these two books. Write down two resources you discovered in these books.

2. Create a list of five classification areas appropriate to your instrument, voice, or area of study. Choose one, browse in that section, and write bibliographic citations for three books that would be valuable to you during or after your graduate studies.

Chapter 9

Databases: Structured for Searching

Preview

- Databases are structured with *records*, for each item, consisting of *fields* for specific types of information. Knowing the field structure of a database improves searching success.
- *Library catalogs* are databases used to identify what a library owns. *Union catalogs* list holdings of many libraries, thus permitting efficient identification of resources.
- While library catalogs do not list articles in journals, special databases called *journal indexes* are available for identifying articles. This chapter gives emphasis to the three major journal databases that cover music journals; others are listed for related disciplines and cross-disciplinary research.
- Field searching, in library catalogs or journal indexes, gives more control and narrower results for a search. It is important to be able to distinguish between two basic search types: *heading* and *keyword*.
- Taking note of the uniform title field may enhance your ability to locate scores and recordings of specific compositions in library catalogs. Problems with variant titles for musical compositions are lessened by knowledge of uniform titles.

9.1 Database Structure

Structure, structure, structure. Understanding the structure of databases, whether they are journal indexes, library catalogs, or Internet resources, is the key to searching successfully. A database is a set of information structured for input, updating, and retrieval. An individual listing in a database, its largest unit, is called a record. The records consist of smaller units called fields, which contain prescribed data. A common example of a database is a telephone directory, where the organizing structure for the white pages is alphabetical order by surname and the structure for the yellow pages is alphabetical order by topic or subject. Each individual listing is a record, and the fields of data in the white pages are surname, forename, street address, state, zip code, and telephone number. Just as the entries in a telephone directory stand for people or businesses, database records in the research arena generally are surrogates for the real information source they represent—the book or journal article or whatever. Each record provides a condensed description that is sufficient to identify a source of information uniquely. It usually requires a second step to procure the information source itself.

It is easy to use a print telephone directory because we readily perceive its organizing structures and may browse through the listings (records) starting at appropriate entry points: surname or type of business (subject). Computerized databases have similar structures but are not so easy to use because the structures and the data are concealed. As a researcher, your understanding of the structures of databases (records and fields) and their access systems will enable you to effectively and efficiently retrieve information.

Here are some examples of the types of databases used in music research. We will investigate many of these databases in later chapters learning how to discover their existence and how they work.

Figure 9.1 Databases for Music Research, Categorized by Type

Type	Examples
Online library catalogs list the holdings of one library	University library catalogs Library of Congress catalog
Union catalogs list the holdings of many libraries	*WorldCat*
Journal indexes list articles in journals. They may be called article indexes or periodical indexes.	*Music Index Online* *International Index to Music Periodicals* *RILM Abstracts* *Education Full Text*
Indexes to current research literature cover journal articles plus sources such as books, chapters in books, research reports or conference proceedings.	*RILM Abstracts* *ERIC* *Academic Search Premier*
Indexes to historical research literature	*RIPM* for music periodicals of 19th and early 20th centuries
Electronic reference sources	*Oxford Reference Online* includes: *The Concise Oxford Dictionary of Music* *The Oxford Companion to Music* *The Concise Oxford Dictionary of Opera* *Who's Who in Opera*

Type	Examples
Internet search engines	*Google* *Google Scholar* *Yahoo!*
Internet web crawlers	*Dog Pile* *Vivisimo*
Internet subject directories	*DW3: Classical Music Resources* (Duke) *Online Resources for Music Scholars* (Harvard University) *Worldwide Internet Music Resources* (Indiana University) *Yahoo!* (subject directory)

There are many types of databases. Some cover many subjects and some specialize in one; some cover many document formats while others concentrate on a single format. It is essential to identify appropriate possibilities and then choose the best ones to suit your need.

HINT for effective use of databases: Evaluate the appropriateness of an online database by reading information on the screen to determine its: (1) purpose, (2) scope—what it covers and for what time periods, and (3) structures for searching, retrieval, and output. Frequently, the help section of a database contains this information.

9.2 Library Catalog Databases

An online library catalog is a database that lists materials owned by a library: its books, scores, sound and video recordings, journals, government documents, theses and dissertations, microforms, and archival collections. These collection items may be physical ones on the library's bookshelves, or they may be electronic or digital versions available, at the click of a mouse, though the Internet. Learning to use library catalogs effectively allows a researcher to discover and locate resources. Search a library catalog early in the research process to identify materials related to your topic. Are there sufficient published materials?

Search your college or university library catalog to identify materials that are most readily available, then go to the stacks to find and evaluate them. A union catalog such as *WorldCat* or that of a regional consortium of libraries will extend your search to a more comprehensive list of resources because it lists the holdings of many libraries. It is efficient to search many libraries with a single search; then, if needed, you may borrow some materials from other libraries using the interlibrary loan service of your library.

There are differences in appearance and functionality from one library catalog to another because libraries make choices from a variety of software. However, the many commonalities between them mean that you can transfer your knowledge of functionality from one to another. Read instructions on the computer screen or select "help" to read specific instructions.

A *bibliographic record* describes each item in the library's collection, and catalog databases are organized around this descriptive information. As in the individual listing in a telephone directory, there are information fields prescribed for bibliographic records in a catalog. This information exists to enable you to identify an item by its author, title, publisher, date, and physical description. Catalogers, who create bibliographic records, follow rules so there will be continuity between records in all library catalogs. They also provide other access points—ways to search a catalog—including subject access terms, call number, and name only or name/title headings for performers, other authors or composers, and the works included.

The process of retrieving information from a library catalog, or from any database for that matter, requires understanding of three steps: (1) searching, (2) retrieval, and (3) output. Database search methods, which can be applied in principle to most databases, require some skill development to find as much information as you need and to do it efficiently. Such methods include field searching by keyword, exact phrase, or controlled vocabulary; general keyword searching using Boolean operators; and advanced Boolean combination searching. These methods are explained thoroughly in subsequent chapters, but here is an overview:

- The initial step is searching. Identify search terms, which fields to search, and what type of search is best—heading or keyword. Decide whether limits such as publication date, language, format, or location might be helpful. Look for an advanced search screen to take control of your search.
- The retrieval step may offer several types of display of search results: a list of headings (names or subjects), brief records, full records, and information about availability (which library, sublocation, availability, due date, volumes and dates owned).
- The output step presents options for handling the retrieved records: sort, select, save, print, or e-mail them. When you use a new database, think about the overall retrieval process and investigate the specific mechanisms used in the database for searching, retrieval, and output.

9.3 Field Searching in Library Catalogs

The primary advantage of field searching is that it restricts a search to particular fields of information. Because fields of data are the building blocks of databases, the ability to search specific fields is a powerful search tool. In field searching, you will retrieve records based on the existence of your search terms in the specified field(s). You can learn which fields exist in a database by examining some of its records. The fields will be labeled, and many of them exist as access points for retrieving the database records. You have greater control of your search if you decide both which words to use as search terms and where (in which fields) to search for them. Typical searchable fields in library catalogs are author fields, title fields, publisher, date, call number, subject headings, and notes. The following bibliographic record, from a library catalog, displays field labels and contents.

Author	Ravel, Maurice, 1875–1937.
Uniform Title	Bolero, orchestra.
Title	Bolero / Maurice Ravel.
Imprint	Paris : Editions Durand ; Bryn Mawr : Theodore Presser, c1932
Call Number	M1049.R25B6 1932
Availability	Music Library = Miniature score * M1049.R25 * B6 1932
Description	1 miniature score (66 p.) ; 22 cm.
Subject	Boleros (Music)–Scores.
Subject	Orchestral music–Scores.
Notes	"Editions musicales."
Publisher No.	D. & F. 11 839 Durand

Field searching is done in one of two ways: as a heading search or as a keyword search. A heading is a specific group of words, like article titles in an encyclopedia. It can refer to a person, place, title, or an idea or subject. In library catalogs "headings" are the access points to catalog records. Name headings, for authors or composers or performers, are access points that must be searched last name first. Word order for title headings must match a title word-for-word from the beginning. Therefore, when entering a heading in a field search, your search terms must match the configuration of the heading. Here are some examples:

1. Use last name first for authors: "copland aaron"
2. Enter titles word-for-word from the beginning: "what to listen for in music." Omit initial articles (in English and in foreign languages; use "young person's guide to the orchestra" instead of "a young person's guide to the orchestra").
3. Learn the exact wording of subject headings: "piano–instruction and study" not "piano pedagogy." You will explore the value of this practice in Chapter 10, "Subject Searching in Library Catalogs: Controlled Vocabulary."

Most catalogs offer basic and advanced search screens. Both interfaces permit searching everywhere in the records or in specific places (fields) where the terms are most likely to occur. Look for the option to choose specific fields to search; frequently, it is a pull-down menu presenting a choice of fields. Here are two examples of basic search screens in library catalogs. They illustrate briefly some types of heading searches and keyword searches in specific fields. Specifics of the search method for "words anywhere" or "general/comprehensive keyword" will be covered extensively in Chapter 12.

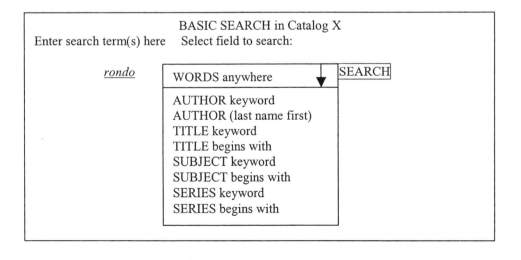

The basic search in Catalog X lets you choose where to search (which field) and a way to search (keyword or exact heading). The basic search in Catalog Y does the same thing but is presented as two separate options: first choose a way to search and within that option make a field choice. The keyword option provides keyword anywhere or keyword in specific fields. The heading option requires a specific field choice.

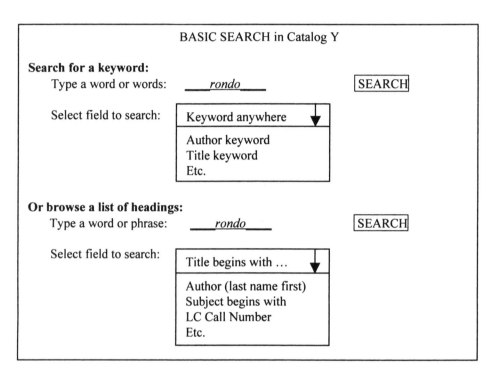

Some catalogs call a heading search a phrase search because of the way you enter words in the search box or a browse search because the search returns an alphabetical display of headings from the specified field. Despite the different names, heading searches operate in the same way: they are "left-anchored" because you enter the words of the heading starting from the left. Note that it is not necessary to include the entire name or title as long as you start from the beginning. A search can even stop in the middle of a word because the catalog matches the character string entered. A heading search always results in a list of headings showing the closest match to the characters entered. For example, a heading search for "what to listen for" retrieves these titles:

What to listen for in jazz
What to listen for in music
What to listen for in rock: a stylistic analysis

After browsing in the results list, you choose an entry from the list to display the bibliographic records. When is a heading search most beneficial?

HINT for a catalog heading search: Use a heading search when you are fairly certain that you know the exact information in a field, the title or author or subject heading, or when you believe you know the beginning of that information. Even if you know only the first words, you will see the alphabetical list and probably recognize the full heading you need.

The second way of searching fields, a keyword search, finds the search terms you use regardless of order and does not require you to enter all of the words for a particular field. You could use "young guide" in a title field search or perhaps "person's guide" instead. A keyword search results directly in a display of the bibliographic records.

HINT for a catalog keyword search: Do field searching with keywords when you do not know a complete title, exact subject heading, or the entire name of an author, performer, or composer.

9.4 Using the Uniform Title Field

When you know the title of a book, it is easy to search for it in a library catalog using a title-heading search. Books have a title page and are published in one language at a time; their titles don't change unless there is a translation of the book. Even new editions frequently bear the same title with only a change in the edition information (2d edition or Revised edition). Book titles remain constant most of the time. If you want to find a copy of a music theory book, *The Cambridge History of Western Music Theory*, it would be a simple matter to do a field search using the exact words of the title, in order, probably omitting the initial article. You could be quite certain that you would find either the bibliographic record for this book because your library owns it, or that no retrieval really means your library does not own it. For a book, using a title search works well unless you are mistaken about the title itself.

For musical compositions, title searching is much more complicated. Music is international in nature, and as compositions are published in various countries, frequently their titles are translated. We encounter *Prélude à l'après-midi d'un faune* and *Prelude to the Afternoon of a Faun* as exactly the same composition bearing different titles due to language in the country of publication. Often popular titles have been given to compositions, such as "Drumroll" or "The Bear" for two of Haydn's symphonies. Furthermore, the same composition, published by different publishers, may list the title in various ways, as for Beethoven's third piano concerto:

Piano concerto no. 3
Concerto for piano and orchestra, no. 3 in C minor
Klavierkonzert Nr. 3, c-moll = c minor = ut mineur, op. 37
Konzert für Klavier und Orchester No. 3 op. 37
Concerto no. III for the piano, op. 37, in C minor
3me concerto, op. 37, en ut mineur pour piano

These title variations are handled in library catalogs by providing an additional, structured title along with the title that occurs on a score's title page or on the cover of a sound recording. This additional access point, created by a cataloger, is called a *uniform title*. Essentially, a uniform title allows you to retrieve all versions of a work in one search despite variations in word order or differing languages of these versions as they have been published. To create uniform titles for compositions, a cataloger must follow specific rules. Whenever a composer's works have been organized and numbered using a thematic catalog, that number becomes part of the work's uniform title. A uniform title will contain a designation if the work is part of the whole or a special format such as excerpts, selections, vocal score, libretto, etc.

It is not important that you learn all of these details, but having some familiarity with the various types of uniform titles can help you decide which title elements are most important to your search. Once you observe the component parts of uniform titles, you can also use these elements when searching in journal indexes or other databases. They can help improve your searching success rate.

Generally in library catalogs, both title-page titles and uniform titles are searched simultaneously when you do a title search. Here are two bibliographic records for Mozart's Symphony, no. 40. Compare the uniform title of each with its title (from the title page). You would not retrieve the first record if you used the search terms "symphony no. 40" in a title-heading search because "40" is not part of the title nor uniform title. When thematic catalog numbers exist (K. 550), use them in your search.

Bibliographic Record 1

Author	Mozart, Wolfgang Amadeus, 1756–1791.
Uniform Title	**Symphonies, K. 550, G minor.**
Title	Symphony in G minor, K. 550. The score of the new Mozart edition, historical note, analysis, views and comments. Edited by Nathan Broder.
Imprint	New York, W. W. Norton [1967]
Edition	[1st ed.]
Call Number	M1001.M92 K.550 .B75
Check Availability:	Music Library / Miniature score: M1001 .M92 K.550 .B75
Description	viii p., miniature score (114 p.) 22 cm.
Contents	Contents: Historical note. –The score of the Symphony. – Analysis. –Views and comments.
Subject	Symphonies–Scores.
Notes	Analysis, etc.: p. 69-114. The score (p. 5-66) edited by H.C. Robbins Landon from the Urtext of the Neue Mozart Ausgabe, 2d version.

Bibliographic Record 2

Author	Mozart, Wolfgang Amadeus, 1756–1791.
Uniform Title	**Symphonies, K. 550, G minor.**
Title	Symphony no. 40 in G minor, K550; Symphony no. 41 in C major, K551 : Jupiter / Wolfgang Amadeus Mozart.
Imprint	Mineola, N.Y. : Dover Publications, 1997.
Check Availability:	Music Library / Miniature score: M1001 .M92 K.550 1997
Description	1 miniature score (106 p.) ; 21 cm.

Subject	Symphonies–Scores.
Notes	Reprinted from Mozart's Werke (Leipzig : Breitkopf & Härtel, 1880–1882)
Series	Dover miniature scores
Other Authors	Mozart, Wolfgang Amadeus, 1756-1791. Symphonies, K. 551, C major.
Variant Title	Jupiter
ISBN	0486298493

There are three general types of uniform titles: (1) form titles, (2) distinctive titles, and (3) collective titles.

Form titles are used when the original name of a composition is a musical form or type of composition such as symphony, concerto, or variations. The uniform title uses these elements of the title: musical form or type of composition, instruments or voices for which it is written, its thematic catalog number or opus number, and the key of the work, for example:

Beethoven, Ludwig van, 1770–1827.
Sonatas, piano, no. 10, op. 10, no. 1, A major

Britten, Benjamin, 1913–1976.
Concertos, violin, viola, orchestra, B minor

Mozart, Wolfgang Amadeus, 1756–1791.
Symphonies, K. 551, C major

Note that words for musical form (sonatas, symphonies, concertos) are given as plurals. The plural of the form name is used if the composer wrote more than one composition in that form. If the composer's output includes only one composition in a specific form, then the form term is singular in the uniform title.

Distinctive titles are used when the composer has provided a title that is not the name of a musical form. Most operas, oratorios, songs and song cycles, and some instrumental music have distinctive titles. Such a title will be listed in a uniform title in its original language. Cross-references in a library catalog help you determine the various languages of musical compositions.

Bach, Johann Sebastian, 1685–1750.
Wohltemperirte Klavier [used for "The Well-tempered Clavier"]

Puccini, Giacomo, 1858–1924.
Bohème [used for "La Bohème."]

Schubert, Franz, 1797–1828.
Dichterliebe

A cataloger constructs *collective titles* for collections that contain multiple works by a single composer. Collections may be any one of three types:

1.   Works in a single musical form

     Schubert, Franz, 1797–1828.
          Songs [Used for his complete songs for various voice types]

     Brahms, Johannes, 1833–1897.
          Concertos [Indicates the complete concertos, all instruments]

2.   Works in a single performance medium

     Brahms, Johannes, 1833–1897.
          Chamber music [Meaning all chamber music for varying instruments]

     Reger, Max,
          Organ music [Includes all musical forms that he wrote for organ]

3.   Works in a mixture of forms and media. *Mixed collective titles* are used for collec-
     tions containing various musical forms for many combinations of instruments or
     voices. Frequently these collections are the scholarly editions of all of the com-
     poser's works. For these sets, the uniform title is simply, "Works."

     Berg, Alban,
          Works

For both form and distinctive uniform titles, additional words are used to designate a
separate publication of a movement of a composition or to define the type of edition. For
part of a large work, the name of the movement or portion is added to the uniform title.
For instance, an aria title will be added after the distinctive title of the opera to which it
belongs; a portion of an oratorio will be added to the name of the complete oratorio—if
these movements are separately published.
     Tosca. Vissi d'arte.
     Messiah. Hallelujah.
     Suite bergamasque. Clair de lune.

The following descriptive terms are added to further identify a work: Selections; arr.
(used for compositions arranged for other instruments); Vocal score or Chorus score;
Libretto or Text; Language of translation.

Understanding uniform titles can also contribute to a logical search strategy when it
comes to finding compositions in a library catalog. Libraries do not always buy scores as
separate publications; frequently, they buy them in collections. For instance, a student
performer might purchase the sheet music for Beethoven's Piano Sonata, no. 10, op. 110.
The library, on the other hand, will probably purchase all thirty-two sonatas by Beethoven in a collection having two volumes. It is more cost effective to purchase the set and
easier to maintain it on the shelves as two large volumes. Likewise, sometimes a single
sonata will occur on a sound recording having a variety of works, or there may be a
sound recording set of the complete sonatas of Beethoven. The uniform title will vary
depending on whether the sonata occurs singly or in a collection in the library.

Therefore, the logical search strategy for musical compositions is to start with the most specific title and then to search again using more general uniform titles that apply to the work. From the title search aspect, we might move in this sequence from specific to general:

Sonatas, piano, no. 10, op. 10, no. 1, A major
Sonatas, piano or Sonatas, piano. Selections
Piano music or Piano music. Selections
Works

HINT: For composition titles, observe the title elements in uniform titles and use that knowledge to improve your searching. A thematic catalog number or opus number will be most helpful. As needed, move from a specific title to a general (collective) title as you search.

There are several reference books that help in resolving problems relating to composition titles. The main section of **Popular Titles & Subtitles of Musical Compositions* by Berkowitz provides alphabetical access to titles of compositions. A composer index lists all works included in the book. Information includes uniform title elements such as thematic catalog number and key so this book is helpful when determining how to do a composition title search in a library catalog. Hodgson's *Music Titles in Translation: A Checklist of Musical Compositions* supplies composition titles in multiple languages in one alphabetical list. Therefore, the *Rite of Spring* is entered under R, under S for *Sacre du printemps*, and under V for *Vesna Sviashchennai*. Another source of information, providing English translations, composer, and date of composition, is Adrian Room's *A Dictionary of Music Titles: The Origins of the Names and Titles of 3,500 Musical Compositions* (2000).

Librarians at Indiana University's music library have created a tutorial that provides more detailed information about using uniform titles: "Making the Most of the Music Library: Using Uniform Titles" http://library.music.indiana.edu/collections/uniform/uniform.html.

9.5 Field Searching in Journal Index Databases

We use journal indexes to identify the existence of articles published in journals. Such indexes are critical finding aids because most library catalogs list only the journals to which the library subscribes, not the contents of those journals (the articles in them). Sometimes called article databases, they also label their fields of information and make them searchable. Here is an example of a full record in *Music Index Online*, one of the important retrieval tools for discovering articles in music journals. Most of its fields are searchable: title, author, periodical, date, language, classification and country of the periodical, and subjects.

TITLE:	Ravel's Bolero: practice techniques for the bassoon solo.
AUTHOR(s):	R. Ramey.
PERIODICAL:	THE DOUBLE REED
VOLUME:	17
ISSUE:	n3

DATE: 1994
PAGE(s):   67–70
LANGUAGE: English
PERIODICAL
CLASSIFICATION: Bassoon, English Horn, Oboe
PERIODICAL
COUNTRY: United States
SUBJECTS: BASSOON Study and Teaching p.67–70 mus
                     RAVEL, MAURICE Works [Bolero] p.67–70 mus

> HINT: Use a field search if you know where your search terms are most likely to oc-
> cur. You will narrow your search if you take the time to decide the best part of the
> record to search.

Review Questions

1. What is an online database? Name some types of databases.

2. Databases are structured with records and fields. Define these structures.

3. Name some searchable fields that are common to both library catalogs and journal
    indexes.

4. In a heading search, how do you structure the search?

5. In a keyword search, what choice of words helps ensure both a focused and compre-
    hensive list of results? Does word order matter? Do you need to use all of the words?

6. Why do the titles of musical compositions vary so much and how does the uniform
    title filed provide guidance with this problem?

7. Can you create a uniform title for this composition: Tchaikovsky's sixth Symphony
    in B minor, opus 74?

Learning Exercises

1. Search in your library catalog for a music journal whose title you know.
    a. Search strategy. What kind of search will be most effective? Which field will
        you search? In your field search, will you use a keyword or a heading search?
    b. Citation information. When you find the full bibliographic record, write down
        the title, imprint information (place of publication, publisher, and date when the
        journal began), and call number. Has this journal ever changed its title?
    c. Holdings information. Determine which volumes the library owns (volume
        numbers and dates). Determine where the journal (older volumes and current is-

sues) is located in the library. What formats of this journal does the library own? Microform? Bound volumes? Current paper issues? Electronic?

2. Evaluate *WorldCat* for its:
    a. Purpose
    b. Scope—what does it cover and for what time periods
    c. Structures for searching, retrieval, and output

3. Search in your library catalog for three complete musical compositions written by different composers.
    a. Write down the composer, title, and uniform title for each. What parts of the uniform title would be helpful to use in a catalog search?
    b. Check the uniform titles in your retrieval list (brief or full records) for different editions of some of these works. Can you use the uniform title to identify arrangements, vocal or choral scores, multiple languages for the text, or selections from the large work? If not, search for the name of an opera or oratorio and look for these terms in the uniform titles. Write down the composers and uniform titles you find.

Chapter 10

Subject Searching in Library Catalogs: Controlled Vocabulary

Preview

- A "controlled vocabulary" is a set or list of authorized subject terms designed to guide subject searching. In library catalogs, the controlled terms are called "subject headings"; in journal databases, however, they may be called "descriptors."
- A controlled-vocabulary list is useful in determining the best search words or phrases to use in subject field searches, to narrow or broaden your topic, or to investigate related terms that may lead to different aspects of a topic. In journal databases, the list may be called a thesaurus.
- Sometimes it is helpful to use the *Library of Congress Subject Headings* in the print version to see the structure and relationships among terms. However, in your online catalog a search for subject headings will probably result in an alphabetical list of headings. Such a browsable results list also lets you see and make choices among headings.

The phrase "controlled-vocabulary searching" may seem intimidating, but actually it is a precise description of a valuable type of subject searching in library catalogs and other databases. When you choose a research topic, you have a subject in mind, and you probably will refine that subject until you settle on a precise and feasible research topic. In that topic-development process and beyond, you start searching various databases for your subject. Subject keyword searching means using likely words for a subject and searching them in title fields or subject fields or everywhere in the records. However, if you learn about the structure of subject headings themselves, the assigned words in subject fields, you will be able to improve your searching ability and your results. Then you can do subject-heading searches to take advantage of the power of controlled-vocabulary searching. The term "subject heading" has a much more precise meaning than the general term "subject." This chapter will lead you through the basics of subject headings in library catalogs and subject field searching in other databases.

Precise, focused searching of a large database is possible when standardized subject headings or descriptors are available. For library catalogs, catalogers assign subject terms to the records for books, scores, journals, and all kinds of library materials. An authoritative body controls these subject headings for the choice of words and the way they are put together. For most university and research libraries in North America, the Library of Congress is responsible for establishing these standardized headings, and the list of them is published as the *Library of Congress Subject Headings* (*LCSH*), five large red books that are available in your library. Journal databases may also use a controlled vocabulary for subject access. Their subject headings are often called descriptors and may be based on *LCSH* or may be established independently. Examples include the *ERIC Thesaurus* and the list of subject headings used by *Music Index Online.*

Why do we need a controlled vocabulary? Natural languages—English, French, and German, etc.—offer a variety of expressions and synonyms to represent a single concept. We need a mechanism to help focus on a single concept despite these various ways of expressing it and without requiring one to think of all the possible words. This mechanism is a list of authorized terms with cross-references to guide us among the various possibilities. Any list of authorized search terms is a controlled vocabulary.

Remember, when using a controlled vocabulary, you need to determine the best search words or phrases to describe your topic according to the authorized system. Consult *LCSH* for library catalog subject headings; consult the database listing of subjects or its thesaurus when searching in a journal index. Not just any word or phrase will work because the whole purpose of a controlled vocabulary is to control the vast array of synonyms and different aspects of a subject. The list or thesaurus provides cross-references from words not used to the authorized words as well as references to broader, narrower, or related terms that are also authorized. It may seem like extra work to consult a list of subject headings or descriptors before starting a database search, but actually the process is very helpful.

HINT: Use a controlled-vocabulary list to:
   1. Determine the best search words or phrases to use in subject field searches
   2. Narrow or broaden your topic
   3. Investigate related terms that may lead to different aspects of a topic

---

10.1 Using the *Library of Congress Subject Headings* (*LCSH*) in Print

Please note the hierarchical system and abbreviations used in *LCSH*:

- **bold** headings are valid search terms
- *may Subd Geog* means that geographic subdivisions may be added to this valid term
- The paragraph following a bold heading is the scope note or explanation of the specific use of the heading
- USE = refers you to the valid heading; look it up to see other relationships
- UF = "Use for" and, therefore, is not a currently valid heading
- BT = broader term, a valid heading that is broader in meaning

- NT = narrower term, a valid heading that is narrower in meaning
- RT = related term, a valid heading that covers a related aspect of the topic or a related topic

An example will help clarify how the *LCSH* controlled-vocabulary list works. To start your research on women in music, consult the *LCSH* print volumes to get a handle on subject searching in a library catalog.

Women in music (*may Subd Geog*)
　　Here are entered works on the portrayal of women in music. Works on all aspects of the practice of music by women are entered under the heading Women musicians.
　　BT　Music

The descriptive paragraph under the heading, "Women in music," is a scope note that describes the specific application of this phrase. If your interest is in how women have fared in making music rather than expressions representing women within musical compositions, you probably won't use this subject heading. Look up the suggested heading instead:

Women musicians (*may Subd Geog*)
Here are entered works on all aspects of the practice of music by women. Works on the portrayal of women in musical works are entered under the heading Women in music.
UF　Musicians, Women [Former headings, no longer used]
　　Women as musicians
BT　Musicians [A broader valid term]
NT　Lesbian musicians [These are narrower valid terms]
　　Nuns as musicians
　　Women accordionists
　　Women bluegrass musicians
　　Women blues musicians
　　Women composers
　　Women conductors (Music)
　　Women country musicians
　　Women drummers (Musicians)
　　Women flamenco musicians
　　Women folk musicians
　　Women jazz musicians
　　Women musicologists
　　Women rock musicians
　　Women singers
　　Women violinists
　　Women violists
－ Japan [This is a geographic subdivision]
－ United States
NT　African American women musicians
　　Women musicians, African American

Women musicians in art (*Not Subd Geog*)
Women musicians in literature   (*Not Subd Geog*)

Also look at adjacent headings in the vicinity of "Women musicians," and you will find other choices before the heading:
Women music critics
BT Music critics
    Women critics
Women music patrons
BT Music patrons
    Women benefactors
Women music teachers
BT Music teachers
    Women teachers

And after the heading:
Women musicologists (*May Subd Geog*)
BT Musicologists
    Women musicians
    Women scholars

Now you have an array of valid search terms to choose among. You don't have to guess about appropriate words but can find phrases that relate specifically to your research interest.

It is important to understand that catalogers assign subject headings to books or other sources at the most specific level possible to describe the contents of the source. They do not use both a specific and a general heading. When multiple subject headings are assigned, it is to reflect various subject aspects of the item. Look for the most specific headings that describe your topic. If the specific heading does not bring the results you wish, then try a broader heading.

Another special feature of *Library of Congress Subject Headings* is that certain subdivisions may be added to authorized headings. There are subdivisions possible for topics, forms of information, geographic places, and time periods. Subject headings become more specific by adding subdivisions to a main topic. The chart below illustrates the types of subdivisions—form, period, geographical, another topic—that are added to valid topical subject headings. Often the topical subdivisions are phrases that distinguish among various aspects of a subject.

Music teachers–Job satisfaction
Music teachers–Training of

Figure 10.1 Types of Subdivisions for *Library of Congress Subject Headings*

Subdivision Type	Example 1	Example 2
Topical	Performance practice–Opera	Musical instruments –Construction
Form	Performance practice –Bibliography	Musical instruments– Dictionaries
Geographical	Performance practice–Austria	Musical instruments–Brazil
Period	Performance practice –17th century	Musical instruments–16th century

Form subdivisions are of great value for library research. If you start with a topical subject heading and then add an appropriate term for the form of information, you can quickly identify specific kinds of sources you need. This approach is especially useful at the start of a research project after you have determined that you need special encyclopedias or dictionaries for background information or bibliographies and discographies that will direct you to other sources. For an extensive list of form subdivisions used for music, see Appendix 1.

Flute–Methods

Music–Bibliography [ML112.8–ML158.8]
Music–Bibliography–Graded Lists [ML132]
Music–Bio-bibliography [ML105–107 (Dictionaries)]
Music–Chronology [ML161]
Music–Dictionaries [ML100–109]
Music–History and criticism [ML159–ML3799]
Music–Manuscripts (May Subd Geog) [ML93–ML98]
Music–Periodicals
Music–Terminology [ML108]
Music–Thematic catalogs [ML134]

Musical Instruments–Catalogs and collections (May Subd Geog) [ML461–ML462]
Musical Instruments–Catalogs, Manufacturers' [ML155]
Musical Instruments–Dictionaries [ML102]
Musical Instruments–Juvenile literature [ML3928–ML3930]

Opera–Dictionaries [ML102.6]

Singers–Biography [ML420]

From the list above, note that many subject headings also provide the Library of Congress classification number that is related to the subject heading. In essence, *LCSH* directs you to an area of the book stacks where you will find materials on this specific subject. So *LCSH* becomes an index to the full-text materials in the library's collection.

Typical period subdivisions are by century for classical music and by decade for popular music.

> Opera–History and Literature–17th century
> Opera–History and Literature–18th century
> Opera–History and Literature–19th century
> Opera–History and Literature–20th century
>
> Jazz–1921–1930
> Jazz–1931–1940
> Jazz–1941–1950
> Jazz–1951–1960
> Jazz–1961–1970
> Jazz–1971–1980
> Jazz–1981–1990
> Jazz–1991–2000
> Jazz–2001–2010

Geographic subdivisions, for continents, countries, states, regions, and cities, may be added to any subject heading bearing the note (may Subd Geog).

> Women musicians–Japan
> Women musicians–United States–New York

Personal names—individuals as subject—are important as subject headings. It would not be possible to list all of the people who might be the subject of books or other writings so *LCSH* gives only some specific examples in different fields of endeavor. Here is the list of valid subdivisions for Richard Wagner. Remember that you may add such subdivisions to any personal name that you wish to search as a subject heading.

> Wagner, Richard, 1813–1883–Aesthetics
> Wagner, Richard, 1813–1883–Anecdotes
> Wagner, Richard, 1813–1883–Anniversaries, etc.
> Wagner, Richard, 1813–1883–Chronology
> Wagner, Richard, 1813–1883–Dictionaries (Not Subd Geog)
> Wagner, Richard, 1813–1883–Discography
> Wagner, Richard, 1813–1883–Dramaturgy
> Wagner, Richard, 1813–1883–Exhibitions
> Wagner, Richard, 1813–1883–Friends and associates
> Wagner, Richard, 1813–1883–Harmony
> Wagner, Richard, 1813–1883–Homes and haunts (May Subd Geog)
> Wagner, Richard, 1813–1883–In literature
> Wagner, Richard, 1813–1883–Indexes
> Wagner, Richard, 1813–1883–Influence

Wagner, Richard, 1813–1883–Language
Wagner, Richard, 1813–1883–Manuscripts
Wagner, Richard, 1813–1883–Manuscripts – Facsimiles
Wagner, Richard, 1813–1883–Museums
Wagner, Richard, 1813–1883–Parodies, imitations, etc.
Wagner, Richard, 1813–1883–Performances (May Subd Geog)
Wagner, Richard, 1813–1883–Performers
Wagner, Richard, 1813–1883–Pictorial works
Wagner, Richard, 1813–1883–Political and social views
Wagner, Richard, 1813–1883–Relics
Wagner, Richard, 1813–1883–Stories, plots, etc.
Wagner, Richard, 1813–1883–Symbolism
Wagner, Richard, 1813–1883–Thematic catalogs
Wagner, Richard, 1813–1883–Written works

There are several advantages to the subdivision structure of *Library of Congress Subject Headings*. They can identify particular kinds of information on a topic, but they also can make a topic narrower by adding layers of specificity to very broad topics. Try to observe and make use of the strings of subdivisions that allow catalogers to build very specific headings, for example:

Music–Italy–Venice–History and criticism–17th century

Women musicians–United States–History–20th century–Encyclopedias

10.2 Using *Library of Congress Subject Headings* in an Online Catalog

So far all of the *Library of Congress Subject Heading* examples in this chapter have been taken from the printed guide that we call *LCSH*. Use the printed source as a starting point to help focus your research topic and to determine which subject headings to use in your search of the online catalog. When you actually do the online search, you will not see the subject headings in exactly the same layout. The ones displayed for you will be subject headings actually used for these items in a specific library. Most computer systems for library catalogs will display cross-references from unauthorized to authorized headings ("see" references), but they may not display the broader, narrower, or related terms. Or, you may need to take one more step to see all of the related terms: in the example below, selecting "LC Authority Record" is the way to see them. Other catalogs employ different language to indicate this capability such as "See related subjects." You will need to discover the appropriate terminology in the catalog you use.

HINT: Taking the time to learn these "behind the scenes" features of your online catalog—subject-heading lists and their cross-referencing system—will lead you to more useful information.

An advantage of the online listing is that it displays all subdivisions in use. So while *LCSH* does not list every geographic subdivision for every heading, all of those used in a particular library are shown in that online catalog's listing. Here is an online catalog display for the subject heading, "women musicians." Remember that this display may look somewhat different depending on the specific library catalog you use. Compare it to the *LCSH* displays previously shown. The numbers on the left indicate the number of records associated with each subject heading. The underscored headings are active links to more information in the online catalog.

24 Women musicians–[LC Authority Record]
Public Note: Here are entered works on all aspects of the practice of music by women. Works on the portrayal of women in musical works are entered under the heading Women in music.
    Women musicians, African American–[LC Authority Record]
      See: African American women musicians
  2 Women musicians–Bibliography.
  6 Women musicians–Biography.
  1 Women musicians–Congresses.
  1 Women musicians–Drama.
  1 Women musicians–England.
  1 Women musicians–England–History–19th century.
  1 Women musicians–Europe, German-speaking–History–19th century.
  1 Women musicians–Fiction.
  1 Women musicians–History–20th century.
  1 Women musicians–Italy–Venice.
  1 Women musicians–Italy–Venice–Biography.
  2 Women musicians–Italy–Venice–History.
  1 Women musicians–Mediterranean Region.
  1 Women musicians–Nigeria.
  2 Women musicians–Periodicals.
  1 Women musicians–Poetry.
  1 Women musicians–Statistics.
  7 Women musicians–United States–[LC Authority Record]
  2 Women musicians–United States–Bibliography.
  1 Women musicians–United States–History–20th century–Encyclopedias.

Did you notice the active link, "LC Authority Record," in the subject-heading list above? Although its layout is different, it contains the same information as the print version of *LCSH*. Consult it when you need to see the scope note (general note) or to explore narrower or broader terms. If there are Library of Congress numbers associated with the subject heading, you will see them listed as call number notes. *LCSH* does not provide a call number note for the heading, "women musicians."

LC Authority Record for "women musicians:"
Heading   Women musicians
Broader term   Musicians

Narrower term	Women rock musicians
Narrower term	<u>Women flamenco musicians</u>
Narrower term	Women blues musicians
Narrower term	Women country musicians
Narrower term	Nuns as musicians
Narrower term	<u>Women composers</u>
Narrower term	<u>Women jazz musicians</u>
Narrower term	<u>Women singers</u>
Use for	Musicians, Women
Use for	Women as musicians
General note	Here are entered works on all aspects of the practice of music by women. Works on the portrayal of women in musical works are entered under the heading Women in music.

In an online catalog, the underlined subject headings are hyperlinks; selecting one of them brings up a display of records for items that have been assigned that subject heading. So a subject-heading search is a two-step process showing: (1) a browsable list of headings, and then (2) records for items with the specific subject heading after you choose it from the list.

If the heading is not underlined, it is not valid. Beneath it there is a cross-reference ("see" reference) to the valid heading.

Women musicians, African American–[<u>LC Authority Record</u>]
    See: <u>African American women musicians</u>

In many catalogs the result of a subject-heading search will be a list of subject headings in use in that specific catalog. You will be able to select narrower terms or related terms for further exploration. Or, you will choose the most appropriate heading to retrieve the bibliographic records that have that subject heading. Remember, the exact appearance and details of operation for online lists of LC subject headings will vary from one library system to another. In fact, a subject search in *WorldCat* results in a retrieval list of the records themselves rather than a list of subject headings.

HINT: The listing of LC subject headings in library catalogs is good place to observe those combinations of topics and subdivisions that identify specific meanings, as Musicians – Massachusetts – Boston – Interviews.

10.3 LC Subject Headings for Musical Compositions

It is helpful to get a sense of the way subject headings of the Library of Congress system work for musical compositions because there are some complications. With a little guidance, the system will make more sense.

First, you need to know that the most specific subject heading for a work is the one that should be used. If a composition for solo flute is a sonata, then its subject heading will be "Sonatas (flute)"; if it is a sonata for flute and piano, the heading will be "Sonatas (flute and piano)." Only if there is no musical form indicated by the title will the heading be "Flute music." You might assume that the subject heading "Flute music" would retrieve at least all solo flute music, but that is not the case at all. Several different types of headings exist.

1. Subject headings that begin with one or more instruments. "Flute and oboe music" is used for duets written for these two instruments; there are headings for "Flute and oboe with" a specified ensemble, etc.

    Flute and oboe d'amore with string orchestra [M1140–1141]
    Flute and oboe music [M288–289]
        UF Oboe and flute music
    Flute and oboe with chamber orchestra [M1040–1041]
    Flute and oboe with orchestra [M1040–1041]
    Flute and oboe with string orchestra [M1140–1141]
    Flute and organ music [M182–186]
        UF Organ and flute music
    Flute and percussion music [M298]
        UF Percussion and flute music
    Flute and percussion with string orchestra [M1140–1141]
    Flute and piano music (May Subd Geog) [M240–244]
        UF Piano and flute music
    Flute and piano with orchestra

2. Subject headings that begin with an ensemble and are qualified by the exact instrumentation in parentheses:

    Brass quartets
    String quartets (May Subd Geog) [M450–454] [Standard instrumentation]
    String quartets–Parts
    String quartets–Scores
    String quartets–Scores and parts
    String quartets, Arranged [M453–454] [Arranged for a different ensemble]
    String quartets (Violas (2), violoncellos (2)) [M450–451]
    String quartets (Violas (4)) [M450–451]
        UF Viola music (Violas (4))
    String quartets (Violin, viola, violoncello, double bass) [M450–451]
    String quartets (Violin, violas (2), violoncello) [M450–451]
        …
    String quartets with jazz ensemble
    String quintets
        …
    Wind quartets
        …
    Woodwind quartets

3. Subject headings that begin with the musical form or genre followed by the instrumentation in parentheses:

    Sonatas (Flute) [M60–64]
    Sonatas (Flute and continuo) (May Subd Geog)
    Sonatas (Flute and guitar) [M296–297]
    Sonatas (Flute and guitar), Arranged [M296–297]

Sonatas (Flute and harpsichord) [M241–242]
Sonatas (Flute and harpsichord), Arranged [M243–244]
Sonatas (Flute and organ) [M182–184]
Sonatas (Flute and organ), Arranged

Variations (Guitar)–[LC Authority Record]
Variations (Guitar)–20th century.
Variations (Guitar), Arranged.
Variations (Guitar with orchestra)
Variations (Guitars (2))

What seems like a small matter—the difference between singular and plural—can mean a lot in a list of subject headings. The singular form of a musical form or genre word refers to sources that discuss the form or genre itself while the plural of the word refers to music in that form or genre. Extracts from two scope notes in *LCSH* clarify this practice.

Sonata [ML1156 (History)] [MT62 (Composition)]
Here are entered general works on the musical form for solo instruments or chamber music combinations, usually in more than one movement and composed between the 17th century and the present....
     UF Sonata-History and criticism
Sonatas-History and criticism
Sonatina
     BT Musical form

Sonatas
Here are entered miscellaneous collections of compositions for one or two solo instruments. Individual sonatas and collections of sonatas for a specific medium of performance are entered under the heading followed by the medium....

This singular-plural difference in meaning applies to similar subject headings such as "String Quartet" and "String Quartets" or "Opera" and "Operas."

HINT: A musical-form subject heading has different meanings in its singular and plural forms. "Operas" retrieves specific compositions that are operas (the music) while "Opera" retrieves books written about the genre and about specific musical compositions in this genre.

10.4 When to Use Controlled-Vocabulary Searching

Each search method has its own advantages and disadvantages, thus making it appropriate for some research needs but not others. There are three major advantages of controlled-vocabulary searching that make it a very important method. (1) Subject headings or descriptors take away much of the guesswork related to synonyms, varying word order, and foreign-language terminology by grouping records according to a uniform subject heading and providing cross-references to that heading. (2) When the subject-heading system provides a structure for types of sources (bibliographies, dictionaries, chronologies, quotations), researchers may recognize materials that they may not have specified with their own search words. (3) For books and other library materials, the print version of *LCSH* also acts as an index to the numbers of the Library of Congress Classification system, thus referring researchers to specific areas of the physical collection for systematic browsing of source materials themselves.

Controlled vocabularies, standardized by editorial groups, are slow to change and may not contain fine enough gradations of meaning to be precisely on target for newer concepts or events. These disadvantages may be overcome by using other search methods. Keyword searching, in both online and print sources, may offer the opportunity for timely vocabulary, for greater precision by combining words in various ways, or for searching in the entire bibliographic record, abstract, or full text of a document. Keyword searching is the next method to be explored.

Review Questions

1. Name the controlled vocabulary used in most academic and research libraries.

2. Identify the meaning of these abbreviations: BT, NT, RT, and UF.

3. What are benefits of using the print version of the LC subject headings? And what are benefits of browsing the list of subject headings in an online catalog?

4. How can you use a list of subject headings to focus or narrow a research topic?

5. From the list below, circle the subject headings that retrieve scores or recordings:
    Flute music
    Flute music–17th century
    Flute music–18th century–Bibliography
    Flute music–20th century
    Flute music–Analysis, appreciation
    Flute music, Arranged
    Flute music–Bibliography
    Flute music–Early works to 1800
    Flute music–Excerpts

6. Match the meaning with its subject heading:
    a. Opera scores   ____ "Opera"
    b. Books about operas   ____ "Operas"

7. How does *LCSH* act as an index to books and scores in the library's physical collection? Why is this index function helpful to a researcher?

Learning Exercises

1. In the library, write down a potential research topic in sentence format, and then use the print version of *LCSH* to find possible subject headings.
    a. Write down a possible valid heading.

b.   Examine the BT, NT, and RT valid headings as well, and write down any that seem to be on target. Be sure to note the relationship to the original term, "BT," etc.

c.   Examine nearby headings that might be useful and write them down.

d.   Look up one of the RT headings and see what possibilities it offers. How does this process help you to narrow a topic or to select subject words that are likely to bring results? Which subject heading will be your first choice to use in a catalog search?

2.   At a computer, use the heading you identified in 1.a. above. Look it up in the online catalog using a subject-heading search. Then browse the list of subject headings displayed in the catalog.

a.   Write down two subject headings that have a main heading and a subdivision (topic, form, period, or geographic).

b.   Write down a subject heading that consists of multiple subdivisions, thus making it much more specific.

c.   Which "compound" subject heading will be your first choice for searching your local library catalog? A compound subject heading includes subdivisions.

Chapter 11

Subject Searching in Indexes and Abstracts

Preview

- A controlled-vocabulary list is useful in determining the best search words or phrases to use in subject field searches, to narrow or broaden your topic, or to investigate related terms that may lead to different aspects of a topic. In journal databases, the list may be called a thesaurus.
- Journal indexes and abstracts may use their own subject vocabulary, as is true for *ERIC* and *Music Index Online*, but some use the *Library of Congress Subject Headings.*
- Some databases offer broad subject categories as a way to limit a search to records in the category. These subject categories are controlled terms and are assigned by an indexer. Subject terms provide more specific subject searching.
- When a database provides a subject index to browse, it lists the subject terms used in the index; they may not be part of a controlled vocabulary or thesaurus.

Searching subject headings is also possible in bibliographic databases that index and abstract materials such as journal articles, essays in books, conference and symposia proceedings, and newspaper articles. Because various commercial firms produce these databases, they may use entirely different controlled vocabularies than that of the Library of Congress. Check the search screen of a new database to see if it offers controlled-vocabulary searching; likely labels are "descriptors," "subject headings," or "thesaurus."

If the only access to a list of subject words is through a "browse" feature, then what you see is a list of exact subject terms occurring in the database. These may not be part of a controlled vocabulary, but you can determine which words might be best to use in the database.

11.1 *Music Index Online* (Harmonie Park Press)

The Expert Search screen for *Music Index Online* provides subject field searching as one of five keyword fields and a Subject List menu choice at the top of the screen. The Help pages, under "Subject," give the simple instruction to "enter one or more words from the Subject List, a name, an organization, a group, etc. in this field." The Music Index Subject List is a controlled vocabulary in two parts: Subject List and Geographic List. One may browse alphabetically in either list to find appropriate subject words or phrases. All valid subject headings are in capital letters, and there are cross-references for "See also" terms (related valid terms) and "See" terms (referring you from invalid to valid headings).

See and See Also References

Concert halls. See AUDITORIUMS AND CONCERT HALLS

By consulting the valid heading, AUDITORIUMS AND CONCERT HALLS, you receive leads to other valid terms that are related:

AUDITORIUMS AND CONCERT HALLS. See also ARENA-TYPE PER-FORMANCES; ARENAS; BANDSTANDS; BROADCASTING STUDIOS; MUSIC TENTS; OPERA HOUSES; PERFORMING ARTS CENTERS; SHELLS; THEATERS

Terms as Main Headings and Subheadings

BIBLIOGRAPHIES. See also CATALOGS; INDEXES; TITLE PAGES; as sub-heading under various subjects
BIOGRAPHY. See also particular individuals; various types (categories) of per-formers, e.g. POPULAR MUSIC PERFORMERS

These form-of-information subheadings may be attached to various subject headings, for instance, to create the heading, "SERIAL MUSIC, BIBLIOGRAPHIES."

Adjacent Headings

BLUEGRASS BANDS
BLUEGRASS MUSIC
BLUEGRASS MUSIC AND FILMS
BLUEGRASS MUSIC AND PHOTOGRAPHY
BLUEGRASS MUSIC AND VIDEO TAPE. See also MUSIC VIDEOS
BLUEGRASS SONGS
. . .
WOMEN
WOMEN AND RADIO BROADCASTING
WOMEN IN INDUSTRY. See also STEREOTYPE
WOMEN IN MANAGEMENT
WOMEN IN MUSIC. See also STEREOTYPE

Examples from the Geographic List

Zaire. See CONGO, DEMOCRATIC REPUBLIC OF
ZAMBIA
Zanzibar. See TANZANIA
ZIMBABWE
Zululand. See SOUTH AFRICA

As a searcher, you may combine valid headings, but it is a good idea first to check the subject list to determine which are preferred. For instance, in a search for factors or people who influenced a composer, try the composer's name and the subject term, "influences," as keywords in the subject field: "copland influences." See Results 1 and 2.

These results indicate that *Music Index* staff assign numerous subject headings to each record and that retrieval can come from words in one heading or words from several headings. When listed in the record, the subject headings also indicate more about the contents of the article. In the second retrieval below, several specific compositions are listed because they are mentioned in the article. The abbreviations, "abst bibliog il musi notes," indicate that the article contains abstracts, bibliographies, illustrations, music [notation], and notes about the compositions.

Result 1:

TITLE   Aaron Copland's America: A Cultural Perspective.
PUBLICATION INFORMATION: (N.Y., Watson-Guptill, 2000)
AUTHOR(s):   G. Levin and J. Tick.
PERIODICAL: MUSIC RESEARCH FORUM
VOLUME: 17
DATE: 2002
LANGUAGE: English
PERIODICAL CLASSIFICATION: Musicology
PERIODICAL COUNTRY: United States
SUBJECTS:
     LEVIN, GAIL M. p.79-82
     TICK, JUDITH p.79-82
     ARTS **Influence** p.79-82
     COPLAND, AARON Exhibitions p.79-82
     COPLAND, AARON General Works p.79-82
     COPLAND, AARON **Influences** p.79-82

Result 2:

TITLE: Aaron Copland and the popular front.
AUTHOR(s):   E. B. Crist.
PERIODICAL: JOURNAL OF THE AMERICAN MUSICOLOGICAL SOCIETY
VOLUME: 56
DATE: Summer 2003
PAGE(s):   409-65
LANGUAGE: English

PERIODICAL CLASSIFICATION: Musicology
PERIODICAL COUNTRY: United States
SUBJECTS:

    CRIST, ELIZABETH BERGMAN p.409-65 abst bibliog il musi notes

    COMPOSERS **Influences** p.409-65 abst bibliog il musi notes

    COPLAND, AARON p.409-65 abst bibliog il musi notes

    COPLAND, AARON General Works p.409-65 abst bibliog il musi notes

    COPLAND, AARON Works [El Salón México] p.409-65 abst bibliog il musi notes

    COPLAND, AARON Works [Fanfare for the common man] p.409-65 abst bibliog il musi notes

    COPLAND, AARON Works [Symphony No. 3] p.409-65 abst bibliog il musi notes

11.2 *International Index to Music Periodicals* (*IIMP*) or *IIMP Full Text*

May be accessed under *Music and Performing Arts Online*
(ProQuest Information and Learning Company)

Besides the Quick Search, available on every page, the primary screen for searching articles is what we would call an advanced search. There you may do a keyword search or you may enter search terms (a phrase) in specific fields, each with the opportunity to "select from a list." Therefore, while *IIMP* does not provide a controlled vocabulary with cross-references among related terms, it does show exactly which terms are used in the database in the various fields.

Two of the fields, available when searching from 1996 on, relate to subjects: "Broad Subjects, e.g. jazz" and "Narrow Subjects, e.g. jazz musicians." The list of broad subjects is a controlled vocabulary, which provides a small number of subjects that serve as a limiting feature. If you choose one of these categories, then you will be searching only those records in the category instead of all records in the database. And remember, once you choose a broad subject, you no longer need to include those words in your search statement.

IIMP **Broad Subjects (examples from the list)**

Blues Music
Chamber Music
Country and Western Music
Dance (with many subdivisions)
Ethnic Music: Africa /Middle East
Ethnic Music: Asia
Ethnic Music: Australia /New Zealand /Oceania
Ethnic Music: Central America /Caribbean
Ethnic Music: Europe
Ethnic Music: General

Ethnic Music: North America (except Mexico)
Ethnic Music: South America
Film
Folk Music
Jazz
Musical Notation
Musical Performance
Musical Sound Sources
Musical Theater
Music and Other Disciplines
Music and Other Literary /Performing /Visual Arts
Music Business
Music Education
Music History
Music in Ritual
Music Reference
Opera
Orchestral Music
Popular Music
Popular Music: Latin Music
Rock Music
Solo Instrument Music
Sound Recording. Processing Systems
Television
Theater
Theory /Analysis /Composition
Vocal Music

IIMP Narrow Subjects

Narrow subjects, by contrast, exist in the thousands. When you "select from a list" of subject terms, *IIMP* provides an option to "Search Subject Terms" that you will want to use. Here is an illustration to see the value of looking up subject terms to determine which words to use in your search. Because a search for "Chopin" returns a list of all names and phrases starting with the composer's name, you may recognize an appropriate specific subject to use. You may choose one or several headings from the list.

Chopin Competition (Warsaw, Poland)
Chopin Competition (Warsaw, Poland: 2000)
Chopin Congress (2nd: Warsaw, Poland: 1999)
Chopin Festival (55th: Duszniki Zdroj, Poland: 2000)
Chopin Festival (55th: Duszniki Zdroj, Poland: 2001)
Chopin in the Colors of Autumn Festival (21st: Antonin, P...
Chopin in the Colours of Autumn International Festi...
Chopin Piano Competition (Warsaw, Poland)
Chopin Society (Czech Republic)
Chopin, Frederic Francois ...

In summary, then, *IIMP* uses broad subject categories to limit an overall search as well as subject terms exactly as they occur in the database. The "select from a list" function allows you to browse in the list of subjects (or other fields) to choose very specific headings and to spell them exactly as they are in the source. These subject terms are not exactly a controlled vocabulary, but the option to browse them and select exact words from the database is still beneficial.

11.3 *RILM Abstracts of Music Literature*

(produced by RILM Abstracts; available from various vendors)

The search interface for *RILM Abstracts* varies greatly because multiple database vendors provide the *RILM* data to libraries. A few vendors provide access to the *RILM Thesaurus*, which like *LCSH* provides its list of authorized subject terms with cross-references. Some libraries also provide a print version of the *RILM Thesaurus*.[1] Some online vendors provide indexes similar to *IIMP*'s "select from a list" approach. For example, by choosing "Subject Headings" from the top of the screen in the EBSCOhost version, one may enter a subject such as "Bernstein" and then browse in the alphabetical list of subjects starting with this name. The results show many specific subdivisions suitable for various aspects of research on the American composer and conductor Leonard Bernstein.

RILM Subject Terms

    Bernstein, Leonard – aesthetics
    Bernstein, Leonard – catalogues
    Bernstein, Leonard – correspondence
    Bernstein, Leonard – discographies
    Bernstein, Leonard – interviews
    Bernstein, Leonard – life
    Bernstein, Leonard – manuscripts
    Bernstein, Leonard – obituaries
    Bernstein, Leonard – performances
    Bernstein, Leonard – periodicals
    Bernstein, Leonard – reception
    Bernstein, Leonard – sound recordings
    Bernstein, Leonard – style
    Bernstein, Leonard – tributes
    Bernstein, Leonard – works
    Bernstein, Leonard – writings

RILM Classification Scheme

RILM Abstracts also addresses the need to limit a search to a large subcategory of music by providing a list of major topics according to their Classification Scheme, which was revised in 2007. Like the subject categories used by *IIMP*, these classifications may be used to limit a search to records associated with a specific classification topic.

01–12	Reference & research materials
14–17	Collected writings
19	Universal perspectives
20–29	Historical musicology (Western music)
30–39	Ethnomusicology
40–48	Sound sources (Instrument families)
50–58	Performance practice & notation
60–69	Theory, analysis, & composition
70–74	Pedagogy
75–79	Music & other arts
80–89	Music & related disciplines
90–99	Music in liturgy & ritual

Review Questions

1. In the indexes *IIMP* and *RILM Abstracts*, what is the difference between (1) a subject category/classification and (2) a subject term?

2. Do journal indexes use *Library of Congress Subject Headings*?

Learning Exercise

1. Write down a potential research topic in sentence format, then try subject searching in one of the major music journal/current literature indexes.
   a. Identify which journal index you are using.
   b. Explain how to find a subject heading or exact words from the subject field in this database.
   c. If subject categories or classifications are available, identify one or more suitable to your research.
   d. List some appropriate subject headings/descriptors or the exact terms used in the subject field. Note: If there is a thesaurus or subject list available, consult it to determine the best subject search terms to use.

Note

1. International Repertory of Music Literature (Organization), *RILM Abstracts of Music Literature: English-Language Thesaurus for Volumes 21–* (1987–), (New York: RILM Abstracts, 1992).

Chapter 12

Keyword Searching

Preview

- Keyword searching is a method for combining terms that represent each concept in your research topic. Unique or unambiguous words are useful; very common words such as "music" or "united" are not. Words applicable to music may also be used in other disciplines, e.g., "instruments" may be medical or statistical or musical. Forgetting about such cross-meanings may lead to "false hits" —retrieval that is technically correct but unrelated to the concept sought.
- Boolean searching allows a researcher to combine keywords in specific ways so that a search can retrieve the most appropriate results. The Boolean connector AND combines terms for different concepts and narrows the search; all terms must exist in the record. OR searches for several synonymous terms at once; it broadens the search because only one term must exist to retrieve the record. NOT excludes records having a term; therefore, it narrows a search. Think carefully before using NOT so you don't exclude records that you actually want.
- Adjacency/proximity operators are used to specify how close together search terms might occur in a record.
- Truncation symbols provide a shortcut to word variation by retrieving words with different beginnings, endings, or internal spelling.
- An advanced search screen puts the searcher in control. It provides Boolean operators to connect search terms in separate fields, limiting options, and sometimes phrase searching.
- Integrated access through a system of metasearching or cross-database searching is efficient, if available. However, the metasearch software may reduce the search capabilities in each database.

12.1 What Is Keyword Searching?

Keyword searching is a technique that is probably very familiar to you; it is the way most people "Google a topic," that is, search the Internet. Keyword searching may be done in most databases whether they are online library catalogs, journal article indexes, or Internet search engines. In a keyword search, you select and input the most significant and unambiguous words related to your topic. The search engine retrieves a record when the specified words occur anywhere—in any searchable field—in the record.

Search terms entered in a search box labeled only "keyword" will search all of the fields of a record; it might result in a search of more than the citation, searching an abstract, full text of the source, or a website if the Internet. Some systems use the label "comprehensive keyword" or "general keyword" to distinguish keyword searching of all fields from the use of keywords in specific fields such as "author keyword" or "subject keyword." In any type of keyword search, the order of words is not important so you may enter them as search terms in any order.

This search method provides flexibility that is missing in controlled-vocabulary searching or in a heading search of specific fields of a record. It is especially effective for:

- Combining concepts that are not likely to be covered by subject headings or descriptors such as newer concepts not yet covered by the controlled vocabulary
- Combining search words that occur in different fields such as author and title
- Limiting a search to specific formats or time periods. Frequently, limiting features are available only in combination with keyword searching.
- Searching when you do not know the author or title, order of words in the title or subject heading, or correct spelling of some part of your phrase

Generally, searching a single keyword is insufficient. It is likely to retrieve far too many items, and many of them will be unrelated to the concepts or materials you seek. These unrelated materials are called "false hits." For instance, in a large and general database, the word "instruments" may occur for medical instruments, scientific instruments, or musical instruments. Most of the time, it is better to use several keywords in combination to retrieve items matching the main ideas or concepts in your search topic. You may combine keywords that you expect to occur in a single field of information (from the title or from the subject), from several fields of information (from the author and title or author and subject), or just use a combination of words related to your topic no matter where they might occur. To combine keywords effectively in a single search, it is necessary to understand several logical structures: Boolean operators, adjacency operators, nesting, and truncation.

Advantages and Disadvantages of Keyword Searching

Keyword searching is particularly effective if concepts are to be combined in an unusual way, that is, if standardized subject headings do not exist for the precise information you need. It is also useful when abstracts or full-text documents are searchable in the database. When there is more information than the standard bibliographic record, there are more chances to find unusual word combinations. And then there is the fact that many databases offer only keyword searching so you need to know how to do it well.

Disadvantages of keyword searching are probably clear by now. Researchers must analyze concepts carefully to determine the various words and word order that writers may have used to describe concepts. Careful planning of the search statement or query is vital to successful keyword searching. If results of a query are too large, consider ways to refine the search—where the words are searched, what limits may be placed, and which words are causing the best retrieval. Keyword searches may need several refinements to bring the best results.

12.2 Boolean Searching

George Boole, an English mathematician of the 19th century, developed Boolean algebra, sometimes called Boolean logic, which includes the logic and symbols for combining sets. *Boolean operators*—they may be called Boolean logical operators, logical operators, connectors, or even conjunctive operators—are the basic tools for most information retrieval systems in use today. The words AND, OR, and NOT are the Boolean operators; use them to connect words representing the main concepts of your research topic.

Why do we need Boolean operators? In most computerized databases each word is indexed as a separate item, and the search system retrieves only the words you request in your search statement. We need these special words or operators to extract database records that contain more than one idea, to account for the use of synonyms in titles and abstracts, or to eliminate records containing unwanted words. The Boolean operators are essential to the keyword search process. They are the means to construct a search query or search statement. Let's see how they work.

Boolean Operators Illustrated with Venn Diagrams

Venn diagrams are pictorial representations of the effect of Boolean operators. Each diagram below shows what will be retrieved (colored gray) using the different operators.

AND Operator using "computer and music"

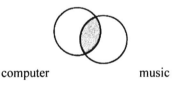

computer   music

When you combine search words with the AND operator, the computer retrieves only those records that contain both words. The shaded area, where the sets overlap, shows that the effect of AND is to narrow a search, reducing the number of references retrieved. Note that AND has the logical meaning that "all of these words" must be present in the record. Use AND to combine different concepts in your search topic.

OR Operator using "Klavier or piano"

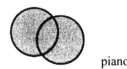

Klavier   piano

The OR operator retrieves all records containing "Klavier," plus all records containing "piano," plus all records that might contain both "Klavier" and "piano." The OR operator helps find similar concepts that may be expressed by a variety of words or synonyms. Use OR to group synonymous terms when at least one of them must be present. Note that OR increases the number of references retrieved because its meaning is that "any of these words" must be present in the record.

NOT Operator using "musical not Broadway"

Broadway   musical

In this example, "musical" must be present, but "Broadway" must be absent for retrieval of a record to occur. Therefore, the shaded area excludes all of the circle representing "Broadway," including the overlap area where records contain both words. The NOT operator eliminates records containing unwanted words. Use NOT to narrow a search, especially where one aspect of a concept is desired while another aspect is unwanted. There is a risk of eliminating useful citations when using NOT, however, so it is a good idea to examine a set of records before using NOT to eliminate some of them. Some databases use AND NOT as the operator.

12.3 Refining a Boolean Search

Nesting: The Use of Parentheses

You may improve your search results sometimes by using parentheses to indicate which words to search first. For example, to retrieve information on the use of computers in teaching rhythm skills, you might have several groups of synonyms to combine with other concepts:

Concept 1: computer and aided or mediated or assisted or based
Concept 2: instruction or learning or training
Concept 3: rhythm

You can do it in one statement if you put the synonyms inside parentheses. The words in parentheses will be searched first, and then those results will be combined with the other terms in the search statement.

computer and (aided or mediated or assisted or based) and (instruction or learning or training) and rhythm

This practice is called nesting. Just nest the synonyms together using parentheses. If such a long search statement seems difficult, many databases let you put together your search in parts with each part posting as a numbered set or line:

1 computer
2 aided or mediated or assisted or based
3 instruction or learning or training
4 rhythm

Then, to arrive at a final search statement, combine the sets: 1 and 2 and 3 and 4. Look for a search history option in a database to see your search statements and retrieval sets.

Proximity and Adjacency Operators

Proximity operators work on the principle that the closer together in a record the terms are, the more likely the retrieval will match the intentions of the searcher. Actually, proximity operators are just specific variants of the Boolean AND operator. As with the AND operator, both terms must be present in the record. Now by using a proximity operator in place of AND, you can specify how close together the terms must be. The most common proximity operators include:

WITH or ADJ retrieves words in same order, side-by-side
NEAR retrieves words in any order, side-by-side
NEAR(#) such as NEAR3 retrieves words in any order within the number specified

In some databases it is possible to specify that the words be in the same sentence, paragraph, field, or descriptor. Proximity operators are important tools for successful retrieval as databases get larger and the records they contain get longer. Using them can help to reduce the number of false hits in a search. Here are some examples of situations where a proximity operator can really help.

1. For compound words. Some expressions may be written either as hyphenated words or as one compound word. Take care of the two options in one statement:
"ground **w** water or groundwater" where the "w" stands for "with"

2. For hyphenated words:
"computer **adj** aided **adj** instruction or CAI"

3. For natural phrases such as place names:
"san **adj** marino"

4. Sometimes the order of the terms is not so important, but it is likely that the closer they are, the more they will match the meaning you intend.
"piano **near** pedagogy" could retrieve the phrase "piano pedagogy" but not "pedagogy of the piano"
"piano **near5** pedagogy" retrieves both terms, in any order, within 5 words as in "modern pedagogy for piano and organ."

Also remember that if a database offers phrase searching, you can choose the phrase search and forget about proximity operators. If you must do a keyword search, for instance in searching an abstract or some other field that doesn't allow phrase searching, you will need these proximity operators to get good, refined results.

Truncation

Truncation is the use of a special character to substitute for one or more characters in a word. These symbols provide a shortcut when variations of a term will all be acceptable. The truncation symbol may vary from one database to another. Frequently an asterisk (*) or question mark (?) is the truncation symbol. Today many databases allow truncation at the beginning of words for prefixes, truncation within words for variant spellings, and truncation at the end of words for various suffixes. This short-cut system may also be called stemming or wildcard. Truncation can bring a long list of records so beware lest you retrieve much more than you expect. Use truncation to solve these kinds of problems:

1. Retrieve both singular and plural forms of the term in one search:
    "conductor *" retrieves "conductor" or "conductors" [right truncation]
    "wom*n" retrieves "woman" or "women" [internal truncation]
    "col*r" retrieves "colour" and "color" [internal truncation]

2. Retrieve many terms having the same stem:
    "music*" retrieves "musician" or "musicians" or "musical" or "musicality" or "musicianship" [right truncation]

3. Retrieve terms having a different prefix: "*ology" retrieves "ethnomusicology" or "musicology" [left truncation]

Whether you wish to use proximity operators or a truncation symbol, you will need to consult online help in each database to determine the specific operators or symbols to use. They do vary significantly so it will help to consult the chart on the next page.

Figure 12.1 Special Operators and Symbols in Music Databases

IIMP	*Music Index*	*RILM Abstracts* EBSCOhost version	*RILM Abstracts* FirstSearch version
Adjacency—Searches words in specific order; may specify number of words			
Followed by or fby	adj	W (within) W3	W W3 (between num ber of words)
Proximity—Searches words in any order; may specify number of words			
near near3	near near3	N (near) N3	N N3
Truncation or Wildcard			
*	? – single character $ – any number of characters	* – right truncation ? – left truncation	* – multiple letters # – single character ?3 – number of letters to replace
Plural automatic	none	none	+ for plurals (–s or –es) – for plural words that change spelling
Phrase "phrase"	"phrase"	"phrase"	"phrase"

12.4 The Advanced Boolean Keyword Search

A keyword search statement using Boolean operators, truncation, or proximity operators may be entered in the text box of a basic search screen in a catalog or other database. However, for a researcher, it may be better to use an advanced search screen to handle the various concepts of the search statement. The advanced search mechanism may be called advanced search, guided keyword search, grid search, advanced Boolean combination search, or possibly an expert search. The search screen just looks like an online form. This search screen allows you to enter keywords for specific fields or anywhere in a record and to combine these field searches using the Boolean operator AND,

OR, and NOT. If any limiting features are available in a database—by language, format, year, or library location—they will show up on the advanced search screen.

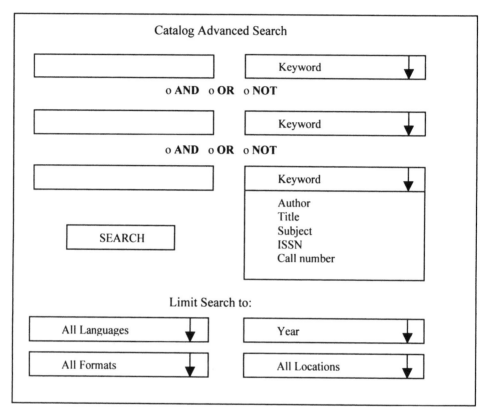

Keyword searching in the *International Index to Music Periodicals, Music Index Online,* and *RILM Abstracts* is similar to the catalog example above. The terminology may differ slightly. Some database creators assume that most searches will be by keyword and may not even label the search boxes for the way to search. Again, between keyword fields if there is no choice of Boolean operators (AND, OR, NOT), the default will be AND. Limiting options may be identified as search options or may be unlabeled entirely. Some limits that are special to journal indexes include the option to search a specific journal, the type of journal or country of publication, a part of the record (citation, abstract, full text), or the type of document, such as reviews, articles, obituaries, or even peer-reviewed articles only.

In library catalogs, journal indexes, or other research databases, it may be possible to enter a phrase to be searched in a field. Sometimes quotation marks around the words will signal treating it as a phrase: "piano pedagogy." At other times, there is an onscreen choice to make such as "Are the words adjacent?" A number of journal indexes offer a "browse the index" feature where you may search an alphabetical list of the field contents. When you see the phrase or phrases you want to use, selecting them puts them into the field search box as an exact phrase. The point is that an advanced search screen may permit phrase or adjacency searching along with keyword searching. Check each database to see how or if it is done.

HINT for effective and efficient use of databases: When given a choice, use an advanced search screen in any database to put yourself in control of your search.

12.5 Integrated Access: The Metasearch

Metasearches are becoming more common as libraries and database producers seek to provide a single point of access to a variety of information sources. These search options use special software to search multiple databases at one time, and have a variety of names: integrated, federated, parallel, simultaneous, broadcast, or cross-database searching. The information sources (databases) covered may be a choice of library catalogs or several indexes of journals or other current literature. Metasearching is also possible with Internet search engines. The following screen shot illustrates a metasearch of two databases at one time.

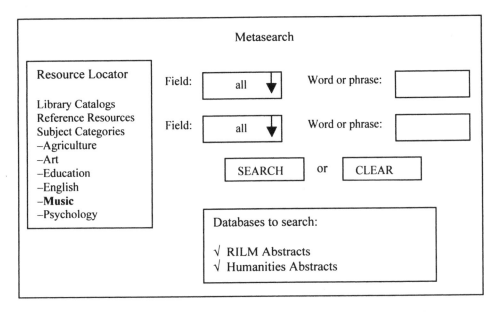

While the name of such a search may vary, the idea is consistent: to increase the efficiency of searching databases by offering one search screen, a choice of databases to search simultaneously, and to provide results which are identified as to source—which catalog, index, or database. The one-stop, totally integrated search is not yet a reality, but it is a goal. At present, where libraries offer integrated searching there may be a maximum number of databases to search simultaneously, or it may be necessary to search specific resources categories: library catalogs, journal indexes, or sound databases, one category at a time. Watch for improvements year by year, but give integrated searching a try when it is available to you.

Results for an integrated search may display in a single list including designations for the source of the information or in separate lists from each source. Sometimes the user may make the choice of how the results are to be displayed. At this time, integrated searching is fairly new. As more and more database producers enable integrated searching of their databases, cross-database searching will increase. There is a limitation to metasearching, however. The search capabilities are limited to the least common denominator among the databases chosen for a combined search. That is, special searching features will be lost if the other databases do not provide the same features. So there may be a gain in efficiency but a loss of refined searching.

12.6 Plan and Implement a Database Search

While improvisation is a wonderful skill for musicians, it is not the best skill for researchers. Successful research results and research reports are more likely to be associated with working methods described as planned, organized, detailed, and iterative. Planning for the kinds of materials needed, where to search for them, how to keep track of and document them—all of these efforts will pay off by saving you time, energy, and frustration. Here is a guide that lays out a series of steps to assemble information resources for your project.

Identify and Select Resources to Search

First, it is important to decide what kinds of information you need. For example, do you need a firsthand account of the premiere of a composition, library books, scores, or recordings? Do you want to read periodical articles, dissertations, or essays in an anthology? The kind of information you need determines what kind of database to use: a newspaper index, library catalog, journal article index, etc.

Where do you search? Next, consider which specific database to search among the many that are available in your library. Libraries must pay for access to databases so the list will vary from library to library. Identify databases appropriate to your subject, but also look for interdisciplinary databases that might include the topic. A music topic might relate to education, literature, psychology, religion, sociology, art, dance, theater, or other subjects.

To determine likely databases, you must know (or find out) the scope and coverage of the database. Does it cover journals in music only or in related disciplines such as the humanities? Does it include chapters in books and dissertations and conference proceedings? Does it include the years of publications you need? And what retrieval results does it provide: citations, citations plus abstracts, or full text? You will probably develop a list of suitable databases and repeat your search in each of them. Some libraries now offer a way to search several databases or several library catalogs at once. These integrated or cross-database search systems were explained briefly in Chapter 9. Are such metasearches available to you for library catalogs, reference resources, or subject databases?

Plan the Search Statement or Query

Finally, formalize your search topic, create a search statement, and determine exactly how to enter that search statement in the database(s) you will use.

1. Write the search topic in phrase form.
2. List the main ideas or concepts.
3. List synonyms, spelling variations, or plurals.
4. Decide on the relationship among the terms: choose Boolean and proximity operators for keyword searching.
5. Formulate a logical search statement.

Then choose the database(s) most relevant to your topic. Verify which operators and symbols each requires. The Database Search Planning Form, on the next page, provides organized guidance for stepping through the search-planning process.

Implement the Information Search in Specific Resources

Now that you are ready to search, log onto your chosen database to implement it. Repeat the following steps in each appropriate database, whether it is a library catalog, research database, journal article index, or the Internet.

1. Plan for input in the specific database.
    a. Records may include the citation (identification and publication information), citation plus an abstract, or full text of the document. Depending on how much information is available, you may need to decide which part to search.
    b. Which search methods work best in this database for this topic? Explore the search interface to determine whether controlled-vocabulary searching is possible. If so, search the thesaurus or browse the subject terms to choose which you will use. Will you use general keyword searching or field searching by keyword or by exact heading?
    c. Check the specific requirements for Boolean and proximity operators, punctuation, truncation symbols, use of exact phrases, etc.
    d. Decide what restrictions or limits to apply such as dates, publication types, or peer-reviewed journals.
    e. Enter your search statement. While you have prepared a comprehensive search query, frequently it is better to start with a simple search and then modify it depending on the results. If this resource allows combinations of results sets, you can enter parts of your search statement, concept by concept, and then combine them. Check for "search history" as the key to such input.

Database Search Planning Form

NOTE: Combine synonyms for a concept with OR. Combine concepts with AND.
Write your Research Topic in a full sentence:

Identify the different concepts in this topic:

Concept 1: connect synonyms with OR	Concept 2: connect synonyms with OR	Concept 3: connect synonyms with OR
	AND	AND

Write a complete search statement. Use appropriate Boolean operators, proximity operators, truncation symbols, and parentheses for nesting.
Example: *computer* and (teaching or instruction) and (music and theory)*

Identify helpful restrictions or limits:

2. Examine your results.
    a.   Evaluate the retrieval. There are many factors to consider. Is the retrieval too large or too small? Are there lots of false hits, where the items retrieved have a different meaning than you intended? Are there many reviews when you wanted articles? Check your results to determine whether you need to improve your search terms, search strategy (where and how you use the terms), or add limits to your search.
    b.   Revise your search as needed. Remember, the more search terms you use, the fewer results you will get. Frequently it is better to start with a simple

search, examine the results, and then add more search terms or limitations to refine your results.

3. Manage the output.
   a. Mark the records that look promising, and print or e-mail them for the next step of acquiring the physical items in your library or through an interlibrary loan request. Remember obtaining each citation in electronic form will help the documentation process for footnotes and bibliographies for your final research product.
   b. If you use bibliographic management software (EndNote, ProCite, etc.), be prepared to use it to handle your working bibliography.
   c. If full text is available, view the text and read it or e-mail it to yourself.

Obtain and Use the Resulting Information Sources

Not all valuable sources will be available in full text online, but through the combination of discovering citations and then placing interlibrary loan requests you can obtain the materials. Libraries want to help both local and remote users by lending materials to them; the cooperative service to lend and borrow materials between libraries is called interlibrary loan. Today, many articles and other text-based resources are scanned and delivered to your computer. Look for an online interlibrary loan request form; complete and submit the form, and library staff will notify you when the material has arrived for your use.

Review Questions

Boolean Operators

1. Keyword searching allows you to search for the occurrence of your search terms anywhere in a database record. It may be called "keyword," "general keyword," or "comprehensive keyword" searching. List two reasons for choosing to do a keyword search.

2. Of course, keywords from an author's name, title, or subject heading may be used in a single field as well. In a field search, you may enter either keywords or a heading. Compare a keyword search with a heading search within a specific field. Consider word order and which words to choose.

3. Identify the three Boolean operators used to combine keywords when searching databases. Why use each? Does it narrow or broaden a search?

Nesting, Adjacency, Truncation

4. List and explain the use of two adjacency/proximity operators. Would you use them instead of AND or instead of OR? What is a key difference between an adjacency term and a proximity term?

5. What are three different ways to use a truncation symbol to retrieve several forms of a word?

6. How might you determine which operators or truncation symbols to use in a specific database?

Plan and Implement a Database Search

7. Distinguish between discovery sources and information sources.

8. Explain the diagram below.

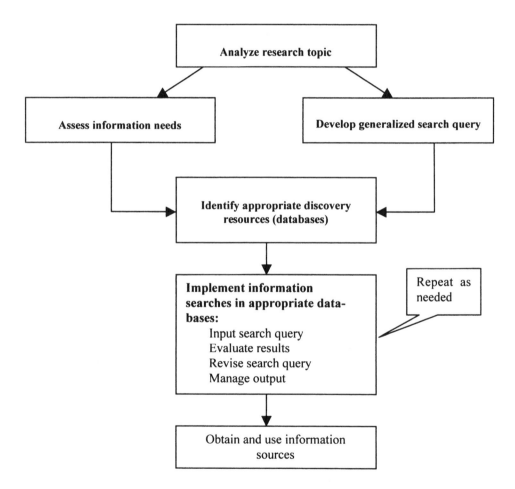

Learning Exercises

1. Write your research topic in a sentence, then make a list of each concept in the topic. Which Boolean operator will you use to combine each of the different topics?

2. Now that you have a list of concepts to search, spend a few minutes considering the various words that authors might use for each concept. Write a list of synonyms for each concept. Which Boolean operator will you use to combine synonyms for a single concept? What other grouping mechanism might you use to let the computer know that all of these words need to be searched in one operation?

3. If you need to search for a phrase for one of your topics, how can you combine the words using Boolean operators? How can you combine them using an adjacency operator? How can you combine them using a proximity operator?

4. What are some advantages of using keyword searching instead of controlled-vocabulary searching? What are advantages of controlled-vocabulary searching?

5. Make a photocopy of the Database Search Planning Form on page 150. Then complete the form based on your research topic. Remember that at this stage of creating a comprehensive search statement, you need to put a Boolean or proximity operator between each search term.

   a. Check your library's list of databases to determine potential resources relevant to your research topic. Use the back of the search form to list the databases that you wish to search.
      • Library catalogs (local, specific libraries, a union catalog such as *WorldCat*)
      • Music journal indexes
      • Other discipline or cross-discipline journal indexes
      • Other databases
   b. For one potential database on your list, determine which operators and symbols are required, and add that information to your Database Search Planning Form.

Chapter 13

Related-Record Searching
and Citation Indexes

Preview

- Related-record searching in its most general form means using subject headings or descriptors in the record of an on-target book or article to find others like it. Selecting active links in a bibliographic record takes you to related materials. Subject headings are best, but you may want to find more works by the same author as well.
- Related-record searching in citation indexes identifies articles that share some of the same footnotes; that is, they cite some of the same works. Therefore, there could be a relationship of interest among the various articles.
- Citation searching is a powerful method of determining which are the major authors for an issue or for narrowing a topic. Citation searching is helpful in preparing a literature review.

13.1 Related-Record Searching

If you have found one excellent source to match and support your research topic, you have an important lead. A shortcut for finding others like it is the related-record search. If your source is a book, and you have it in hand, search for its record in an online catalog. By examining the full record for the item, you can see which subject headings have been assigned to the book. Then select the subject headings in turn if they are active links, and you will retrieve records for other books or materials having the same subject heading. The journey from the known item, through its subject links, to other items is one type of related-record searching. This method is a very efficient way to find on-target sources. If the subject headings listed are not active links, just return to the search screen and enter (use copy and paste for improved accuracy) the subject heading in the subject-heading search area. Another application of this search method is possible in journal indexes. Find one suitable article, check its descriptors or subject headings, and use them to find other articles on the same specific topic or subtopic. Most of the time the article descriptors are not active links, thus requiring you to manually input a new subject search to find the related records.

HINT for related-record searching: Use a known source to find others like it. Search for the known source in a database, and then check its bibliographic record for subject headings. Use those subject headings to find similar materials.

As you examine the footnotes in a suitable book or article, you will learn which sources the author used as a basis for her work. Finding and examining these cited works allows a researcher to trace ideas back as they developed in the research conversation or to find seminal articles in the discipline. In fact, there are special databases called citation indexes, which specialize in tracking citations both forward and back.

13.2 Citation Indexes

The Institute for Scientific Information (ISI) produces three databases, known collectively as the *Web of Science*,[1] that provide keyword searching plus citation searching for journal articles:

Science Citation Index (SCI), 1970–
Social Sciences Citation Index (SSCI), 1970–
Arts & Humanities Citation Index (A&HCI), 1975–

Any of these indexes could be useful for various investigations in the subareas of music research, for instance, research on vocal cords or music therapy in *SCI*, music teaching or psychology and testing in *SSCI*, or just about any aspect of music in *A&HCI*. As with other journal indexes, one may use the general search in these citation indexes to identify journals having keywords for the topic in their titles or subject headings.

But there is an entirely new aspect to citation indexes: they also include the bibliography (or footnotes) for each indexed article. So if you start with a known item—book, conference paper, or journal article—and then do a cited reference search, the retrieval will be a list of journal articles that cite the original source in a footnote. Other authors writing on this topic have found something of value in the works they cite. These later works are likely to have some relationship, and perhaps a strong relationship, to the relevant known item where you started. Sometimes the research dialogue becomes quite evident as various scholars refute, expand, or comment on the work of other scholars. Citation searching helps the researcher to track the thread of discussion as it goes forward in time: who has cited this source? If necessary, it is possible to track cycles of citations, the first set that cited an original source, then articles that cited this set, and so on. Please note that *A&HCI* goes even deeper in its indexing. Its citation index will retrieve a person, composition, poem, or other work if mentioned in the text of an article, not just in a footnote.

HINT for a review of the literature: Citation searching is a powerful method of determining the major authors for an issue or to narrow a topic. Use it in preparing a literature review.

Citation searching is particularly useful for cross-disciplinary topics, to identify frequently cited works that might be seminal to a research problem, and to track the influence of particular scholars. For example, in the combined ISI citation databases, called *Web of Science*, a general search for "ravel and bolero" retrieves this article in the *European Journal of Neurology* published in January 2002: "Maurice Ravel and Right-hemisphere Musical Creativity: Influence of Disease on His Last Musical Works?" by Amaducci, Grassi, and Boller. For the researcher studying a topic on music and the brain, having retrieved this article, it is now possible to check:

> *Cited references* for previous research (the footnoted sources in the Amaducci article),
>
> *Times cited* for subsequent research (articles citing the Amaducci article), or
>
> *Related records* (articles sharing footnotes with the Amaducci article).

Citation Index Example, part 1

A sample search, as it might occur in *Arts & Humanities Citation Index*, will show how a citation database offers more than regular journal databases. Rick's topic is vague at this point: an investigation of shape-note hymnals. He wants to identify some articles or other resources and determine some of the authors who have written on this topic. Rick understands that finding some relevant authors who are cited by others indicates that some value has been placed on their work. Rick tries "General Search" using the term "shape-note" in the topic field. His other choice is "Cited Reference Search," but he doesn't know an author or title on this topic so he can't use this one. The results are 11 records including:

Sutton, B. "Shape-Note Tune Books and Primitive Hymns." *Ethnomusicology* 26, no. 1: (1982), 11-26.

The full record for this article includes information and links not normally present in a journal index:

Cited References   18
Times Cited   2
Find Related Records

Rick selects "Cited References" to see all 18 of the sources that Sutton cited, or footnoted, in his article. Because he may want to find and read some of these books or articles later, he selects and saves the most promising ones. All of these documents were written prior to Sutton's article and were important to his discussion in some way. The cited-references results include:

Cited Author	Cited Title	Year	Vol	Page
HORN D	SING TO ME OF HEAVEN	1970		
JACKSON GP	ANOTHER SHEAF WHITE	1952		
TALLMADGE WYB	INTERAMERICAN MUS	1975	2	106

When he selects "Times Cited," the system displays two articles that cite Sutton's article. Obviously these articles were written after that of Sutton so "Times Cited" provides access to related subsequent literature.

1. Gross, S., Berg, W., "Singing It 'Our Way': Pennsylvania-German Mennonite Notenbuchlein (1780-1835)," *American Music* 19, no. 2: (2001): 190-209.
   Times Cited: 0

2. Titon, J. T., "Stance, Role, and Identity in Fieldwork among Folk Baptists and Pentecostals," *American Music* 3, no. 1 (1985): 16-24.
   Times Cited: 5

13.3 Related-Record Searches in Citation Indexes

The phrase "related-record searching" has a specific meaning in citation indexes. It retrieves articles that share some of the same footnotes; that is, they cite some of the same works. The assumption is that these articles will have a subject relationship even though their titles and abstracts may not share the same keywords. Such a search is more efficient than keyword searching because it takes away the guesswork of which terms might be in titles. It may be easier than a controlled-vocabulary search because you do not need to determine an exact subject heading or descriptor.

Citation Index Example, part 2

In Rick's search for "shape-note" materials, above, he could choose to go one step further by following the link to "Find Related Records." The results list consists of records for sources that have some citations (footnotes) in common with the original record he chose. Articles with shared citations occur in the same year as or after the original work.

Related Records
1. McKenzie, W., "Anthems of the Sacred-Harp Tunesmiths," *American Music* 6, no. 3 (1988): 247-263.
   Times Cited: 0   Cited Refs: 18   Shared Refs: 2

2. Patterson, D. W., "Hauser, William 'Hesperian Harp' and 'Olive Leaf': Shape-Note Tunebooks as Emblems of Change and Progress," *Journal of American Folklore* 101 (Jan-Mar 1988): 23-36.
   Times Cited: 2   Cited Refs: 26   Shared Refs: 2

From these records, Rick will probably want to see the shared references and may do so by selecting the link under the number of shared references. Again, he may examine the footnotes from related records (Cited Refs) or go to records for articles that cite these (Times Cited), continuing to cycle forward in the research conversation. The "Shared References" choice displays sources that use some of the same footnotes as the original work.

Shared References

Cited Author	Cited Work	Year
Cobb, B.	Sacred Harp Tradition...	1978
Jackson, G. P.	White Spirituals, So...	1933

Other databases that offer citation searching include *JSTOR* and, for full-text articles on the web, *Google Scholar*. Librarians at Harvard College Library have created an excellent guide entitled "Searching the Citation Indexes (*Web of Science*)," available at http://hcl.harvard.edu/research/guides/citationindex/.

Review Questions

1. Identify two reasons to use citation searching.

2. In the *Web of Science* citation indexes from ISI, records include the number of cited references and the number of times cited. What do these two phrases mean?

3. What is a related-reference search
   a. As it may be done in almost any database?
   b. As it may be done in a citation index?

4. Name two reasons to use a related-reference search.

Learning Exercises

1. Identify a book or article relevant to your research topic. Examine footnotes (cited references) in this source, and list several that you would want to add to your preliminary bibliography. This procedure takes you back in time to previous research.

2. In either a library catalog or a journal index, find one record relevant to your research. Use related-record searching to find "more like this." Print your original record and at least one that you discover through the related-record method.

3. Use citation searching in a citation index to find a known item, and then identify works written subsequently that cite the known item.

4. Use a related-record search in a citation database to identify articles that share footnotes (cite the same sources).

Note

1. Data in sections 13.1 and 13.2 came from a search of *Arts & Humanities Citation Index*; however, the information shown here is neither complete nor an exact replica of displays in the database.

Chapter 14

Other Discovery Methods:
Experts and the Internet

Preview

- Experts in the field—researchers, professors, and practitioners—can provide unpublished information or guidance in planning your research. Style manuals include guidance for properly citing interviews or correspondence.
- Specialized music directories are available to identify experts and professional or commercial organizations. Usually part of a reference collection, they are classed in ML12–ML18.
- As with online catalogs and journal indexes, advanced search screens in search engines and metasearch engines enable power searching of the Internet.
- Internet subject directories or subject trees provide hierarchical access—from general to more specific topics—and frequently retrieve websites where human intellect has contributed to the selection.
- Useful digital content for music study such as primary materials (manuscripts or photographs), scores, or recorded music, is increasing exponentially as libraries and archives digitize unique holdings.
- The "Deep Web" is that part of the Internet where websites cannot be found by search engines or which require a password to be accessible. Advances are underway to enable better searching of the hidden Internet through services such as *Google Scholar*.
- Evaluation of sources is an essential part of research. Typical criteria include an assessment of authority, currency, accuracy, objectivity, and documentation.

14.1 Ask Experts

The idea of using people as resources doesn't occur to every researcher, but consulting with an expert can save a lot of time and possibly direct your efforts when print and electronic sources aren't working so well. They can provide shortcuts by directing you to resources, helping to clarify your research topic, or providing unpublished information.

Exactly how can people, who know your research area, help you? Sometimes the latest information resides with individuals doing research and has not been published yet. Journalists rely on people as sources all the time, but most academics fail to realize the potential gains from contacting other experts. Talking about your research with appropriate people may result in:

- Valuable feedback on your thinking, methods, and unresolved problems
- An overview of the field
- More questions or more specific questions to consider
- Identification of valued authors or researchers or works to read
- Tips on areas that need more research

How can you identify people to contact? Two categories are very easy: professors in your institution or other nearby colleges or universities and local librarians. Professors are in a position to summarize the state of research in a field and to recommend specific publications for you to read. They are generally very pleased to assist in this way because, of course, teaching and directing research are primary responsibilities for them. Besides music professors, and especially if yours is a cross-disciplinary topic, you may need to consult with professors in other subject disciplines. Ask music professors you know for recommendations or consult sources at your university to identify appropriate individuals. Try departmental websites for individual biographies that sometimes list research interests. Look at the university catalog for departmental faculty listings. Call the departmental secretary to ask which faculty member specializes in your area. Librarians, likewise, are in a position of knowing, through everyday experience, how to identify, obtain, and evaluate resources in many subject areas. Remember that there are likely to be one or more librarians, who have specialized educational backgrounds in music, at your institution or at others nearby. Be sure to determine whether a music librarian is available to assist you.

What about other experts, whether or not they are located nearby? Consider authors of books that you have found useful in the initial stages of your research. Use directories such as the College Music Society's *Directory of Music Faculties in Colleges and Universities, U.S. and Canada* or *Musical America* to identify people who might have expertise to share. Then use the telephone or e-mail to contact them. Directories in the music library reference collection are classed in ML12–18. Certain among these are essential because they cover multiple subdisciplines in music. Identify others by browsing in these classification areas or by doing a subject-heading search using a valid topical heading plus the subdivision, "–directory." Two music biographical dictionaries, *International Who's Who* (Classical and Popular), contain directory sections for both North American and international resources.

Look for directories among the databases available from your library, or ask a librarian to recommend multidiscipline print directories to you. Some of the general print directories in most libraries include:

Encyclopedia of Associations (Gale Research)
Encyclopedia of Associations: International Organizations (Gale Research)
Directory of British Associations (CBD Research)
Directory of European Professional and Learned Societies (CBD Research)

On the Internet, use search engines and online directories to find contact information for individuals. Online telephone directories and staff lists or "people-finder" features on most websites are useful also. The following online directories are a few examples of many that are available.

The College Music Society also provides its online *Directory of Music Faculties for U.S. and Canadian Institutions* offering music programs as well as a database for music organizations worldwide. The online versions provide less information than the print versions but are quick and useable from any computer. The institutions and organizations database is searchable by institution/organization name, city, state or Canadian province, country, area code, or zip code. The information returned includes organization name (in the original language), address, phone and fax numbers, e-mail address, and website.

General online telephone directories include *AT&T Directories* for phone numbers and addresses in the United States and *Yahoo! Phone Numbers and Addresses* for links to numerous directory sites including its own, *Yahoo! People Search*.

It is essential that you be prepared for a conference with a professor or librarian or for a phone or e-mail conference with a remote expert. Do the background reading to give yourself a foundation for discussion or to help frame your questions. Be sure to introduce yourself and explain what you are trying to do. Identify how you will use information you obtain. To make best use of your contact's time, ask specific, targeted questions. Always credit your sources by learning how to footnote an interview. Ask your expert for further sources of information, either in print or other people to contact. And, finally, send a thank-you note to the individual who assisted you.

14.2 Standard Directories for Music: ML12–18

The purpose of a directory is to identify individuals, groups, organizations, or institutions and to provide contact information for them. You may need them for access to products or services, but remember that expert individuals could assist you with leads, ideas, or advice on a research project as well. When it comes to travel to a library for access to specialized materials, contacting a librarian at the institution is useful for planning purposes.

**Musical America: International Directory of the Performing Arts* is reissued on an annual basis, which is important to the currency of its directory information. For many years it was a special issue of the journal *Musical America*, published from 1898–1992. Divided into two sections, the United States and Canada, and International, it provides contact names, addresses, telephone numbers, e-mail addresses, and websites for individuals and organizations. Listings cover such categories as agents and managers, opera companies, choral groups, symphonies, professional organizations, music schools, contests, festivals, foundations and awards, publishers, and record companies. The only remnant of the journal that remains is the musician-of-the-year feature articles naming an outstanding composer, conductor, instrumentalist, ensemble, and educator. On their website, free access is available to news stories about the international music industry, people in the news, competitions and awards, reviews, a career center, calendar of events, press releases, the feature articles from the print directory, plus e-mail and website addresses for any organization listed in the print edition.

Another standard directory is the **Directory of Music Faculties in Colleges and Universities, U.S. and Canada* published annually by the College Music Society. Its print version provides directory information for institutions and lists faculty by name, institution, and teaching areas. It is possible also to search the CMS Database, at no cost, for institutional information only. Finally, the directory sections of two bibliographic dictionaries are quite useful: *International Who's Who in Classical Music* and *International Who's Who in Popular Music*. Both include extensive international directory sections for organizations, publishers, libraries, etc.

14.3 What Is the Internet?

The Internet is essentially a network of computer networks around the globe. In practical terms, it is a way of connecting and providing access to information stored on millions of computers. In the 1990s, due to the development of a common language and common communications protocol, the Internet became available to anyone with a computer and service provider. The language is HTML, HyperText Markup Language, and the communications system is http, HyperText Transfer Protocol. What we call the World Wide Web is the system of organized access to websites available through the Internet. If you need more information on terms or mechanisms relating to the Internet, see http://www.learnthenet.com/English/index.html.

Each website has a unique address called a URL, for uniform resources locator. A naming convention was developed, the Domain Name System, to permit categorization by types of organizations. This domain name is the last part of the URL in the following pattern: "www.server.domain." It is helpful to recognize these domains because they can be used as a limiting factor in a search of the web. For the URL "www.menc.org," the second and third parts of the address represent the domain: some form of name of an organization (MENC, the National Association for Music Education) and a suffix (org) for the type of organization. When you know an Internet address, you can simply type it into the address box of your Internet browser (Mozilla, Firefox, Internet Explorer, etc.). Some of the most frequently used domain suffixes are:

.com   Commercial businesses
.edu   Educational institutions
.gov   United States government agencies
.net   Networks such as Internet service providers
.org   Non-commercial organizations

14.4 Search Engines

Web search engines are generally produced by commercial companies but are made available at no cost to users because they carry sponsored advertising. A search engine consists of three parts: (1) the spider or crawler, which is a program that identifies and reads pages on the web, (2) a database of web pages gathered by the spider, and (3) a search engine mechanism or software that permits users to search the database and receive results in a ranked order. Relevancy ranking used to be based solely on the frequency with which search terms appeared in web pages. Today, second generation search engines use more sophisticated ranking systems including concept, keyword, site, links, or popularity, and sometimes with human intervention in the ranking process.[1] There are many search engines available; some of the most effective are listed here along with a summary of their searching requirements. It is vital to read help pages to learn the rules for formulating search queries in each search engine.

Fast and effective, *Google* is the famous leader in the world of search engines. It ranks results based on the number of links from pages ranked high by the service, a type of popularity ranking that does seem to display the most relevant sites in about the top twenty listed. Search rules include:

- Default AND
- Type OR in all caps, if needed, but parentheses are not allowed
- Use quotation marks for phrases
- No truncation
- Advanced search allows complex Boolean searching, limit by language, file format, domain, or most recent sites. Newer additions to advanced searching include SafeSearch (with or without filtering), Froogle product search, page-specific searching to find similar pages or pages that link to the page, and topic-specific searches including university websites and *Google Scholar* for scholarly papers.

The *Ask.com* site is a merger between *Ask Jeeves* and *Teoma* and produces excellent retrieval. It uses *Teoma*'s ranking system: a "subject-specific popularity" ranking based on the number of same-subject pages that reference it, rather than general popularity. Search rules include:

- Default AND
- Type OR in all caps, if needed, but parentheses are not allowed
- Use quotation marks for phrases or select the checkbox next to "Find this phrase."
- No truncation
- Use + before a common word that is excluded normally: +the +who
- Use – before a word to indicate NOT
- Advanced search allows complex Boolean searching, limit by place on page, language, domain, geographic region, or date page was modified.

14.5 Metasearch Engines

To retrieve results from a variety of search engines using a single search statement, use a metasearch or metacrawler. Metasearching is the generic name for this type of simultaneous searching. You complete a single onscreen search form and the results are returned in a single list with duplicate hits removed. Sometimes you may choose to have the results displayed in groups from each of the separate search engines. Returning the top ten relevancy-ranked results from each of the search engines involved, *Ixquick* currently uses 12 search engines. It reports both which search engines retrieved the website and the relevancy ranking that search engine gave it. *Clusty* performs document clustering (based on titles, URLs, and short descriptions) to permit examination of results in categories that are generated automatically. For instance, a search using the keywords, "teaching rhythm computers," offers at least ten categories including "Lesson, Plan," "Music & Computers," "Music Teacher," "School," and "Software, Music."

Figure 14.1 Terminology for Boolean Operators in Internet Search Engines

Boolean Operator	**Search Engine Terminology Possibilities**
AND / and	All the words+ (plus sign) AND, and
OR / or	Some of the words At least one of the words OR, or
NOT / not	None of the words Without the words – (minus sign) NOT, AND NOT
For a phrase	"words of a phrase" in quotation marks Exact Phrase

14.6 Subject Directories or Subject Trees

Sometimes called subject trees because of the branching from general to specific subjects, these Internet directories provide a collection of links at each subject level. The major advantage to a subject directory is that someone, not a computer, has evaluated the sites for quality. You stand a better chance of finding useable information because of this evaluation process. Similar sites may be called portals.

Music Directories

DW3 Classical Music Resources provides links to music websites in seven categories: chronologies and necrologies, composer homepages, databases, electronic journals and newsletters, genres, national and regionally oriented pages, organizations and centers for scholarly research. Staff of the Music Library at Duke University compile the directory. Created and maintained by staff of the Edna Kuhn Loeb Music Library at Harvard, *Online Internet Resources for Music Scholars* provides links in the following categories: Online Tools for General Reference, Online Journals and Newsletters, Music Databases and Information Resources, Digital Music Collections, Music Information Meta-Sites, Scholarly Societies and Organizations, and Music Departments and Libraries. The site provides referrals to music information on meta-sites of educational institutions including:

- DW3 Classical Music Resources (Duke University).
  www.lib.duke.edu/dw3/index.php
- *Music Resources* (Sibelius Academy).
  www2.siba.fi/Kulttuuripalvelut/music.html

- Scholarly Societies Project–Music (University of Waterloo).
  www.lib.uwaterloo.ca/society/music_soc.html
- Worldwide Internet Music Resources (Indiana University).
  www.music.indiana.edu/music_resources/
- WWW Sites of Interest to Musicologists (AMS).
  www.sas.upenn.edu/music/ams/musicology_www.html

General Directories That Include Music

Librarians' Internet Index, subtitled "websites you can trust," is a searchable directory of websites, publicly funded and maintained by librarians. Organized into 14 main topics and nearly 300 related topics,[2] it is useable as a hierarchy or by direct searching. Compiled at the University of California, *Infomine: Scholarly Internet Resource Collections* includes websites of interest to scholars and provides a description of each site retrieved in a search. *Infomine* provides keyword searching or browsing by subjects: *LCSH* or LCC, authors, titles, resource types, and new resources added within the last 20 days. *Intute*, formerly *RDN* (*Resource Discovery Network*), is international in scope and indicates the source of websites using national flag icons. The Music and Performing Arts section is further divided into major subjects: conservation, history and theory, opera, dance, music, theater and drama. Selection and description of websites is supported by a network of institutions in the UK arts and creative industries and managed by a team at the Manchester Metropolitan University. Their policies and subject headings are accessible. Finally, *Yahoo! Directory* gives music listings under the heading, "Performing Arts/Music," accessible directly at http://dir.yahoo.com/entertainment/music/.

14.7 The "Deep Web"

Scholarly information on the Internet is hard to locate among the quantities of self-publishing and commercial information there. However, new techniques are under development to help the researcher search the "Deep Web." Also termed "Hidden Internet" or "Invisible Web," this part of the internet contains websites that cannot be found by search engines or which require a password to be accessible. For instance, a search engine can locate university library catalogs but will not be able to search for records within those catalogs. Many individual items—images, sounds, or documents—that are part of digital libraries are not fully retrievable via search engines. Of course, search engines cannot enter password-protected databases such as fee-based indexes (including most that are available to a university community while enrolled or employed there), corporate intranets, banking information, and so on. One approach to accessing the hidden Internet was introduced in 2004 by Google and is called *Google Scholar*.

> *Google Scholar* enables you to search specifically for scholarly literature, including peer-reviewed papers, theses, books, preprints, abstracts and technical reports from all broad areas of research. Use *Google Scholar* to find articles from a wide variety of academic publishers, professional societies, preprint repositories and universities, as well as scholarly articles available across the web.[3]

Use of *Google Scholar* can be one of the fastest ways to locate full-text sources supplied by your own library. One of its features, "group of," results in a display of various available links to journal articles, both commercial versions and those on major open access (free) repositories. So you may use *Google Scholar* to locate both print and electronic resources. When viewing an article, use the "cited by" feature to access abstracts of articles being cited in the article. This citation indexing was discussed in Chapter 13.

Because *Google Scholar* is in its Beta form, its results may not be complete or current. At this time it is strongest in coverage of science and technology. *Google Scholar* may lead to a publisher's website where access to a full-text article requires payment. Do not pay for full text if you are affiliated with an academic library; instead, search for the article in the library's databases, its catalog (for a subscription to the electronic journal), or place an interlibrary loan request. It is likely that the library already has a subscription that can provide the article to you at no cost. Use *Google Scholar* to supplement searches in your library's bibliographic databases.

Also, in 2004, OCLC began a free program entitled *Open WorldCat* or *World-Cat.org*, which permits a search engine user to discover which nearby library owns certain materials. If the web search matches the title of a library-owned item, the search results include a link to the "Find in a Library" search. Following that link and specifying geographic information helps to locate the item at a library in your city, region, or country. These interactions between database vendors and search engine creators are helping to open the hidden Internet.

14.8 Digital Libraries

Useful digital content for music study is increasing exponentially as libraries and archives digitize unique holdings. Examples include primary materials (manuscripts or photographs), scores, and recorded music. Streaming audio databases (requiring subscriptions) are listed in Chapter 3 with other types of databases. A number of libraries have embarked on sheet music digitization projects and some commercial entities publish collections of scores.

- *Choral Public Domain Library* includes music, text, and translations at http://www.cpdl.org, and is part of ChoralWiki.
- *Sheet Music Consortium* is a collaborative library project of Duke, Johns Hopkins and UCLA, now including more than 120,000 titles at http://digital.library.ucla.edu/sheetmusic.
- *Online Sheet Music* from Ebrary
- *Classical Scores Library* from Alexander Street Press

Multimedia websites are being used to publicize special collections of unique scholarly resources. They truly help bring primary materials to individual researchers around the world. While the lead has been taken by major national libraries, a growing number of universities, museums, and historical libraries are contributing to the wealth of sources in varied media formats: images of art and manuscripts, photographs, audio, scores, and video. Besides their important scholarly use, they bring cultural and social history to the desktop of anyone with an interest in exploring them. National sites presenting music content include:

- *American Memory* (Library of Congress), http://memory.loc.gov
- *Digital Collections* (Library and Archives of Canada), http://www.collectionscanada.ca/musicindex-e.html#h
- *Online Gallery* (British Library), http:www.bl.uk/onlinegallery/homepage.html

14.9 Evaluating Internet Resources

When using the Internet for research, it is essential to remember that the Internet has become a self-publishing medium. Anyone having access to a server and who has learned to create a web page can publish on the Internet. The self-publishing nature of web pages is very different from traditional publications—books, magazines, sound recordings—which have been selected for publication and edited by someone other than the creator. web documents also may change fairly continuously or remain available even when their content is out of date. Be a skeptic about the quality and reliability of such information on the web. There is a wide range of information on the web, from facts and statistics to opinions; and it has been created for various purposes, from informing to persuading to selling. It is vital to evaluate the documents you discover on the web.

Evaluation is always an essential part of research, but how might it be done for Internet documents? And how does evaluation of web-based information compare to evaluation of print-based resources? The following comparison provides the bare bones of evaluation for print versus web-based resources. The differences are primarily a matter of where to look in the resource. Evaluate on the basis of criteria for authority, currency, accuracy, objectivity, and documentation for each information source you consider in a research project or even in daily life.

Evaluation Criteria

Authority and credibility

First the question is, can you trust the source? Who is the author (editor, contributors), what are her credentials, and has she written much on this subject? Who is the publisher or organizational support? What do other people say? Can you find reviews of the source?

Print: For a book, check the title page, preface, and foreword for the name of the author and publisher, author's credentials and other publications. It might be necessary to use reference books or databases to determine credentials, other publications, or to seek evaluative reviews. For journals, there is usually an identification of the author, his organizational affiliation, and possibly other writings on the subject. Who is the publisher? Does the company have a track record in this field? Is its reputation good? Does it publish scholarly materials?

Web: Examine the URL to determine whether the source is a personal page (personal name) or an Internet provider of personal pages (aol.com), or is it a page residing on an institutional or organizational web server? For personal pages, there is no institutional "publisher" vouching for information provided. Is the domain appropriate and reliable for your information need? Domains of .edu or .gov or .org might be more reliable than the commercial domain, but it does depend on the information needed. Is an author or name of the organization or agency listed for the page? Is there an explanation of why the page exists? Look for the page creator's credentials.

Currency

Consider the date of publication and date of contents. How important is currency for this topic? In the arts and humanities, recent writings are not the only ones that may have value.

Print: Check the copyright date and look for a date at the end of a book's preface. The preface or "how to use" section may date the contents explicitly.

Web: Can you find a date on the page or website? Look for "latest revision." Many times undated information, especially facts or statistics, simply should not be used.

Accuracy and verifiability

These qualities refer to the basic soundness of the information. If you cannot determine how the information was gathered or what research methodology was used, you should be suspicious of the results.

Print: Examine the table of contents or article subheadings to assess completeness and method of coverage of the subject. In a research document, look for an explanation of data-gathering and interpretation methods. Scan a few sections of the book or article; from your own knowledge, does the information seem accurate? You might need to compare it to other sources to check accuracy. If the book is a new edition, it may be helpful to compare it with a previous edition to determine if material has been omitted. Frequently the new edition contains prefaces to earlier editions for the purpose of comparison.

Web: Try comparing information from a website to a trusted print resource. Do links to additional or related sites verify information on the original website? Are these referred sites reputable or scholarly? Do they actually exist? Use an Internet directory that evaluates content to check on the quality of a website. Search for the site's title in *Librarians' Internet Index* or *Infomine*.

Objectivity

Look for evidence of fairness and lack of bias in treatment of the subject. Are statements of opinion identified as such or simply stated as fact? Is coverage of the topic inclusive of appropriate ethnic, national, gender, or topical groups, for instance representing both art music and popular music? For controversial issues, are both sides presented? Is language appropriate for the audience and topic?

Print: Examine portions of the book or article looking for language that indicates bias or inclusiveness and for balanced arguments.

Web: There isn't a real difference between evaluating the objectivity of a web resource versus that of a printed one. Read the content. However, it is also important to determine a reason for the web publication. Is it there to persuade, influence, sell, or inform? Does the sponsoring organization or author have a special agenda?

Documentation or referral to other sources

Scholarly documentation, notes, and bibliographies are essential mechanisms used to credit the ideas and opinions of others. They are vital to the conversational process of research reporting.

Print: Be certain that the author is crediting others through notes and bibliographic citations. Even in more popular treatments, you should find references in the text giving attributing statements and opinions that are not original with the author.

Web: Does the page list sources or corroborative sites? Does it provide footnotes or a bibliography? How authoritative are the sources cited? Are they merely other unedited websites? It is a good idea to find at least two other sources that support the conclusions of a web-based resource as corroboration of findings and information reported.

For more guidance on the Internet side, check these web pages from the University of California, Berkeley Library, http://www.lib.berkeley.edu/TeachingLib/Guides/Internet/Evaluate.html and from Johns Hopkins University Libraries, http://www.library.jhu.edu/researchhelp/general/evaluating/index.html.

Review Questions

1. Identify at least three reasons to use people as a discovery strategy.

2. What kind of reference book or online source is used to provide contact information for individuals or organizations?

3. Describe how to prepare for and conduct an interview with an expert.

4. Why is it good practice to start an Internet search at an advanced search screen? What are some likely limits that will be available?

5. How does a metasearch engine differ from a search engine?

6. What is an Internet subject directory or directory tree? What does it offer that is different than keyword searching?

7. Give five examples of kinds of information likely to be hidden from most search engines; that is, what is on the "hidden Internet"?

8. Describe ways of checking Internet resources for authority, currency, accuracy, objectivity, and documentation.

Learning Exercises

1. Compare the results of a *Google* search for living people or current organizations in music with a search of a print directory: *Directory of Music Faculties in Colleges and Universities, U.S. and Canada* or *Musical America* [ML13]. Comment on currency of information, validity, authority of the source, etc.

2. Using your research topic, search an Internet music subject directory, a search engine, and a metasearch engine. Describe the nature of your searches and your results. Which Internet searching mechanisms worked best for your topic?

3. Evaluate one of the sources for your research topic that you have found on the Internet. Describe what you have learned about its authority, currency, accuracy, objectivity, and documentation. Are you still willing to use it for your research?

Notes

1. Laura Cohen, "Conducting Research on the Internet," University Libraries, University at Albany, State University of New York, July 21, 2004, revised May 10, 2005. http://library.albany.edu/internet/research.html, (accessed 25 August 2007).

2. "Librarians' Internet Index," The Califa Library Group, http://lii.org, (accessed 12 July 2008).

3. "About Google Scholar," Google Scholar, http://www.googlescholar.com, (accessed 25 August 2007).

Chapter 15

Using Thematic Catalogs

Preview

- A thematic catalog is a special type of bibliography for the works of an individual composer. To qualify as a thematic, rather than a descriptive, catalog of works, it must provide notation for the beginning of movements or sections of each work—the incipits.
- A complete bibliography of a composer's works without provision of musical incipits may be called a descriptive catalog of works or a *catalogue raisonné*.
- The way to locate up-to-date listings of thematic catalogs is through a subject search of *WorldCat* for the phrase, "thematic catalogs."
- The standard bibliography of thematic catalogs is by **Barry Brook and Richard Viano: *Thematic Catalogues in Music: An Annotated Bibliography*, 2d ed., 1997. Use this book to identify whether a thematic catalog exists for a composer.

A thematic catalog is among the most important and unique tools available to music researchers. The compiler of a thematic catalog arranges a body of music in a systematic order, assigns a unique identification number to each work, and using musical notation for the beginning measures of each movement (the incipit), provides positive identification of the compositions.

Barry Brook, a musicologist known for research on thematic catalogs, provides some background information helpful to understanding this unique type of resource.

The thematic catalogue is superior to the non-thematic one as a research aid since its incipits provide identification in a minimum of space and symbols. For most music an incipit of about a dozen pitches suffices. When rhythmic values accompany the pitches, the incipit is almost inevitably unique. While the non-thematic list may identify a work by its composer, title, opus number, key, instrumentation, movement headings, first line of text, date, publisher, dedicatee, plate number etc., no one of these, indeed no combination of these, can normally provide as certain an identification as an incipit. Even transposed works can be readily identified in properly organized incipit files. In dealing with works that are anonymous or of disputed authorship, incipits become indispensable.[1]

So, exactly what does "thematic" mean in the phrase, "thematic catalog"? It refers to the opening music (and words) of a composition or of the movements (sections) of the composition; thus, it presents incipits along with other information regarding the work. Brook explains that in the 18th century "because compositions almost always began with their main theme, the words 'theme' or 'themata' were treated as synonymous with what has only recently come to be called '*incipit.*'"[2]

15.1 Uses beyond Identification of a Composition

While the incipit is the key to identification of a musical work, thematic catalogs provide much more information about each composition. This concise presentation of authoritative information provides an invaluable starting point for research and information gathering. Much of the following information will appear in the entries for each composition in a thematic catalog.

Information in thematic catalogs for each composition:
- *Incipit* (initial bars of notation for each movement, segment)
- Title
- Opus number or thematic catalog number
- Key
- Instrumentation
- Movement headings (tempo markings)
- First line of text
- Author of text
- Dates (written, published, sometimes first performance)
- Dedication
- Publisher's plate number
- Autograph—existence, location
- First and subsequent publications
- Location in complete works
- Bibliography

Once you can locate a specific work in a thematic catalog, there may be a very valuable piece of information in the work's entry. That information is the coding for the composition's location in the composer's complete works edition. Often the information is very near the top of the entry, but you may need to recognize or decipher a code for the complete works followed by the series, part, volume, and page numbers. In the case of Mozart, the listing will be *MW* (Wolfgang Amadeus Mozart's *Werke*) for the old edition of Mozart's works and *NMA* (Wolfgang Amadeus Mozart: *Neue Ausgabe sämtlicher Werke*) for the new edition. Similarly for Johann Sebastian Bach, the old edition is referred to as the *Bach Gesellschaft Ausgabe* (*BGA*) while the newer one is the *Neue Bach-Ausgabe* (*NBA*). Look for a list of abbreviations to decode the complete works references.

Organization of Thematic Catalogs

Entries for compositions in a thematic catalog are generally ordered either chronologically, according to composition date, or in a classified order, by instrumentation or genre. For instance:

- *Chronological order* is used for thematic catalogs of Mozart and Schubert.
- Analogous to chronological order is *opus number* order followed by compositions without opus number (WoO–*Werke ohne Opus*, German for "works without opus"). This organizational pattern is used for the works of Beethoven in the thematic catalog compiled by Kinsky.
- *Classified order* is used in thematic catalogs of J. S. Bach, Vivaldi, and others. Sometimes, within the classifications—cantatas, operas, songs, symphonies, concerti, keyboard works, etc. —the works are ordered chronologically.

While the centerpiece of every thematic catalog consists of entries for each composition, there are other parts of the catalog that offer great assistance to researchers. The table of contents indicates the overall organization, and therefore may assist in locating specific compositions. Remember that some foreign publications place the table of contents at the end of the book (especially French and Italian publications).

There may be a number of indexes that are useful for locating compositions within the catalog. Frequently you will find a thematic index, which uses musical notation and provides a reference to the catalog number; first line and title index to vocal works; classified index to works by instrument or genre name; an index to all individuals referenced in the entries; or several separate name indexes for dedicatees, lyricists, etc.

Notice the variety of appendices or supplementary lists. Often they contain very important information, such as a concordance of different number systems used for the composer's works, a list of misattributed works giving more recent scholarly evidence as to the actual composers, a list of lost works, fragments, or sketches, or a chronology of the life and works of the composer.

15.2 Value of Thematic Catalog Numbers

Note that thematic catalogs are useful for solving problems associated with locating scores or recordings. The unique numbering of compositions, provided by the compiler of a thematic catalog, is frequently the key to finding the work in a library's online catalog. Thematic catalogs are usually referenced by the name or initial of their compilers, occasionally by an abbreviation of their titles. The thematic catalog numbers consist of the appropriate abbreviation plus the numeric designation for each composition. For example:

- K. refers to Köchel, the compiler of W. A. Mozart's thematic catalog, for instance, K. 550 is used for Mozart's Symphony no. 40.
- S. refers to Wolfgang Schmieder. S. numbers used to be used by the Library of Congress in its cataloging of Bach's works, but now B.W.V. is used, standing for *Bach Werke-Verzeichnis*, which is the title of the catalog compiled by Schmieder. B.W.V. 1006 is an example of a thematic catalog number for Bach.
- D. refers to Otto Erich Deutsch, Schubert's compiler.
- L. is used to refer to Longo, one of Domenico Scarlatti's catalogers.

- RV refers to *Ryom Verzeichnis*, the catalog of Vivaldi's works compiled by Ryom.

If you know the thematic catalog number (or opus number), try using it in the title portion of a combined author and title keyword search. Rules of the specific database will determine whether you should include the compiler or title abbreviation along with the work numeral in your search.

15.3 Building Vocabulary

The majority of thematic catalogs are in German, having been produced by German musicians and musicologists. To improve your ability to make use of thematic catalogs, spend some time becoming familiar with German bibliographic terms that are used. Here is a short list of some helpful words that occur frequently in thematic catalogs.

Abschrift (Abschr.)	Reprint or copy
Anhang (Anh.)	Appendix or supplement
Anmerkung (Anm.)	Footnote
Ausgabe (Aus.)	Edition
Bearbeitung (Bearb.)	Arrangement, compilation
Erstausgabe	First edition
Erstdruck	First printing
Gesamtausgabe (GA)	Complete edition(s), complete work(s)
Also *Gesammelte Werke (GW),*	
Sammelwerk, or *Sämtliche Werke*	
Inhalt	Table of contents
Literatur	Bibliography
Register	Index
Thematische Verzeichnis	Thematic catalog
Verzeichnis (Verz.)	Catalog

Review Question

1. What is a thematic catalog and how does it differ from a "descriptive catalog" or "catalogue raisonné"?

Learning Exercise

1. Choose the most current edition of a thematic catalog for a composer of interest to you. Study the catalog to learn how to use it, and then answer the following questions.
   a. Citation and Subject Heading. Give a complete citation for the thematic catalog. List the exact subject heading for this book.
   b. Sample Thematic Catalog Numbers. List the full thematic catalog number and title for each of two compositions. Remember the thematic catalog number consists of one or more letters and a number.
   c. Organization. What is the overall organizational plan of the thematic catalog: chronological, opus number, or classified? Describe any suborganization that you observe.
   d. Complete Works Indexing. Does this catalog index the composer's complete edition; that is, are locations given for the compositions in the complete works? If so, provide an example by listing the composition title and its location information in the complete works.
   e. Numbering Systems. Determine whether various numbering systems have been used for this composer. If so, list them.
   f. Indexes. List the indexes provided.
   g. Appendices. List the appendices provided.
   h. How to Locate a Composition. Identify one composition and write instructions on exactly how to locate the entry for that composition.
   i. Same Title for Multiple Works. If vocal/choral works are included, find one title that is used for more than a single work. Identify the kinds of vocal works these are, for example, mass, cantata, oratorio, chorale, aria, etc. Do their manuscripts exist? Where? Who is the poet or librettist for each?
   j. Thematic Index. If there is a thematic index, explain how to use it.

Notes

1. Barry S. Brook, "Thematic Catalogues," in *Grove Music Online*, edited by L. Macy, http://www.grovemusic.com (accessed 30 August 2007).
2. Brook, "Thematic Catalogues."

Part 3

Resources: The Literature of Music

Part 3

Resources: The Literature of Music

Besides the many information-searching strategies explored in Part 2, there is one more way of understanding the materials available for research in music. That way is the type-of-literature method of teaching and learning about resources. As the traditional way that music faculty passed on their knowledge of the field, it still has an important place. In fact, this method of exploring literature is the reason that some introductory courses in music research are named "Music Bibliography." Just knowing that certain categories of information and publication exist will alert you to possible sources to seek when you have a new research project or information need.

This part of the book takes the form of a bibliographic essay, presenting a highly selective list of resources with comments about their usefulness in the text. The bibliography at the end of the book provides full citation information for each resource. Note that what have been called "starting-point resources" have already been presented in Part 1: The Short Course because they are important for early explorations of a research topic and thesis development. Already covered were standard bibliographies for the field of music, union catalogs, dictionaries of many types, journal literature, and the databases used to access current literature.

This section presents resources according to type—directories, music histories, books on performance practice, those for teaching music, etc.—in Library of Congress Classification order. This arrangement is designed to promote understanding of the classification system as a way to improve your access to library collections by browsing. Coverage includes electronic materials as well as those in print. Emphasis is placed on resources published from 2000 to the present plus essential standard resources of varying dates, which all music researchers need to know and use. For more complete listings, refer to *Music Reference and Research Materials: An Annotated Bibliography* by Duckles and Reed, the standard bibliography for the discipline of music, and the recent book by Laurie Sampsel, *Music Research: A Handbook* (see Chapter 2, p. 14).

Many music libraries offer an extensive collection of reference books, intended primarily for consultation rather than cover-to-cover reading. In many cases, the most recent books and standard sources from ML12–54, ML100–ML159.9, and some other classifications are housed in a designated reference area. Older editions in these classifications may be found in the book stacks, where they are available for checkout. Be sure to observe specific location information when using a library catalog.

NOTE: Throughout this section, two asterisks (**) indicate key resources.

Chapter 16

M: The Music—Scores and Recordings

Preview

- Scores come in a variety of formats. Do you know them all—full score, chorus score, conductor's score, miniature score, piano reduction, vocal score, score and parts, parts?
- Critical, *Urtext*, performing, and facsimile editions have substantive differences. Consider edition types when looking for a score.
- Critical editions are scholarly versions of compositions based on careful examination of all available sources. They use editorial procedures that distinguish between the composer's notation and editorial additions or changes.
- Two large groups of critical editions are available to scholars and performers. Each series classified in M2 contains the works of many composers related by time, geography, or musical style. The M3 classification is used for the complete works of individual composers.
- There are several ways to locate specific compositions in large critical editions. Learn to use *Grove Music Online* composers' works lists, thematic catalogs, and both online and print bibliographies: *Index to Printed Music* (2004–) and the print bibliographies by Hill and Stephens (1997) and Heyer (1980).
- When it comes to call numbers for sound recordings, many libraries use a simple numbering system to identify shelf location; others use systems based on record label numbering, and a few use classification systems such as that of the Library of Congress.

16.1 Score Formats

You probably know the following types of scores, but to be certain, check the definitions of the formats of scores that are commonly available.

Conductor's score. Also called condensed score. Here the separate parts from an original full score are combined on a minimum number of staves to provide the structure of the work, its melodies and harmony. Cues are inserted to indicate points of entrance for soloists or instruments. Frequently used for band music.

Chorus score. A score containing each choral part on a separate staff with no accompaniment or with instrumental lines (orchestra or chamber ensemble) reduced for keyboard. Used for vocal works containing chorus.

Close score. As with hymns, such a score is used for vocal music and puts all vocal parts on two staves.

Full score. A score that displays the complete music of a composition with each part on a separate staff. Normally used for conducting ensembles such as orchestras, bands, or choirs.

Miniature score. Also called study score or pocket score. A photographic reduction of a full score, used for instrumental and vocal works. These scores are designed for easy use in studying or listening to music.

Parts. Separately issued music for a single voice or instrument from a larger work. A symphony requires parts for each instrument as does a string quartet. In libraries, the parts may be assembled in a single container for shelving purposes.

Piano reduction. Also called piano score. Whether originally for orchestra, chamber ensemble, opera, or other genre, the critical factor here is that a large number of parts are arranged or reduced to two staves, playable at a piano, plus a line for the soloist. Piano reductions are used frequently for concertos to allow the soloist to rehearse with an accompanist instead of a full orchestra.

Score and parts. Chamber music, from duet to nonet or larger, is often issued with a score, having all of the parts, for the conductor plus each individual part for the performers. In libraries they may be offered together with the score in a binder and a pocket for the parts.

Vocal score. Also called piano-vocal score or organ-vocal score. Similar to the piano reduction, this type of score presents separate lines for vocal soloists and choral parts but reduces the instrumental lines to be playable at the piano. It is used for vocal works that use large instrumental forces such as operas or choral works with orchestra.

16.2 Musical Editions

An overview of historical music editions is important for our understanding of editing practices over time and the rise of critical scholarly editions. Explaining music editing before 1850, from 1850 to 1950, and after 1950 is the *Grove Music Online* article, "Editions, historical," by Robinson, Hill, Stephens, and Woodward. Of primary importance is their comprehensive list of historical music editions in three categories: (1) single-composer complete editions, (2) other collected editions, and (3) anthologies.

Definitions

Complete edition, also known as *collected edition, complete works, Gesamtausgabe* (Ger.), *Sämtliche Werke* (Ger.), *opera omnia* (Lat.). A critical edition of the complete works of an individual composer. Classified under M3, these large, multivolume sets may take twenty to thirty years to complete. Today, most are guided by an international committee of scholars along with the publishing company issuing the set. Complete editions fall under the category of critical or scholarly editions.

Critical edition, also known as a *scholarly edition*. An edition intended as an accurate, authentic reading of the composer's intentions. Scholars responsible for these editions make a careful comparison and evaluation of the primary sources: autograph manuscript, manuscripts in the hand of contemporary copyists, sketches, or publications (proof copies with corrections, first edition, etc.) supervised by the composer. They keep editorial additions to a minimum and clearly distinguish between original notation or comments and those added by the editor. Volumes of critical commentary or *Kritische berichte* (Ger.) are published as part of a critical edition to describe differences among primary sources and to explain editorial decisions.

Facsimile. A photographic reproduction that replicates the original manuscript or printed source. An entire edition of a composition or group of compositions in facsimile conveys the composer's work, as written, to a modern audience. Frequently a sketch or single page of a manuscript will be reproduced in facsimile at the beginning of a performing or critical edition. At least one set of complete works is being issued in facsimile: *Gustav Holst: Collected Facsimile Edition*. Used for study rather than performance, facsimile editions are normally classed in ML96.5.

Historical set, monument, Denkmal (Ger.). A large, multivolume critical edition that includes compositions of many composers who are related by geography, time period, or genre; classified in M2. Examples that gather music of a country include *Denkmäler deutscher Tonkunst* (Monuments of German Music), *Musica Britannica*, and *Recent Researches in American Music*. Others are organized by time period, such as *Recent Researches in the Music of the Baroque Era*, or use a combination of criteria such as *Tudor English Church Music* or *English Lute Song*.

Performing edition, also known as a *practical edition*. An edition intended for performance rather than scholarly study. Such an edition may not indicate the source(s) on which it is based and may not differentiate between editorial additions and original markings. These editions vary greatly in quality. Performing editions are much less costly than scholarly editions. Yet, in the 20th century, a number of publishers have brought music scholarship to bear on performance editions by issuing *urtext* editions or by providing performance editions based on critical editions. Some of these publishers are Henle, Vienna Urtext, and Bärenreiter.

Urtext edition. The word "Urtext" literally means original source. While its use denotes a critical performing edition based on a single authoritative primary source, that may be misleading. Most musical works have multiple primary sources, which need to be compared to reconstruct the composer's intentions. Essentially, an *urtext* edition has the purpose of giving the composer's intentions without later editorial additions. If there are editorial additions, they should be clearly distinguishable through devices such as a smaller font, asterisk, or footnote.

16.3 Critical Editions (M1–M3.1) and Their Indexes

Because critical or scholarly editions are based on intense scholarly investigation, they are authoritative scores. Conductors, performers, musicologists, and theorists use them to verify possible errors in performing editions or as the authoritative score for analysis and study. The first questions to answer about critical editions are where are they located and which sets have been published?

The historical sets or monuments of music are classed in M2 for "musical sources." Composers' complete works are classed in M3, and for sets including partial contents of a composer's output, termed "selections," the classification is M3.1. First editions of compositions are shelved together in M3.5. To complete the picture, M1 is used for general collections or anthologies, which may or may not be critical editions. The following examples illustrate these types of special editions.

M1   *The International Library of Piano Music*
M2   *Denkmäler der Tonkunst in Österreich*
M3   *Carl Philipp Emanuel Bach Edition* or under its uniform title:
        Bach, Carl Philipp Emanuel, 1714–1788. Works.
M3.1   *Richard Strauss Vocal Works*

Checking a specialized bibliography is the best way to determine which of these large multivolume sets and series have been published. There are two print bibliographies plus a new database providing the means of locating specific compositions in the critical editions of music.

Heyer's monumental work, *Historical Sets, Collected Editions, and Monuments of Music: A Guide to Their Contents* (1980), is published in two volumes. The first is a bibliography listing historical sets and series by title and complete works by composer name, all interfiled in alphabetical order. For the complete works, explicit listings of series and volume contents give users a way to locate individual compositions. For the historical sets, the composer or topic of each volume is provided. The second volume is an index. It is especially useful for composer access to compositions in the M2 collections. Heyer's bibliography is still useful for critical editions published before 1980 and for volume access for those libraries that do not subscribe to the database, *Index to Printed Music* (*IPM*).

Published in 1997, *Collected Editions, Historical Series & Sets, & Monuments of Music: A Bibliography* by Hill and Stephens updates Heyer's work. It provides "a comprehensive list of important editions of historically significant music."[1] Under composer name, the bibliography lists separate editions of M3 complete works (or "collected editions" as they are called here) with the newest edition first. Contents of the sets are not included. For the M2 collections, every volume title is listed because each covers different composers, genres, or time periods. Users have direct access to composers' works, even when they are part of multicomposer M2 sets, so there is no need for an index. Complementary to this bibliography is a database, *Index to Printed Music: Collections & Series* (*IPM*, 2004–), that serves as an index to M2 and M3 sets. Its purpose is to assist users in finding individual compositions in standard scholarly critical editions. The database is expected to be complete in about 2008; it is searchable by composer, title, series name and number.

Actually, when it comes to determining the location of a composition in the composer's complete works (M3), there are three different ways to proceed.
- Consult the composers' works lists in *Grove Music Online* or *The New Grove's Dictionary of Music and Musicians*. Look for the abbreviation for the series title (*NBA* for *Neue Bach Ausgabe*, etc.) followed by series and volume numbers.
- Find the work in the composer's thematic catalog. Again, there will be abbreviations for the complete works and numbers for location within.
- Use the *Index to Printed Music* (*IPM*) or browse the volume listings for the complete edition in Heyer's *Historical Sets, Collected Editions, and Monuments*

of Music to obtain the specific series, volume, and page number for the work in the complete edition.

16.4 Performing Editions

The music (scores and parts) used for performance and study purposes is organized in the same ways as are the ML and MT books, from general collections to individual works by genre. Therefore, the rest of the M-subclass is divided into discrete classifications using specific numbers for instrumental music and vocal music. Further, vocal music is separated into secular and sacred categories.

M5–M1490	Instrumental music
M5	Collections of instrumental music of varying forces and instruments
M6–M175.5	Music for solo instruments
M177–M990	Music for two or more solo instruments [chamber music]
M1000–1420	Music for ensembles [orchestra, band, jazz ensembles]
M1375–M1420	Instrumental music for children
M1450–M1490	Various types of instrumental music [dance, aleatory, electronic]
M1495–M2199	Vocal music
M1495	Collections of vocal music of varying forces and types
M1497–M1990	Secular vocal music
M1999–M2199	Sacred vocal music

With a few pointers, it will be easier to make sense of the logic of the classification system as applied to printed music. Depending on the library's practice, the very same system may be applied to sound and visual recordings as well. Note, however, that most libraries use numeric schemes for sound recordings rather than LC subject classification.

Instrumental Music: M5–M1490

For solo instrumental music, the order of instruments is the same as in the ML and MT classes: keyboard (organ, piano, other), stringed, wind, plucked, and percussion instruments. By examining just a few examples, you will see some of the patterns that occur for instrumental music.

Solo string compositions are grouped together from M40 through M59.5 with separate numbers being assigned to each instrument in score order: violin, viola, violoncello, and double bass. Within the classes used for each instrument, collections come before separate works; and the order of works is miscellaneous, original works, arrangements. This pattern—shown for violin—occurs again and again for viola, violoncello, double bass, and then for each instrument in other instrument families.

M40–M59.5	Stringed instruments
M40–M44	Violin
M40	Miscellaneous collections

M41	Original works: collections
M42	Original works: separate works
M43	Arrangements: collections
M44	Arrangements: separate works
M44.3	Simplified editions
M45–M49	Viola
M50–M54.3	Violoncello
M55–M58	Double bass
M59.A–M59.Z	Other instruments by name, A–Z

Looking at solo and duet piano music, in M20–39, the same overall pattern occurs: miscellaneous collections, original compositions subdivided by collections and separate works, and then arrangements subdivided by collections and separate works. The patterns shown for piano apply in a similar way to other instruments and ensembles. That is, when it comes to original works there are divisions for the forms of composition most used for that instrument or ensemble. For piano, you see M23 for sonatas, M24 for suites, M25 for pieces, M27 for variations, M28 for marches, and M30–32 for dances. The specific forms will change depending on the instrument or ensemble.

M20–M39	Piano
M20	Miscellaneous collections
M21–M32	Original compositions
M21–M22	General collections
M23–M24	Special collections. Separate works
M23	Sonatas
M24	Suites
M25	Pieces
M25.2	Double keyboard, Janko keyboard, etc.
M25.3	Two pianos, one performer
M26–M26.2	Piano, 1 hand
M26	Left hand
M26.2	Right hand
M27	Variation forms
M28	Marches
M30–M32	Dances
M30	General
M31	Two-rhythm (polka, etc.)
M32	Three-rhythm (waltz, etc.)
M32.8–M39	Arrangements
M32.8	General collections
M33–M39.6	Special collections. Separate works
M33–M33.5	Operas, oratorios, cantatas, etc.
M34	Transcriptions, paraphrases
M35–M35.5	Orchestral music. Band music
M37–M37.5	Concertos, etc.
M38	Chamber music, part-songs, and music for one instrument
M39	Potpourris. Medleys

M39.5   Works for two pianos, one performer
M39.6   Works for piano, 1 hand

Chamber music, called "music for two or more solo instruments," comes next in M177–M990. This category is very easy. The 100s include collections of two or more different combinations and then duets for keyboard instruments. Most duets are M200s, trios M300s, and so on to nonets in M900s. Of course, within each of these large categories there are class numbers for specific instruments. For example, exact trio numbers depend on the types of instruments in the trio:

M315–M319   Piano and two wind instruments
M320–M324   Piano, one stringed, and one wind instrument
M325–M329   Piano and two plucked instruments

Works for orchestra comprise the next large grouping:

M1000–1075   Standard orchestra
    M1001   Symphonies
    M1002   Symphonic poems
    M1003   Suites; variations
    M1004   Overtures
    M1005–1039   Concertos for one instrument and orchestra
    M1040   Concertos for two or more different solo instruments
    M1042   Concertos for orchestra

It is helpful to observe that for the concertos for one solo instrument, there will be one number for the full score and then the very next number for a piano reduction of the score. For instance, piano concertos in full score are classed ML1010 while the piano reductions are classed ML1011. The same thing happens for violin with M1012 and M1013.

The exact numerical pattern used for standard or chamber orchestra is then repeated for string orchestra using M1100–1175. These logical structures continue, with some changes for the nature of the ensemble, through the rest of the instrumental music area.

M1200–M1269   Band
M1270   Fife (bugle) and drum music, field music, etc.
M1350–M1353   Reduced orchestra
M1355   Jazz ensembles
M1356–M1365   Dance orchestra and instrumental ensembles
M1375–M1420   Instrumental music for children

Final instrumental categories include these.

M1450   Dance music
M1470   Aleatory music
M1473   Electronic music
M1480   Music with color or light apparatus
M1490   Music printed before 1700 or copied in manuscript before
                 1700

Vocal Music: M1495–M2199

Patterns for vocal music again replicate the order of subclasses in ML and MT. The overall division is between secular and sacred music. For vocal music, the divisions relate to the kind of score and to the forces in the performance: solo; vocal chamber music as duets, trios, etc.; choirs with men's or women's voices: SSA, SATB, TTBB, etc.

Under dramatic music, M1500–M1527.8, the classifications used for opera scores illustrate well the classification distinctions for type of score.

M1500–M1508.2	Operas
M1500–M1503.5	Scores
M1500	Complete works
M1501	Concert arrangements
M1502–M1503.5	Vocal scores. Chorus scores
M1502	Without accompaniment
M1503–M1503.5	Piano accompaniment
M1503	General
M1503.5	Concert arrangements
M1504	College operas
M1505–M1508.2	Excerpts
M1505	Original accompaniment
M1506–M1508	Arranged accompaniment
M1506	Orchestra or other ensemble
M1507	Piano Collections
M1508	Separate works. By title

It is not important to memorize classification numbers, but as you use various scores start to notice their classifications. For singers, it becomes easy to remember that M1500 is the place to find complete operas in full score and M1503 is the place to find them in vocal score. Excerpts are found in other classifications. The type of accompaniment helps determine which number is assigned to each score. Art songs, primarily in collections, are classed from M1611–M1624.8. Remember to consult song indexes to locate specific song titles within published collections. National, regional, popular songs, and topical songs are found in classes M1629–1978.

Choral musicians will be interested in the two major categories for choral music: secular in M1530–M1610 and sacred in M1999–M2199. Patterns for the order of choral music rest on types of voices for the choral work (mixed, men's or treble) and accompaniment type.

M1530–M1610	Choruses
M1530–M1546.5	Choruses with orchestra or other ensemble
M1530–M1537	Mixed voices
M1530–M1531	Full scores
	With separate numbers for type of accompaniment: orchestral, other, and with recitation
M1532–M1533	Vocal and chorus scores unaccompanied or with piano accompaniment
M1534–M1537	Excerpts with original or arranged accompaniment, orchestra, piano collections and piano separate works

The grouping of vocal music for children includes songs suitable for the classroom, school music textbooks (M1994), dramatic, and choral music.

Vocal music for children

M1990–M1998	Secular vocal music for children
M1990	Kindergarten
M1992–M1994.6	Primary and secondary schools
M1992	Miscellaneous collections
M1993	Action songs. Drill songs. Musical games
M1994	School songbooks
M1994.5–	
M1994.6	School songs of particular schools. By school, A–Z
M1995	Dramatic music
M1996	Cantatas
M1997–M1998	Choruses, songs, etc.
M1999–M2199	Sacred vocal music
M1999	Collections
M2000–M2007	Oratorios

Specific classifications follow expected patterns:

M2000	Full scores
M2001	Vocal and chorus scores without accompaniment
M2003	Vocal scores with piano or organ accompaniment
M2004–M2007	Excerpts with original accompaniment, arranged accompaniment, orchestra, piano or organ, collections, and separate works.
M2010–M2017.6	Services, by religion and denomination subarranged by type of music such as masses
M2018–M2019.5	Sacred vocal chamber music
M2020–M2101.5	Choruses
M2102–M2114.8	Songs
M2115–M2188	Hymnals. Hymn collections
M2190–M2196	Sacred vocal music for children

16.5 Sound Recordings

Using a library catalog to find sound recordings works much like finding scores, but there are several factors to keep in mind. Just as printed music may be published in collections of several works, frequently there are many compositions included on a single recording. The title of a recording may not cover all of its contents and may not even list the composers. Here are a few search hints for sound recordings.

- Use an author search for performers as well as composers.
- Searching for a specific work will probably require a combination of composer name and composition title information.
- Start with a specific title (using thematic catalog or opus numbers as appropriate) and move to more general titles. For example, search for "Beethoven sonata 110," but if you don't find it try "Beethoven sonatas piano."

- Look at the full record to see the contents listing for the recording. It will have composers and titles most of the time.
- The full record will also display the names of performers.
- See Chapter 10 under "LC Subject Headings for Musical Compositions" for a discussion of specific types of subject headings to use.

Many libraries use a simple numbering system to identify shelf location for sound recordings; others use systems based on record label numbering, and a few use classification systems such as that of the Library of Congress.

Distribution methods for sound recordings have started to change in the last few years. Today libraries purchase physical recordings, mainly compact discs, but they are also beginning to subscribe to online sound databases that provide access to music from websites and deliver it via web streaming. The following sound databases, or music-listening services, became generally available in 2004 and 2005: *Classical Music Library*, offering more than 50,000 audio tracks from over 30 labels in 2007; *Naxos Music Library*, which includes the entire catalog of Naxos, Marco Polo, and DaCapo recordings plus others and provides access to over 263,000 tracks from thousands of complete compact discs; and *Smithsonian Global Sound*, covering traditional music of the world, natural sounds, and folk music from published recordings owned by Smithsonian Folkways Recordings, and archival collections of Folkways, Cook, Dyer-Bennet, and other labels. Another scholarly online source for recordings is *DRAM* (*Database of Recorded American Music*), which began in 2001 and includes over 1,500 CDs (9,800 compositions), liner notes, and essays from New World, Composers Recordings, and several other labels. A source for jazz recordings from the Naxos and Fantasy catalogs is *Naxos Music Library Jazz* (2005).

Review Questions

1. List and define four different formats used for printed music.

2. Distinguish between the contents of M2 and M3 critical editions.

3. Describe the underlying process for creating a critical edition; that is, what are the sources or bases for such an edition?

4. List two of the three ways to determine the location of a specific composition in a composer's complete works.

Learning Exercise

Compare two editions of a composition: a performing edition and a critical edition in the composer's complete works. Your goal is to observe differences in the published editions but not at the measure-by-measure level of detail. First, identify a composition to study, then find the work in the composer's complete works and in a performing edition.
NOTE: The two editions should be of different publishers.

Supply the following information based on your comparison:

1. Composer and title of work

2. Explain how you found the two editions

3. Performing edition:
    a. Call number
    b. Editor
    c. Is this an *urtext* edition? How do you know? What does *urtext* mean?
    d. Are facsimiles of primary sources included? Of what?
    e. Is critical commentary included anywhere in the score? How much and of what type?

4. Critical edition in complete works:
    a. Title of the complete works set and complete call number of the volume that contains this composition
    b. Is there a volume of critical commentary to accompany this volume of the music? Please list its call number. If not, are critical comments included in the volume with the score? How much and of what type?

5. Comparison: Explain differences between the two scores.
    a. Dynamics and articulation markings
    b. Is instructional information present such as realization of ornaments?
    c. Do editorially added markings appear to be differentiated from the originals? How?
    d. Are there footnotes to offer explanations?

6. For performance, which edition would you choose and why?

Note

1. George R. Hill and Norris L. Stephens, *Collected Editions, Historical Series & Sets, & Monuments of Music: A Bibliography* (Berkeley, CA: Fallen Leaf Press, 1997), p. ix.

Chapter 17

ML: Music Literature

Preview

- Books of vocal texts, usually with translations, are essential to singers and choral musicians. Find them in the reference collection or in the general book stacks in ML47–49 and ML54. For the full libretto of an opera, go to ML50.
- Histories of music demonstrate a variety of approaches: surveys, chronologies, music iconographies, outline music histories, and source readings. Some cover music of a specific time period; others treat music of a country or region.
- Biographies are written to portray an individual historically in time and to assess his or her contributions. Biographies of musicians are issued collectively, covering a number of people related in some way, or for individuals: composers, performers, music publishers, and others.
- Books on performance practice are of interest to performers, conductors, and musicologists; they present scholarly findings about instruments, styles, and ways of playing that document the performance of music in various times and places. Today performance research informs the playing of most performers, who seek "authenticity" in historical works they play.
- The ML (Music Literature) and MT (Instruction and Study) subclasses organize books and other materials by subject. Patterns in the classifications for instrumental and vocal music present a logical structure across the areas for music history, analysis, instruction and study, and techniques for children.

17.1 Translations: ML47–49 and Texts: ML54

Books providing word-for-word and poetic texts and translations are useful to vocalists, conductors, and music historians. The LC Classification area for libretti (the words) and scenarios of dramatic vocal works is ML47 through ML54.8. As is usual in the classification schemes, the organizational pattern moves from general to specific. In this case, the major subclasses for vocal texts line up as follows:

ML47   Miscellaneous collections
ML48–50.7 Opera
      ML48–49   Collections of opera texts
      ML50   Separate works [Individual libretti]
ML54.6–54.8   Solo songs and cantatas

For choral directors, especially, Jeffers' *Translations and Annotations of Choral Repertoire* is a useful set of translations covering sacred Latin texts and German texts in two volumes. In many libraries, these may be classed in BV, for religious texts.

A valuable and recent series of translations of opera libretti has been edited by Nico Castel in conjunction with various opera singers and published by Leyerle in Geneseo, NY. Each is a separate publication with no series title. These books include International Phonetic Alphabet transcriptions and word-for-word translations along with notes on phonetics of the language involved or the specific translation. Individual volumes cover opera libretti of Puccini, Verdi, Mozart, *bel canto* and *verismo* Italian operas, Strauss, Wagner's *Ring* cycle, and a selection of German operas.

There are books in abundance providing the texts to solo songs and cantatas. Most provide poetic or word-by-word translations into English and are classed in ML54. For instance, there are *Schubert's Complete Song Texts* (1996) by Glass, *Lieder Line by Line, and Word for Word* (1996) by Phillips, and *The Singer's Debussy* (1987) by Rohinsky.

17.2 Music History and Chronology

A good place to find an overview of the study of music history is Stanley Glenn's entry "Historiography" in *Grove Music Online*. Glenn reviews trends and issues both prior to the existence of music history as an academic study and from 1750 to the end of the 20th century. His bibliography covers works from 1310 through 1997.

On library shelves, books on music history extend from LC Classifications ML159 to ML360. General histories fall in ML159–ML160, then histories by period in ML161–ML197, followed by histories centered on a geographic region or country in ML198–ML360. In addition to the classifications that allow us to browse at the shelves, it is enlightening to examine music history books that have a specific orientation or those that offer specific kinds of information. The following groupings and examples illustrate some of these different approaches to the publication of historical information about music.

Surveys: ML160

A survey of music history usually attempts to cover music as created and experienced in all time periods and regions of the world. These surveys range from single-volume textbooks for undergraduate music courses to multivolume works presenting lengthy and detailed explanations of events or concepts in specific periods or geographical regions. **A History of Western Music* (2006) by Burkholder, Grout, and Palisca, a comprehensive music history, has become the standard college textbook. Its publisher, W. W. Norton, also offers both a collection of scores, *Norton Anthology of Western Music*, 7th ed., and the *Norton Recorded Anthology of Western Music*, a set of audio compact discs. The current edition offers expanded coverage of social and cultural history and of previously underrepresented music from the 20th century, the Americas, and popular music in all time periods. Two historically significant books illustrate a change in emphasis from chronological facts of music history to survey approaches that feature stylistic or social analysis. Crocker's *A History of Musical Style* (1966) was the first to concentrate on the style of music over time. It is not classed with the general music histories but with books on composition and performance in ML430.5. Noteworthy as the first historical survey to emphasize the place of music in society, Lang's *Music in Western Civilization* (1941) influenced the writing of music history in the second half of the 20th century.

Music History Series: ML160

The history of music, from ancient times to the 21st century, can be given more in-depth treatment when separate volumes are prepared to cover specific time periods. Publishers' series exist to do this very thing. Note that the publisher's name is part of the title. Publishers set a standard format, length, audience, and general organization for books in their series and recruit specialist authors to write each book. The latest editions of several major series are listed here. *The Oxford History of Western Music* (2005), edited by Taruskin, includes five period volumes and one on resources including chronology, bibliography, and master index. It will be available as an online source in 2009 as part of the *Oxford Music Online* gateway. *The Norton Introduction to Music History* (1978–2005) replaces the earlier *Norton History of Music* series (1978–2001). This publisher's series covers European and American music by period and offers a companion score anthology for each book. Titles in this series are frequently used for period courses in music history. Period and regional volumes in *The Prentice-Hall History of Music Series* (1991–2002) are suitable for use as textbooks for advanced undergraduates. Of seven current volumes, five cover periods of music history and two are geographically oriented.

Chronologies: Classed by Topic or Period

It is certainly easy to understand that chronologies present information in date order. However, many people do not realize the value of modern music history chronologies. Some offer information on premiere performances and the critical reception of musical works. For instance, ****Music since 1900** (2001), edited by Slonimsky and Kuhn, was first published in 1937. The latest edition was completed by Laura Kuhn after Slonimsky's death in 1995. It continues the four-part organization of recent editions, including a descriptive chronology, a collection of letters and documents, a dictionary of terms, and an index. The day-by-day listings cover January 1900 through 14 December 2000. While uneven in areas such as women's contributions to music and jazz, music at the end of the 20th century is well covered. Other types of chronologies offer only brief information on composers and other musical events. *A Chronicle of American Music: 1700–1995* (1996) by Hall lists musical events with some reference to other arts, politics, and society in general. Kendall's *The Chronicle of Classical Music: An Intimate Diary of the Lives and Music of the Great Composers* (2000) is an illustrated chronology of musical events over four centuries.

Music Iconography: ML85–89

Music history, as represented pictorially or in other visual art forms, is the basic interest of those who study music iconography. In *Grove Music Online*, Tilman Seebass defines iconography as "the study of visual representations, their significance and interpretation."[1] Music iconography, therefore, relates to representations of objects used to make music, places for making music, and musicians. These representations may be in any type of visual art, illustrations or drawings, photographs, paintings, cartoons, and more.

Iconographical studies gained prominence in music during the 1970s and 1980s. At this time the formation of an international project occurred, the *Répertoire International d'Iconographie Musicale (RIdIM)*, to develop methods to study, classify, and catalog visual material relating to music for scholarly and practical purposes. Established in 1972, *RIdIM* is sponsored by the International Musicological Society and International Association of Music Libraries, as well as the International Council of Museums. A number of bibliographies have been published under its auspices. The official organ of *RIdIM* is a yearbook, *Imago musicae: International Yearbook of Musical Iconography*, which began in 1984. It is a journal that disseminates articles relating to music and art or research on music images. The LC subject heading, "Music in Art–Periodicals," retrieves such journals.

George Kinsky wrote *A History of Music in Pictures* in 1929, reprinted by Dover in 1951. This classic work provides, in chronological order, portraits of musicians; music in the visual arts of painting, drawing, and sculpture; early instruments; and facsimiles of compositions and theoretical works. It was a groundbreaking work for iconography. An ongoing series entitled *Musikgeschichte in Bildern*, edited by Besseler and Schneider, began in 1961 and today consists of 26 volumes in four series:

> Band I. *Musikethnologie* [Music in Societies and Cultures of the World]
> Band II. *Musik Altertums* [Music of Antiquity]
> Band III. *Musik des Mittelalters und der Renaissance* [Music of the Middle Ages and Renaissance]
> Band IV. *Musik der Neuzeit* [Music of Modern Times]

Individual volumes concentrate on specific subjects or geographical areas. The set is retrievable under the LC subject heading, "Music–History and criticism–Pictorial works."

Outline Histories: ML161

The outline histories of music present information in a narrative outline form and are used primarily as study aids. The following examples have been published in many editions: Miller and Cockrell's *History of Western Music* (1991) and *An Outline History of Western Music* by Wold (1997).

Source Readings: Classed According to Topic

Source readings provide the documentary foundation of music history and have been assembled generally for a particular topic or focus. In these collections, primary sources are presented for study and often are accompanied by commentary and contextual statements. Much of the time primary sources are referred to simply as "sources." A Library of Congress subject heading for them is "Music–History and criticism–Sources."

Many primary-source collections have appeared also to serve specific needs: composers writing on music or the process of composing; travelers writing on non-Western music as they observed it; writings on performance, music education, or women in the practice of music. These letters, documents, diary entries, performance reviews by music critics, or classical writings enliven our understanding of music history from the viewpoint of those who were present at the time.

For General Music History

An indispensable primary source reader for musicians, both students and practitioners, is **Source Readings in Music History* (1998) by Strunk and Treitler. It is published in one volume and is also available in seven separate volumes issued to cover specific time periods. Another example is Weiss and Taruskin's *Music in the Western World: A History in Documents* (1984).

For Special Topics

As a student or researcher, you should look for special-topic source readings or documentary histories. They will enrich your understanding of your field of interest. The following titles illustrate the variety of subject coverage existing in this genre: *Time, Place and Music: An Anthology of Ethnomusicological Observations c.1550 to c.1800* (1973) by Harrison; MacClintock's *Readings in the History of Music in Performance* (1982); *Music Education: Source Readings from Ancient Greece to Today* (2002) by Michael Mark; Neuls-Bates' *Women in Music: An Anthology of Source Readings from the Middle Ages to the Present* (1996); *Music Education: Source Readings from Ancient Greece to Today* by Mark (2002); and Southern's *Readings in Black American Music* (1983).

17.3 Biographies

Some biographies are written to include groups of musicians in different categories such as pianists, conductors, or singers. These collective biographies are located in LC classifications ML385–406. Remember that you may discover them using a subject-heading search, for instance, "Pianists–Biography" or "Conductors (Music)–Biography," or "Singers–Biography."

Books about the lives and works of individual composers comprise the largest section of any music library's biographical section. They are easy to browse; just find ML410 and look for the subject of the biography by surname, A–Z. Individual biographies of performers and other musicians follow the same pattern established for the collective biographies. The list below compares the classification order for both collective and individual biographies.

Other reference books that aid in the search for biographical information include bio-bibliographies and biographical indexes. Use this book-type terminology in subject-heading searches; for instance, "Composers–Bio-bibliography" retrieves *A Directory of Composers for Organ* (1999) by Henderson. And the subject heading "Composers–Biography–Indexes" retrieves *Composers on Record: An Index to Biographical Information on 14,000 Composers Whose Music Has Been Recorded* (1985) by Greene.

Online databases also are available to aid in the search for biographic information. *Biography and Genealogy Master Index (BGMI)* accesses biographies on over 4 million people from the beginning of time through the present. This database helps identify which reference books include entries on the individual you are researching. *BGMI* covers both current and retrospective reference books containing multiple biographies; it does not index periodical articles or books of biography about a single individual.

Check your library's list of databases to determine if you have access to this or another biography database. Finding death dates of musicians who lived since the middle of the 20th century is a challenge. Gaylord Music Library of Washington University provides an online necrology based on compilation work of Nathan Eakin. The online version currently covers deaths between 1999 and 2005 and is available at http://www.library.wustl.edu/units/music/necro/.

Figure 17.1 Classification Numbers for Collective and Individual Biographies

Collective	**Individual**	**Biography Category**
ML385	—	General works [various types of musicians]
ML390	ML410	Composers
ML395	—	Instrumentalists, general works
ML396	ML416	Organists
ML397	ML417	Pianists
ML398	ML418	Stringed instrument players
ML399	ML419	Other instrumentalists
ML400	ML420	Singers
—	ML421	Vocal and instrumental performing groups
ML402	ML422	Conductors
ML403	ML423	Theoreticians, historians, critics, etc.
ML404	ML424	Manufacturers of instruments
ML405	ML425	Music publishers, printers, dealers
ML406	ML426	Others

Biographies in Series

Two current publishers' series are issuing new and revised biographies of composers. These are well-respected series, but it is not necessary to list all of the composers included because it is easy to locate them in library catalogs. Use a subject keyword search for the composer's last name. *The Master Musicians*, originally published by J. M. Dent and Sons in London, began in 1948. The American edition began with Schirmer Books and continues under Oxford University Press. More than 40 composers' biographies have been published in the series. New editions and new titles published since 2000 include: Britten, Musorgsky, Puccini, Rachmaninoff, Ravel, and Schumann. *The New Grove Composer Biography Series* consists of composer biography articles from the second edition of *The New Grove Dictionary of Music and Musicians* with substantial additions and updates to both text and bibliographies. Published since 2000 are volumes on Beethoven, Mozart, and Stravinsky. A number of earlier volumes are collective in nature such as *The New Grove Twentieth-Century American Masters*: Ives, Thomson, Sessions, Cowell, Gershwin, Copland, Carter, Barber, Cage, Bernstein; *The New Grove Russian Masters*; and *The New Grove French Baroque Masters*: Lully, Charpentier, Laland, Couperin, Rameau.

17.4 Performance Practice

The study of performance practice is concerned with how music was performed historically and how it is performed today. The subject is of great interest to modern performers. Aspects of the topic include how musical notation is realized in performance including ornamentation, improvisation, tempo, rhythm, and articulation; playing of instruments and production of the voice; size, arrangement, and conducting of ensembles; and pitch and temperament.

LC classifications ML430–ML458 are used for books on composition and performance as a part of music history. The earlier numbers in the category cover style, improvisation, notation, rhythm, melody, use of continuo, harmony, counterpoint, musical form, and instrumentation. ML457 covers interpretation and performance practice while ML458 is used for conducting. Books classed in these areas are not instructional, but instead they deal with historical development of these aspects of music.

Library of Congress subject headings for performance practice are fairly obvious. "Performance practice (Music)" is the primary heading and is used for books that deal with styles of performance in particular periods, places, or groups. A broader term is "Music–Performance." Narrower terms that may be of interest are "Musica ficta" and "Embellishment (Music)." Note that books on performance aspects of specific instruments are given more specific subject headings. For instance, when it comes to the piano there are two primary headings: "Piano–Performance" and "Piano music–Interpretation (Phrasing, dynamics, etc.)." These more specialized performance guides are likely to be shelved in classification areas with other books about the instrument or its music. Such piano performance materials are shelved in classes ML700–742.

Reference Books on Performance Practice

A new dictionary on the topic in general is classed in ML100: *Performance Practice: A Dictionary-Guide for Musicians* (2005) by Roland Jackson. It provides alphabetical access to performance practice topics related to instruments, genres, tuning, etc. It includes articles on individuals important to the study of authentic performance. While there are not many published bibliographies covering performance practice, the few that exist give you a starting point for identifying primary and secondary sources on the topic. Also by Roland Jackson is *Performance Practice, Medieval to Contemporary: A Bibliographic Guide* (1988). Covering writings published from 1960 to 1986, the bibliography is arranged by historical period and subarranged by categories and includes 20th-century performance practice. Vinquist and Zaslaw compiled an earlier bibliography of both primary and secondary sources written between 1100 and 1900: *Performance Practice: A Bibliography* (1971). Of course, you can identify more recent articles, books, or book reviews in online journal or current literature databases.

General Performance Practice Books: ML457

Two stellar works on historical performance are Donington's **The Interpretation of Early Music* (1989) for Baroque music and ***Performance Practices of the Seventeenth and Eighteenth Centuries* (1993) by Neumann and Stevens. Neumann has written many books on performance practice including *Essays in Performance Practice* (1982); *New Essays on Performance Practice* (1989); and others on Bach and Mozart. Some of the most recent books on the topic include: *Playing with History: The Historical Approach to Musical Performance* (2002) by John Butt; *A Performer's Guide to Medieval Music* (2000) by Duffin; and *Performing French Classical Music: Sources and Applications* (2001) by Schultz.

Early Music Revival and "Authenticity"

An important part of the study of performance practice relates to the effort to discover what was an "authentic" style of performance during an historical period. While there had been various episodes of revival of earlier music, such as Mendelssohn's performances of works of J. S. Bach, after World War II early music became a popular commodity. Long-playing records and independent labels spurred the interest in early music. New music scholarship influenced performers such as Alfred Deller, Denis Stevens, and Thurston Dart; conductors like Nikolaus Harnoncourt and Gustav Leonhardt; and new ensembles such as the Monteverdi Choir, the Ensemble Clément Janequin, and the Hilliard Ensemble. These and other leaders demonstrated a strong interest in using historical instruments and information from recent scholarship to perform music in a manner that was as close as possible to the original style. Harry Haskell, author of "Early Music" in *Grove Music Online*, has documented this movement in *The Early Music Revival: A History* (1988, reprinted 1996).

17.5 Music Theory and Composition: ML and MT

A variety of books are used in support of the study of music theory and composition. One special category is that of facsimiles of composers' manuscripts [ML95.5–96.5]. These photographic reproductions of original music manuscripts may be published as anthologies of excerpts from several composers or may consist of the full manuscript of a single composition reproduced to show exactly how each page appeared. Useful for demonstrating aspects of the compositional process, facsimiles are of special interest to conductors and performers as well as composers, theorists, and musicologists.

Early music treatises, in their original languages and in translation [ML170], are primary sources for the theorist and musicologist. *Corpus Scriptorum de Musica (CSM)*, a series published by the American Institute of Musicology, presents treatises on music written between the 11th and 16th centuries. Two database projects are meeting the need for access to treatises. *Thesaurus Musicarum Latinarum (TML)* at Indiana University eventually will contain the full corpus of Latin music theory from the Middle Ages and early Renaissance. It permits users to access the unedited texts of these sources plus various printed editions. Utrecht University's *Thesaurus Musicarum Italicarum (TMI)* provides Italian music treatises from the second half of the 16th to the early 17th century.

Rather than list numerous examples of resources for music theory, let's consider how the LC Classification system groups books for composition and music theory. The following chart illustrates the logical and consistent arrangement of these topics, whether they fall in the area of history and literature (ML) or study and teaching (MT).

Figure 17.2 Books for Music Theory and Composition

Subject Matter	History	Appreciation and Analysis	Technique / Instruction and Study
Music manuscript facsimiles	ML96–96.5		
Music treatises, medieval & Renaissance	ML170		
General works	ML430	MT6.5 or MT91	
Style	ML430.5		
Improvisation; Accompaniment; Transposition	ML430.7		MT68
Notation	ML431–432		MT35–39
Rudiments; Music theory for children			MT7
Composition			MT40–41
Rhythm	ML437		MT42
Solmization			MT44
Scales			MT45
Melody	ML440		MT47
Continuo	ML442		MT49
Harmony	ML444	MT90–146	MT50
Counterpoint & polyphony	ML446		MT55
Music forms & genres	ML448		MT58–67
Instrumentation & orchestration	ML455		MT70–74
Interpretation; Performance practice	ML457		MT75
Embellishment			MT80
Memorizing			MT82
Conduction; Score reading and playing	ML458		MT85

Books covering the history and construction of instruments, and the forms of instrumental and vocal music over the centuries are numerous. They are classed from ML459 to almost the end of the ML subclass, ML3265. It is useful to have some knowledge of the arrangement of these books and journals on the shelves and to understand some of the common subarrangements for them.

17.6 Instruments and Instrumental Music: ML and MT

There are four large groupings for books and journals about instruments, their history and construction, and on music written for instruments: (1) instruments in general; (2) instrumental music and playing of instruments; (3) ensembles: chamber music, orchestra, band; and (4) electronic and computer music. The major categories and subdivisions follow a pattern as well: periodicals, societies, and general works, studies by period, books by region or country, and then specific categories such as the families of instruments and specific instruments one by one. Again it is possible to make comparisons between the history and literature subclass (ML) and in various parts of the instruction and study subclass (MT).

Figure 17.3 Books for Instrumentalists

Instruments / Instrumental Music	History	Appreciation and Analysis	Technique / Instruction and Study	Instruction and Study for Children
General	ML459–548	MT90	MT170–172	MT740–801
Collections for Analysis		MT6.5 or 91		
Composers		MT92		
Keyboard	ML549–747		MT179–258	
Bowed Stringed	ML749–927		MT259–338	
Wind	ML929–990		MT339–538	
Plucked	ML999–1015		MT539–654	
Percussion	ML1030–1049		MT655–728.3	
Mechanical, other, and electronic	ML1049.8–1093			
Ensembles				
Chamber	ML1100–1165	MT140–145	MT728	MT810
Orchestra	ML1200–1270	MT125–130	MT730	MT810
Band	ML1299–1354	MT135–136	MT733–735	MT810
Percussion			MT736	
Electronic and Computer	ML1379–1380		MT56	

17.7 The Voice and Vocal Music: ML and MT

Vocal music resources, for both singers and choral directors, are also arranged in four groups: (1) general works on vocal music, (2) choral music, (3) secular vocal music, and (4) sacred vocal music. Each major area is subdivided for periodicals, societies, and general works; time periods; regions or countries; and forms or types of music. There are some special categories for books on private pedagogy and school music instruction such as physiology and care of the voice, history of vocal instruction and study, systems and methods of teaching, special teaching techniques, and studies and exercises. Forms and types of secular vocal music include opera, musicals, cantatas, and songs.

While not surprising, it is useful to note that sacred vocal music has patterns of sub-division by religion and even by specific denomination. Some of the sacred forms and types of music include oratorio, cantata, chorale, Gregorian chant, Psalmody and hymnology, liturgy and ritual, mass, Gospel music, and contemporary Christian music.

Figure 17.4 Books for Singers

Instruments / Instrumental Music	History	Appreciation and Analysis	Technique / Instruction and Study	Instruction and Study for Children
General vocal music	ML1400–1460		MT820	MT898
Choral music	ML1499–1554		MT875	MT915
Secular Vocal Music	ML1600–2881			
Dramatic music: opera, musicals, etc.	ML1700–2110	MT95–100		
Cantatas	ML2400			
Songs	ML2500–2881	MT120–121		
Sacred Vocal Music	ML2900–3275			
Oratorios	ML3201–3251	MT110–115		
Cantatas	ML3260	MT110–115		
Chorales	ML3265	MT110–115		
Other				
Physiology; Care of the voice			MT821	
History of vocal instruction & study			MT823	
Systems & methods			MT825–850	MT900
Special techniques			MT855–883	MT905
Studies & exercises			MT885–893	

17.8 Program and Dance Music

Books on these subjects are classed from ML3300 through ML3465 to include those focusing on periods, regions or countries, and specific types such as ballet or pantomime.

After all the music history and literature areas that concentrate on art music, the ML subclass turns to popular and national music and then to other aspects of music that do not necessarily rest on the classical music tradition. These types of literature will be discussed briefly and not totally in LC Classification order.

17.9 Popular and National Music

This growing segment of music book publishing includes popular music of all types including jazz, blues, and rock as well as national (folk and world) music. Note that specific types of popular music, from jazz to rock and beyond, have distinct numerical divisions assigned to them.

ML3469–3541	Popular music
ML3505.8–3509	Jazz
ML3519–3520	Bluegrass music
ML3520.8–3521	Blues. Rhythm and blues
ML3523–3524	Country music
ML3526–3532	Disco, Doo-wop, Funk, Honky-tonk, House, Industrial, Klezmer, New Age, Novelty songs, Ragtime, Rap, Reggae
ML3533.8	Rock music
ML3535–3541	Rockabilly, Salsa, Skiffle, Soul, Swamp pop, Techno, Underground dance music, Western swing

For national music, geographic subarrangements parallel those for other types of materials: continent, country or region, and city or locality. Countries that have greater quantities of publications are given discrete classification numbers, such as ML3563 for Canada; others are given decimal groupings, such as South America: ML3575.A3–Z, organized alphabetically by region or country.

ML3544–3775   National music by region or country

17.10 Music Industry

Books in this classification range, ML3790–3795, encompass music publishing, the sound recording industry, careers in music, copyright and licensing, and other business aspects of music. **This Business of Music: The Definitive Guide to the Music Industry* (2003) is now in its ninth edition, written by Krasilovsky, Shemel, and Gross.

17.11 Guides to Research and the Discipline

For the disciplines of musicology and ethnomusicology, much has been written defining the nature of these areas of study, their methods, and research needs. Practitioners in these fields study music history in art music and popular music as well as music practiced in societies around the world. Books that cover the disciplines treat the methods, techniques, and issues of these two related scholarly fields.

Musicology: ML3797

For an overview of musicology as a scholarly study of music, consult "Musicology" by Duckles and others in *Grove Music Online*. It includes aspects of the discipline: historical method, theoretical and analytical method, textual criticism, archival research, lexicography, organology, iconography, performance practice, aesthetics, criticism, sociomusicology, psychology and hearing, gender and sexual studies. Recent books on the nature of the field include *Empirical Musicology: Aims, Methods, Prospects* (2004) by Clarke and Cook, Kivy's *New Essays on Musical Understanding* (2001), Korsyn's *Decentering Music: A Critique of Contemporary Musical Research* (2003), and *Constructing Musicology* (2001) by Alastair Williams.

Ethnomusicology: ML3797.6–3799

The *Grove Music Online* article, "Ethnomusicology," by Carole Pegg and others defines the field as "the study of social and cultural aspects of music and dance in local and global contexts."[2] Authors of the article list contemporary theoretical issues in these categories: theory and culture, communities and their musics, ethnicity, nationalism and globalization, race, sexuality and gender, new historicism, practice theory, and music theory and analysis.

Two books of interest here are *The Cultural Study of Music: A Critical Introduction* (2003) edited by Clayton, Trevor, and Middleton and Myers' *Ethnomusicology: Historical and Regional Studies* (1993).

17.12 Philosophy and Physics of Music: ML3800–3920

The study of music crosses into other fields when the sciences of sound and perception come into play. Books in these areas cover such major topics as acoustics and physics, ML3805–3817; physiology, ML3820; psychology, ML3830–3838; music and color, ML3840; aesthetics, ML3845–3877; criticism, ML3880–3915; social, political, therapeutic, and religious aspects, ML3916–3921; and music therapy, ML3919–3920.

17.13 Juvenile Literature on Music

Books written for children on types of music, instruments, orchestras, composers, and more are shelved together in these classification areas: ML3928–3930.

Review Questions

1. Identify at least three types of music history books and give examples of each.

2. What was the early music revival of the 20th century? Name some of its proponents.

3. What does "performance practice" mean? Why is it important to performers, conductors, musicologists, ethnomusicologists?

Learning Exercises

1. Prepare annotated citations for three history books, each from a different category: surveys, historical series, chronologies, music iconography, outline histories, or

source reading. Choose books that you expect to use in your graduate studies or in the future.

2. Use the catalog or browsing to select three history books that treat your area of concentration as a graduate student. They might relate to the history of an instrument, ensemble, voice, music written for it, or genre histories on opera or jazz. Others might choose histories of music education or books about the study of history in musicology or ethnomusicology. Prepare annotated citations for these books.

3. General books on performance practice are classed in ML427. Those for specific instruments may be identified using a subject-heading search. Choose one general book and one for your instrument, voice, or ensemble; then prepare annotated citations for each.

4. Consult the classification charts in this chapter for books on instruments and instrumental music or voice and vocal music. Make your own list of LC Classifications and what they contain for your area of applied music or ensemble. Determine, for piano and piano music or for chamber music, etc., what classifications are used for history, analysis, technique, and instruction.

Notes

1. Tilman Seebass, "Music Iconography," in *Grove Music Online*, ed. by L. Macy, http://www.grovemusic.com (accessed 30 August 2007).
2. Carole Pegg, "Ethnomusicology," in *Grove Music Online*, ed. by L. Macy, http://www.grovemusic.com (accessed 30 August 2007).

Chapter 18

MT: Instruction and Study

Preview

- The ML (Music Literature) and MT (Instruction and Study) subclasses organize books and other materials by subject. Patterns in the classifications for instrumental and vocal music present a logical structure across the areas for music history, analysis, instruction and study, and techniques for children. See Chapter 17 for comparisons of classifications in ML and MT on music theory, instruments and instrumental music, voice and vocal music.
- The third major subclass, MT, is used to arrange materials published for teaching purposes whether for preschool, grades K–12, higher education, applied music, the adult learner, or music theory and composition.
- The literature of education in general is provided in class L of the Library of Congress Classification. Obviously, many education reference books and journals are essential to study and research in music education. Some education databases have been mentioned in Chapter 3.

18.1 Instruction and Study in the Schools: MT1–5

The Library of Congress classification for music education, from preschool through high school, provides only a limited number of subclasses, MT1–5. These classifications contain the books on theory and history of professional music education. MT1 is for general works of theory and history of music education, such as North and Hargreaves' *Musical Development and Learning: The International Perspective* (2001). MT3 includes such books for specific regions or countries so they are subarranged geographically, with MT3.U5 as the classification for music education in the United States. Two histories of American music teaching found there are *Music Education: Historical Contexts and Perspectives* (1997) by Labuta and Smith and **A History of American Music Education* (1999) by Mark and Gary. This classification, MT3, includes books that are guides to teaching music at various levels: elementary, middle school, secondary school; books aimed at the ensemble director whether for choir, band, or orchestra; books on supervision and administration. MT4 and MT5 organize books on teaching institutions in the United States, by city and in other countries, by city. Because there are not finer delineations, for topics or grade levels, within the professional music education area, it is not a classification section arranged for easy browsing.

Subject headings become important, then, for identifying specific types of music education books. The most important one for professional music education is "School music" which relates to classification MT1. "School music supervision" relates to MT3 for the United States, to MT10 for teachers' and supervisors' manuals, and to MT170 for instrumental techniques for children. For historical works on music teaching in the United States, the basic LC subject heading is "School music–Instruction and study–United States–History." The broadest subject heading for the field of music education, "Music–Instruction and study," is applicable in one way or another to all materials classed in the MT subclass. Since both browsing and subject headings are not quite specific enough for some music education topics, title keyword searching may be used to good effect.

18.2 Guides to Research and the Discipline: Music Education: MT1

Summary essays on research findings in music education can provide background and direction for new research projects or inform the student or practicing teacher. A number of textbooks are available, as well, to delineate the various types of research that are applied to music education—historical, descriptive, experimental—and to present the methods and tools used. Outstanding books for this purpose are Colwell's **Handbook of Research on Music Teaching and Learning: A Project of the Music Educators National Conference* (1992) and its sequel, **The New Handbook of Research on Music Teaching and Learning: A Project of the Music Educators National Conference* (2002) edited by Colwell and Richardson. Both handbooks are of value because they provide an overview of research interests and findings in music education at an interval of ten years. A variety of researchers report on the state of research; the 2002 version reports on ten broad areas: policy and philosophy; curriculum; musical development and learning; musical cognition; social and cultural contexts; music teacher education; music education connections or partnerships; neuroscience, medicine, and music; outcomes in general education; and research design, criticism, and assessment in music education. Valued textbooks on music education research are *A Guide to Research in Music Education* (2005), now in its fifth edition by Phelps, Sadoff, Warburton, and Ferrara and *Research in Music Education: An Introduction to Systematic Inquiry* (1987) by Rainbow and Froehlich.

18.3 Music Theory, Appreciation, and Analysis

The specific classifications for these areas are illustrated well in the tables on pages 203–205. Refer to them to see the logical approach to subclasses that applies to books on music history, analysis or appreciation, and instruction and study.

18.4 Pedagogy—Individual Instruments, Voice, Ensembles

Because there are individual classes assigned to pedagogical materials for each individual instrument, families of instruments, and ensembles, there are many MT subclasses used for this purpose, generally termed: instrumental techniques, MT180–810. And, a fair number of subclasses are used for singing and vocal techniques, MT820–915. Again, examine the classification tables on pages 202–205 for books on your areas of interest across the types of literature from histories to analyses, to instruction and study.

Subject headings that are more specific than "School music–Instruction and study" are likely to retrieve the books about teaching ensembles in the schools and practical materials to use with students. For example, "Choral music–Instruction and study" retrieves: Phillips' *Directing the Choral Music Program* (2004) [MT932]. "Instrumental music–Instruction and study" will retrieve books that deal with band and orchestra programs such as *The Teaching of Instrumental Music* (2002) by Colwell and Goolsby [MT170].

Of course there are manuals and methods available for the private music teacher as well, identified by using the subject heading for a specific instrument. For example, "Piano–Instruction and study" retrieves recent guides to pedagogy and technique: *Practical Piano Pedagogy: The Definitive Text for Piano Teachers and Pedagogy Students* (2003) by Baker and Fraser's *The Craft of Piano Playing: A New Approach to Piano Technique* (2003) [MT220].

18.5 Ballet, Opera, Theater Music, and Production: MT950–960

Books in these areas may be directed to teaching at any level or to matters of production history or practice. Included are such different books as *Musicals! Directing School and Community Theater* (1997) by Boland and Argentini, *Opera in Context: Essays on Historical Staging from the Late Renaissance to the Time of Puccini* (1998) by Radice, and *Singing, Acting, and Movement in Opera: A Guide to Singer-getics* (2002) by Mark and Lynn Clark.

Review Questions

1. Which classification numbers are used for professional music education books? What problems keep us from browsing effectively in this area?

2. What topical subdivision is appropriate for books about teaching almost any kind of music?

3. Which MT class numbers would contain books about teaching band? Teaching orchestra? Teaching choir?

Learning Exercises

1. Prepare annotated citations for three music education books, one each for philoso-
    phy, band, and administration of music in the schools.

2. When looking for an LC subject heading, what topical subdivision is appropriate for
    books about teaching almost any kind of music?

Appendix 1

Form Subdivisions: A Selective List from the Library of Congress Subject Headings

These form headings—indicating a form of information—have been selected as most applicable to the field of music. Add them to topical subject headings for a search focused on the type of resource needed. For the full list of what are called "free-floating sub-divisions," see the *Library of Congress Subject Headings.*[1]

Relating to Text Resources

– Abstracts
– Atlases
– Autographs
– Bibliography
– Bibliography – Catalogs
– Bibliography – Early
– Bibliography – First Editions
– Bibliography – Graded lists
– Bibliography of bibliographies
– Bio-Bibliography
– Biography
– Biography – Dictionaries
– Calendars
– Catalogs
– Catalogs, Manufacturers'
– Catalogs and collections
   (May Subd Geog)
– Catalogues raisonnés
– Chronology
– Computer programs
– Concordances
– Congresses
– Conversation and phrase books

  (for musicians, musicologists, etc.)
– Correspondence
– Description and travel
– Diaries
– Dictionaries
– Dictionaries – Early works to 1700
– Dictionaries – French [Italian]
– Dictionaries – Juvenile
– Dictionaries – Polyglot
– Directories
– Discography
– Discography – Methodology
– Dissertations
– Encyclopedias
– Gazetteers
– Handbooks, manuals, etc.
– History – [period] – Chronology
– History – [period] – Sources
– Humor
– Hymns–Texts
– Illustrations
– Indexes
– Instruction and study

(May Subd Geog)
- Instruction and study – Fingering
- Instruction and study – Juvenile
- Instruction and study – Pedaling
- Interviews
- Juvenile
- Juvenile – Instruction and study
- Newspapers
- Notebooks, sketchbooks, etc.
- Obituaries
- Outlines, syllabi, etc.
- Pamphlets
- Periodicals
- Periodicals – Bibliography
- Periodicals – Indexes
- Photographs
- Pictorial works
- Poetry
- Popular works
- Portraits

- Posters
- Prayer-books and devotions
- Programmed instruction
- Programs
- Quotations
- Reviews
- Software
- Sources
- Spurious and doubtful works
- Statistics
- Stories, plots, etc.
- Study guides
- Surveys
- Tables
- Textbooks
- Texts
- Thematic catalogs
- Translations
- Union list

Relating to Music Resources (Scores and Recordings)

- Cadenzas
- Chord diagrams
- Chorus scores with organ
- Chorus scores with piano
- Chorus scores without accompaniment
- Excerpts
- Excerpts – Arranged
- Facsimiles
- Fake books
- Folklore
- Hymns
- Instructive editions
- Instrumental settings
- Juvenile – Instruction and study
- Methods
- Methods – Group instruction
- Methods – Juvenile
- Methods – Self-instruction
- Methods – (Jazz [Rock, Bluegrass, etc.])
- Music
- Musical settings
- Orchestral excerpts
- Orchestras
- Organ scores
- Parts
- Parts (solo)

- Piano scores
- Piano scores (4 hands)
- Scores
- Scores and parts
- Self-instruction
- Simplified editions
- Solo with harpsichord
- Solo with harpsichord and piano
- Solo with organ
- Solo with piano
- Solo with pianos (2)
- Solos with organ
- Solos with piano
- Solos with piano (2)
- Songs and music
- Songs and music – Discography
- Songs and music – History and criticism
- Songs and music – Texts
- Sources
- Studies and exercises
- Studies and exercises – Juvenile
- Studies and exercises – (Jazz [Rock, Bluegrass, etc.])
- Studies and exercises (Left hand)
- Studies and exercises (Right hand)
- Teaching pieces

Note

1. Library of Congress, Cataloging Policy and Support Office, *Library of Congress Subject Headings*, 5 vols. (Washington, DC: Library of Congress, Cataloging Distribution Service, 2004).

Appendix 2

Outline of the Library of Congress M–Class

This summary listing of classification numbers for music and books on music is an adaptation of the full classification schedule, *M. Music and Books on Music* (1998).[1] It provides an outline of the three music subclasses:

M: Music (scores and recordings)

ML: Literature on Music (books and journals)

MT: Musical Instruction and Study (books, journals, instructive editions of music)

For an online version of the M, ML, MT classifications in brief outline form, consult http://www.itsmarc.com/crs/LCSO0013.htm. See Appendix 3 for a topical guide to LC classifications for music. It is designed to help you quickly identify LC Classification areas for your own instrument or area of study for both books and scores.

M: Music (Scores and Recordings)

Collections, Critical Editions: M1–5

M1	Anthologies
M2	Collections of musical sources by two or more composers (historical sets or monuments)
M3	Collected works of individual composers
M3.1	Selections, as in all of a composer's vocal music
M3.5	First editions

Instrumental Music: M5–1490

M5–190	Solo instruments
M191–990	Chamber music
M1000–1160	Orchestra
M1200–1270	Band
M1350–1366	Dance orchestra; Jazz

M1376–1420	Instrumental music for children
M1450	Dance (ballet, folk)
M1470–1480	Aleatory, Electronic, with color

Vocal Music: M1495–2199

| M1495 | Collections |

Secular vocal music:

M1497–1527.8	Dramatic music
M1528–1529.5	Vocal chamber music
M1530–1610	Choruses
M1611–1626	Songs
M1627–1685	National music
M1686–1985	Popular music
M1990–1998	Secular vocal music for children

Sacred vocal music:

M1999	Collections
M2000–2007	Oratorios
M2010–2019.5	Services: solo and chamber music
M2020–2114.8	Choruses
M2115–2188	Hymnals, Liturgy
M2190–2199	Sacred vocal music for children

ML: Literature on Music

Various topics; many are reference books
ML1–5	General music periodicals
ML12–21	Directories
ML25–28	Society publications
ML29–33	Special collections
ML35–46	Festivals, congresses, programs, scrapbooks
ML47–54.8	Librettos and lyrics
ML55–60	Addresses, essays, lectures
ML82–83	Women and children in music
ML85–89	Visual and pictorial
ML90	Writings of musicians (collections)
ML93–96	Manuscript studies
ML96.4–96.5	Facsimiles
ML100–109	Dictionaries, Encyclopedias
ML111–112.5	Music librarianship, printing, publishing
ML112.8–158.8	Bibliographies
ML128	By topic
ML132	Graded lists
ML134	Individuals (composers, performers; includes thematic catalogs)
ML136–152	Catalogs
ML156–158.8	Discographies, videographies
ML159–360	History and criticism

ML161–197	By period
ML198–360	By region or country
ML385–429	Biography
ML430–455	Composition and performance; includes history of theory, form, instrumentation, performance practice, conducting

Instruments and Instrumental Music: ML459–1380

ML459–497	Instruments
ML465–471	By period
ML475–497	By region or country
ML600–1093	Music and playing
ML603–607	By period
ML610–642	By region or country
ML645–647	Forms, types
ML649–1093	Families and individual instruments
ML 1100–1165	Chamber music
ML 1200–1270	Orchestral music
ML 1300–1354	Band music
ML 1379–1380	Electronic music; Computer music

Vocal Music: ML1400–3275

ML1400–1451	Vocal music: general, by period, by country
ML1460	Vocal technique
	See also MT823 History of vocal instruction & study
ML1499–1554	Choral music
ML1600–2881	Secular vocal music
ML2900–3275	Sacred vocal music

Other: ML3300–3930

ML3300–3354	Program music
ML3400–3465	Dance music
ML3545–3775	National music; includes folk, popular, world
ML3790	Music industry
ML3797	General works on music history and musicology
ML3800–3923	Philosophy and physics of music
ML3830	Psychology
ML3845–3877	Aesthetics
ML3880–3923	Criticism
ML3930	Literature on music for children

MT: Musical Instruction and Study

MT1–5	Theory and history of music education through high school
MT1	General works
MT3.A–Z	By region or country
MT4.A–Z	Institutions–U.S.
MT5.A–Z	Institutions in other countries

Theory and History of Music Education; Music Theory

MT5.5–7	Includes Anthologies of analysis and Rudiments of theory
MT10	Teachers' manuals
MT17	Special education
MT18	In higher education
MT20–32	Specific methods, e.g., Kodaly, Orff
MT35–38	Notation
MT40–67	Composition
MT58–67	Forms & genres
MT68	Improvisation, accompaniment, transposition
MT70–71	Instrumentation & orchestration
MT73	Band & instrumentation
MT75–82	Interpretation, embellishment, memorizing
MT90–145	Analysis and appreciation of compositions; listener's guides
MT165	Tuning

Instrumental Techniques: MT170–810

MT180–255	Keyboard
MT259–338	Strings
MT339–538	Winds
MT539–654	Plectral
MT655–722	Percussion
MT728	Chamber music instruction & study
MT730	Orchestral instruction & study
MT733	Band instruction & study
MT740–810	Instruction & study for children
MT820–949	Singing and voice culture
MT825–850	Systems & methods
MT855–883	Special techniques
MT885–893	Studies & exercises
MT898–949	Techniques for children
MT950–960	Ballet, opera, theater music, production

Other Classifications That Relate to Music

A	General works
B	Philosophy & Psychology
D	History
GV	Dance
K	Law; copyright
L	Education
N	Art
NZ	Architecture
P	Languages & Literature
Q	Science
T	Technology
Z	Bibliography

Note

1. Library of Congress, Cataloging Policy and Support Office, Library Services, *Library of Congress Classification, M. Music* (Washington, DC: Library of Congress, Cataloging Distribution Service, 2007).

Appendix 3

Topical Guide to Music in the Library of Congress Classification[1]

Revised and Updated by Margaret Kaus[2]

Using the Guide

Look up an instrument, ensemble, or genre alphabetically to find LC class numbers that apply to scores and recordings (M), literature of music (ML), or instruction and study (MT). Make note of the class numbers, and then go to the appropriate area of the library's book stacks to browse. Examples of topical entries are: Band, Flute, Choral Music (Sacred), Choral Music (Secular), Oratorio, Music Education, or Suites.

Accompaniment

M14 Organ accompaniments to hymns, etc. (collections)
MT68 General: including improvisation, transposition
MT190 Organ: accompanying Gregorian chant and other liturgical music
MT191.A3 Organ accompanying techniques
MT236; MT239 Piano accompanying techniques (including sight-reading and transposition)
MT950 Accompanying dance and rhythmic movement

Ballets

M1520 Full scores
M1523 Piano reductions
M1524–M1526 Excerpts
ML52–ML52.6 Librettos
ML128.B2 Ballet–Bibliography
ML3460 Literature, history
MT95–MT100 Analytical guides
MT950 Accompanying dance and rhythmic movement

Band

M1200–M1249 Band music, original
M1201 Symphonies
M1203 Suites

M1204 Overtures
M1205–M1206 Solo instrument & band
M1242 Concertos (no soloist)
M1245–M1249 Pieces
M1254–M1266 Arrangements for band
M1269 Marching routines
M1270 Fife and drum, field music
M1420 Band music for children
ML128.B23 Band music–Bibliography
ML132.B3 Band music–Graded lists
ML1300–ML1354 General: history, special
periods, by country
MT733, MT735, MT810 Instruction and study

Bassoon

M75–M79 Bassoon alone
M253–M254 Bassoon and piano
M1026 Bassoon with orchestra (full score)
M1027 Bassoon with orchestra (piano reduc-
tion)
M1126 Bassoon with string orchestra (full
score)
M1127 Bassoon with string orchestra (piano
reduction)
ML128.B26 Bassoon music–Bibliography
ML128.W5 Woodwind music–Bibliography
ML950–ML953 General: history and construc-
tion, music and playing
MT400–MT408 Bassoon techniques (including
orchestral excerpts)

Cantata

M1530–M1610 Secular cantatas (included in
Choruses, secular)
M1611–M1624.8 Solo cantatas (original and
arranged)
M1629.5 National
M2020–M2036 Sacred cantatas (included in
Choruses, sacred)
M2102–M2114.8 Sacred solo cantatas (original
and arranged)
ML54 Librettos
ML128.C15 Cantatas–Bibliography
ML2400, ML3260 History and criticism
(Secular/Sacred)
MT110–MT115 Analytical guides, choral
MT120–MT121 Analytical guides, solo voices

Chamber Music

M180–M299 Duets
M300–M399 Trios
M400–M499 Quartets
M500–M599 Quintets
M600–M699 Sextets
M700–M799 Septets
M800–M899 Octets
M900–M986 Nonets (or larger ensemble of
strictly chamber music)
M990 With instruments of 18th century or
earlier
M1413–M1417 Chamber music for children
ML128.C4 Chamber music–Bibliography
ML132.C4 Chamber music–Graded lists
ML156.4.C4 Chamber music–Discography
ML1100–ML1165 General: history, special
periods, by country, kinds and forms
MT140 Analytical guides, two or more com-
posers
MT145 Analytical guides, one composer
MT728, MT810 Methods

Chant

M2011 Masses
M2148 Propers
M2150.2; M2153.2 Collections of chants
M2149 Antiphonaries
ML102.C45 Dictionaries
ML3082 History and criticism
MT190 Accompaniment
MT860 Techniques of chant singing

Children and Music / School Music

M1375–M1420 Instrumental music for children
(including music with words)
    M1375–M1385 Solo instrumental music
    M1389–M1417 Duets, trios, etc.
    M1420 Orchestra or band
M1546.5 Choruses (secular) for children's
voices with orchestra
M1990–M1998 Vocal music (secular) for chil-
dren (including school music texts)
ML83 Children and music; Children as musi-
cians
ML128.J8 Juvenile music–Bibliography
ML128.S25 School music–Bibliography
ML132 Graded lists of music (by medium)

ML156.4.C5 Children's music–Discography
ML156.4.S4 School music–Discography
ML3928–3930 Children's literature about music
MT740–MT810 Instrumental music–Instruction and study for children
MT898–MT948 Vocal music–Instruction and study for children

Choral Music (Sacred)

M2000–M2007 Oratorios
M2010–M2017.6 Services
M2020–M2036 Cantatas
M2060–M2101.5 Choruses or part-songs with keyboard, with solo instrument, or unaccompanied
ML128.V7 Vocal music–Bibliography
ML132.C5 Choral music–Graded lists
ML1500–ML1554, ML2900–ML3275 General: history, special periods, by country, kinds and forms
MT110–MT115 Analytical guides
MT88 Choirs
MT875 Choral techniques
MT915 Choir training for children

Choral Music (Secular)

M1530–M1546.5 Choruses with orchestra or ensemble
M1547–M1609 Choruses or part-songs with piano, with solo instrument, or unaccompanied
ML128.V7 Vocal music–Bibliography
ML132.C5 Choral music–Graded lists
ML1500–ML1554 General: history, special periods, by country, kinds and forms
MT110–MT115 Analytical guides
MT88 Choirs
MT875 Choral techniques
MT915 Choir training for children

Clarinet

M70–M74 Clarinet alone
M248–M250 Clarinet and piano, original
M251–M252 Arrangements for clarinet and piano
M1024 Clarinet with orchestra (full score)
M1025 Clarinet with orchestra (piano reduction)

M1124 Clarinet with string orchestra (full score)
M1125 Clarinet with string orchestra (piano reduction)
ML128.C58 Clarinet music–Bibliography
ML156.4.C6 Clarinet music–Discography
ML945–ML948 General: history and construction; music and playing
MT380–MT388 Clarinet techniques (including orchestral excerpts)
MT801.C6 Instruction and study for children

Composers

M3–M3.3 Collected works (A–Z by last initial of composer)
ML90 Writings of composers (prose)
ML105–ML107 Biographical dictionaries
ML134 Thematic catalogs of individual composers
ML156.5 Discographies of individual composers
ML390 Collected biographies
ML410 Individual biographies
MT92 Analytical guides to works of individual composers

Concertos

M1005–M1039.5 Various solo instruments with orchestra
M1040–M1041 2 or more different instruments with orchestra
M1042 Orchestra (no soloist)
M1105–M1139.5 Various solo instruments with string orchestra
M1140–M1141 2 or more different instruments with string orchestra
M1142 String orchestra (no soloist)
M1205 Concertos with band
M1242 Concertos (no soloist)
ML128.C84 Concerto–Bibliography
ML1263 History and criticism
MT125 Analytical guides to orchestra music
For single instrument concertos, *see* heading for that instrument.

Dance Music

M1047–M1049 Dances, orchestra
M1147–M1149 Dances, string orchestra
M1247.9–M1249 Dances, band

M1450–M1459 Music for dance classes
M1356 Dance orchestra [big band]
M1520–M1526 Ballets
ML128.B2 Ballets–Bibliography
ML128.D3 Dances–Bibliography
ML3400–ML3465 History and criticism
MT95–MT100 Analytical guides
GV400–GV750 Dance in education

Double Bass

M55–M57 Double bass alone
M58 Arrangements for double bass
M237–M238 Double bass and piano
M1018 Double bass with orchestra (full score or piano reduction)
M1118 Double bass with string orchestra (full score or piano reduction)
ML128.D6 Double bass music–Bibliography
ML920–ML925 General: history and construction; music and playing
MT320–MT334 Double bass techniques (including orchestral excerpts)
MT801.D65 Instruction and study for children

Electronic Music

M1473 Electronic music
ML73–ML74.7 Music software and data processing methods
ML1092 Electronic musical instruments
ML3805 Music–Acoustics and physics
MT41 Computer composition
MT723 Computer sound processing
QC220–QC246 Sound
TK7800–TK7895 Applications of electronics

Ethnomusicology

ML128.E8 Ethnomusicology–Bibliography
Music (art music): history and criticism by region/country
    ML198–ML239 Americas
    ML240–ML325 Europe
    ML330–ML345 Asia
    ML350–ML355 Africa
    ML360–ML360.6 Australia, Oceania, etc.
ML3545 General (including ethnomusicology texts)
National music (folk, popular, etc.): history and criticism
    ML3549–ML3575 Americas

ML3580–ML3730 Europe
ML3740–ML3758 Asia
ML3760–ML3760.6 Africa
ML3770 Australia
ML3771 New Zealand
ML3774–ML3775 Oceania, other
For musical scores *see* entry for "Popular music."

Euphonium

M110.B33 Baritone/Euphonium music
M270.B37 Baritone/Euphonium and one other instrument (e.g., piano), collections
M271.B37 Baritone/Euphonium and one other instrument (e.g., piano), single work
M1034.B37 Baritone/Euphonium with orchestra (or large ensemble; full score)
M1035.B37 Baritone/Euphonium with orchestra (or large ensemble; piano reduction)
ML128.B24 Baritone/Euphonium–Bibliography
MT496–MT497.8 Baritone/Euphonium techniques (including orchestral excerpts)
See also listings for Tuba

Flute

M60–M64 Flute alone
M240–M242 Flute and piano, original
M243–M244 Arrangements for flute and piano
M1020 Flute with orchestra (full score)
M1021 Flute with orchestra (piano reduction)
M1120 Flute with string orchestra (full score)
M1121 Flute with string orchestra (piano reduction)
ML128.F7 Flute music–Bibliography
ML132.F58 Flute music–Graded lists
ML156.4.F43 Flute music–Discography
ML935–ML937 General: history and construction; music and playing
MT340–MT348 Flute techniques (including orchestral excerpts)
MT801.F5 Instruction and study for children

Guitar

M125–M129 Guitar alone
M276–M277 Guitar and piano
M1037.4.G8 Guitar with orchestra
M1137.4.G8 Guitar with string orchestra
M1623 Songs with guitar accompaniment

ML128.G8 Guitar music–Bibliography
ML156.4.G8 Guitar music–Discography
ML1015.G9 General: history and construction;
music and playing
MT580–MT589 Guitar techniques
See also M1627–M1844 for piano-vocal scores
of songs (folk, popular, etc.), many of which
include chord symbols or tablature for guitar.

Harp

M115–M119 Harp alone
M272–M273 Harp and piano
M1036–M1037 Harp with orchestra
M1136–M1137 Harp with string orchestra
M1623.4; M1624.4 Songs with harp accompa-
niment
ML102.H38 Dictionaries
ML128.H3 Harp music–Bibliography
ML1005–ML1008 General: history and con-
struction; music and playing
MT540–MT548 Harp techniques

Horn

M80–M84 Horn alone
M255–M257 Horn and piano, original
M258–M259 Arrangements for horn and piano
M1028 Horn with orchestra (full score)
M1029 Horn with orchestra (piano reduction)
M1128 Horn with string orchestra (full score)
M1129 Horn with string orchestra (piano re-
duction)
ML128.H67 Horn music–Bibliography
ML128.W5 Wind instruments–Bibliography
ML156.4.H7 Horn music–Discography
ML955–ML958 General: history and construc-
tion; music and playing
MT420–MT428 Horn techniques
MT801.H7 Instruction and study for children

Jazz

M1356 Big band music; Dance orchestra music
M1366 Jazz; blues; ragtime
M1630 American popular music
ML102.J3 Dictionaries
ML105 Biographical dictionaries (general)
ML128.J3 Jazz–Bibliography
ML156.4.J3 Jazz–Discography
ML200.8 American music history, by city
ML385 Composers–Biographies–Collections

ML394 Instrumentalists–Biographies–Collec-
tions
ML410 Composers–Biographies
ML417 Pianists–Biographies
ML420 Singers–Biographies
ML3505.8–ML3543 History and criticism, by
country

Jewish Music

M1850–M1853 Secular vocal music
Sacred vocal music
        M2017.6 Music for worship services
        M2079.5; M2099.5 Choral music
        M2114.3 Solo songs
        M2144 Hymnals
        M2186–M2187 Liturgy and ritual
ML102.J4 Dictionaries
ML128.J4 Jewish music–Bibliography
ML156.4.J4 Jewish music–Discography
History and criticism
        ML166 General/ancient Hebrew music
        ML3195 Sacred music
        ML3776 Secular music

Liturgy and Religious Music

M14 Organ accompaniments to hymns
M14.3 Liturgical music for organ
M2000–M2007 Oratorios & excerpts
Religious services
        M2010–M2014.6 Roman Catholic
        (masses & excerpts)
        M2015 Orthodox
        M2016–M2017.2 Protestant
        M2017.6 Jewish
        M2102–M2114 Solo songs (sacred)
        M2115–M2146 Hymnals
Liturgy and ritual
        M2147–M2155 Catholic
        M2156–M2160 Orthodox
        M2161–M2184 Protestant & other Chris-
        tian churches
        M2186–M2187 Jewish
        M2188 Other non-Christian religions
M2190–M2196 Sacred music for children
ML128.S17 Sacred music–Bibliography
ML3000–ML3197 Religious and denomina-
tional music–History & criticism
MT88 Liturgical instruction, church choirs, etc.
MT190 Organ accompaniment of Gregorian &
other liturgical music

Music Education (Schools, K–12)

M1985 Musical games
M1990–M1998 School music textbooks
ML128.J8 Juvenile music–Bibliography
ML128.S25 School music–Bibliography
ML3930 Literature on music for children
MT1–MT5 Theory, history of musical instruction
MT740–MT810 Instruction and study for children
MT825 Systems and methods of instruction
MT878–MT892 Techniques
MT898–MT949 (especially MT918–MT936) Singing techniques for children, schools

Music History (General overview of ML class)

ML100–ML109 Dictionaries/encyclopedias
ML112.8–ML158 Bibliography
ML159–ML360.6 Music history
    ML162–ML197 Special periods
    ML198– ML360.6 By region or country
ML385–ML429 Biography
ML459–ML1380 Instruments and instrumental music
    ML475–ML548 By region or country
    ML549–ML1092 By instrument
ML1100–ML1165 Chamber music
ML1200–ML1270 Orchestral music
ML1300–ML1354 Band music
ML1400–ML3275 Vocal music
    ML1500–ML1554 Choral music
    ML1600–ML2881 Secular vocal music
    ML2900–ML3275 Sacred vocal music
ML3545–ML3776 National music (folk, popular, etc.)
ML3800–ML3923 Philosophy, physics, and aesthetics of music

Music Theory

ML171–ML360.6 Literature on, treatises, in music history
MT5.5–MT10 General, rudiments, exercises
MT35 Notation, dictation, ear training
MT40–MT67 Composition
    MT50 Harmony
    MT55 Counterpoint
    MT58–MT64 Musical forms
    MT67 Composition texts

MT68 Improvisation, accompaniment, transposition
MT70–MT74 Orchestration, instrumentation
MT75 Interpretation
MT80 Embellishment
MT90–MT146 Analytical guides to musical works

Music Therapy

ML128.M77 Bibliography
ML3920 Literature, history

Musicians

ML81 Musical prodigies
ML82 Women and music
ML83 Children and music
ML85–ML89 Portraits, caricatures, etc.
ML93–ML97 Manuscripts, autographs, etc.
ML105–ML107 Biographical dictionaries
ML134 Thematic catalogs of composers' works
Collected biographies
    ML385 General
    ML390 Composers
    ML394–400 Performers
    ML402 Conductors
Individual biographies
    ML410 Composers
    ML416–ML419 Instrumentalists
    ML420 Vocalists
ML421 Vocal/instrumental groups
ML422 Conductors
ML3790–ML3795 Music industry/Music as a profession/Musical life

Oboe

M65–M69 Oboe alone
M245–M246 Oboe and piano, original
M247 Arrangements for oboe and piano
M1022 Oboe with orchestra (full score)
M1023 Oboe with orchestra (piano reduction)
M1122 Oboe with string orchestra (full score)
M1123 Oboe with string orchestra (piano reduction)
ML128.O2 Oboe music–Bibliography
ML128.W5 Wind instrument music–Bibliography
ML940–ML943 General: history and construction; music and playing

MT360–MT368 Instruction and study (including orchestral excerpts)

Opera

M1500 Operas (full score)
M1503 Operas (piano-vocal score)
M1505–M1508.2 Operas, excerpts
M1527 Operas (film, radio, television)
ML48–ML50.7 Librettos
ML102.O6 Dictionaries of opera
ML128.O4 Opera–Bibliography
ML1754–ML1950 History and criticism, special periods, by country, forms and kinds
MT95–MT100 Analytical guides, opera plots
MT955 Opera production (instruction and study)
MT956 Opera performing (instruction and study)

Oratorio

M2000–M2007 Oratorios
    M2000 Full scores
    M2002–M2003 Piano-vocal scores
    M2004–M2007 Excerpts
ML52.85–ML53.6 Librettos
ML128.O45 Oratorios–Bibliography
ML3201–ML3251 History and criticism: special periods, by country, kinds and forms
MT110–MT115 Analytical guides

Orchestra

M1000–M1075 Orchestral music
M1001 Symphonies
M1002 Symphonic poems
M1003 Suites
M1004 Overtures
M1005–M1075 Concerti, etc.
M1100–M1160 String orchestra music (subdivided as above)
ML128.O5 Orchestral music–Bibliography
ML132.O68 Orchestral music–Graded lists
ML1200–ML1270 General: history, special periods, by country, kinds and forms
MT730 Instruction and study
MT810 Instruction and study for children

Organ

M6–M14.5 Organ alone

M12–M13 Arrangements for organ
M14 Accompaniments (hymns, liturgical works)
M180–M186 Duets (organ and other instruments)
M300–M304 Trios with organ
M400–M404 Quartets with organ
M500–M504, etc. Quintets, etc. with organ
M1005 Organ with orchestra
M1108–M1109 Organ with string orchestra
ML128.O6 Organ music–Bibliography
ML132.O7 Organ music–Graded lists
ML156.4.O6 Organ music–Discography
ML550–ML649 General: history and construction; music and playing
MT170–MT208 Organ techniques
MT801.O7 Instruction and study for children

Percussion

M145–M175 Percussion solos (including some electronic instruments)
M284 Percussion and piano, original
M285 Arrangements for percussion and piano
M1038 Percussion with orchestra (full score)
M1039 Percussion with orchestra (piano reduction)
M1138 Percussion with string orchestra (full score)
M1139 Percussion with string orchestra (piano reduction)
ML102.P4 Encyclopedias
ML128.P23 Percussion music–Bibliography
ML156.4.P4 Percussion music–Discography
ML1030–ML1049 General: history and construction; music and playing
MT655–MT722 Percussion techniques
MT736 Instruction and study, percussion ensembles
MT801.X9 Xylophone–Instruction and study for children

Piano

M20–M39.6 Music for piano alone
    M23 Sonatas
    M24 Suites
    M27 Variations
    M32.8–M39 Arrangements for piano
M200–M204 Piano, 4 hands, Original
M207–M211 Arrangements for 4-hand piano
M214–M216 2-piano music
M1010 Piano with orchestra (full score)

M1011 Piano with orchestra (2-piano reduction)
M1110 Piano with string orchestra (full score)
M1111 Piano with string orchestra (2-piano reduction)
ML102.P5 Encyclopedias
ML128.P3 Piano music–Bibliography
ML132.P3 Piano music–Graded lists
ML156.4.P5 Piano music–Discography
ML649.8–ML747 General: history and construction; music and playing
MT220–MT255 Piano techniques (including teaching materials)
MT130–MT145 Analytical guides to piano music

Plucked Instruments (guitar, harp, etc.)

M115–M142 Solo plectral instrument music
M272–M283 Piano and one plectral instrument
M292–M293 2 plectral instruments
M325–M329; M425–M429; etc. Trios, quartets, etc. of piano and plectral instruments
M365–M369; M465–M469; etc. Trios, quartets, etc. of plectral instruments
M1036–M1037.4 Solo plectral instrument with orchestra
M1136–M1137.4 Solo plectral instrument with string orchestra
M1623–M1623.5; M1624–M1624.5 Songs accompanied by a plectral instrument
ML1000–ML1015 General: history and construction, music and playing
MT539–MT654 Plectral instrument techniques

Popular Music (including folk, ethnic, rock, jazz, etc.)

M1628–M1677.3 United States
M1678–M1679.2 Canada
M1680.2 North and South America collections
M1681 West Indies and Bermuda
M1682–M1683.3 Mexico
M1684–M1685 Central America
M1686–M1694.2 South America
M1698–M1789 Europe
    M1730–M1733 France
    M1734–M1735.2 Germany
    M1738–M1747.2 British Isles
M1795–M1825 Asia
    M1804–M1805 China

    M1808–M1809.2 India
    M1812–M1813.2 Japan
M1828 Arab countries
M1830–M1838 Africa
M1840–M1843.2 Australia, New Zealand
M1844 Pacific islands
For history and criticism of popular music *see* entry for "Ethnomusicology."

Saxophone

M105–M109 Saxophone alone
M268 Saxophone and piano, original
M269 Arrangements for saxophone and piano
M1034.S4 Saxophone with orchestra (full score)
M1035.S4 Saxophone with orchestra (piano reduction)
M1134.S4 Saxophone with string orchestra (full score)
M1135.S4 Saxophone with string orchestra (piano reduction)
ML128.S247 Saxophone music–Bibliography
ML128.W5 Wind instrument music–Bibliography
ML156.4.S3 Saxophone music–Discography
ML975–ML978 General: history and construction; music and playing
MT500–MT508 Saxophone techniques
MT801.S4 Instruction and study for children

Songs (Sacred)

M1999 Sacred vocal collections
M2018–M2019.5 Duets, trios, etc.
M2102–M2114.8 Songs for one voice
M2190–M2196 Sacred music for children
M2198–M2199 Gospel, revival, temperance songs, etc.
ML128.S2 Sacred vocal music–Bibliography
ML128.S3 Songs–Bibliography
ML128.V7 Vocal music–Bibliography
ML132.S6 Songs–Graded lists
ML2900–ML3275 General: history and criticism, special periods, by country, kinds and forms, by denomination
MT820–MT893 Vocal instruction and vocal techniques

Songs (Secular)

M1528–M1529.5 Duets, trios, etc.

M1611–M1624.8 Songs for one voice
M1625–M1626 Recitations, accompanied
M1627–M1853 National music (includes folk, patriotic, popular, etc.)
M1900–M1985 Songs of special character
M1990–M1998 Children's songs/School music textbooks
ML128.S3 Songs–Bibliography
ML128.V7 Vocal music–Bibliography
ML132.S6 Songs–Graded lists
ML2500–ML2881 General: history and criticism, special periods, by country, kinds and forms
MT820–MT893 Vocal instruction and vocal techniques
MT898–MT948 Techniques for children (including schools)

String Instruments

M40–M59.5 Solo string instrument music
M217–M239 Piano and one string instrument
M286–M287 Duets of string instruments
M349–M353 String trios
M450–M454 String quartets (Quartets of 2 violins, 1 viola, and 1 violoncello are classed under M452)
M550–M554 String quintets, sextets, etc. (Groups larger than 9 are M650–M654, etc. usually classed as string orchestras; *see* the entry "Orchestra")
M1012–M1019 Solo string instrument with orchestra (or two or more like wind instruments, e.g., violin duet and orchestra)
M1112–M1119 Solo string instrument with string orchestra
ML128.S7 String instrument music–Bibliography (For the individual instrument, *see* the instrument)
ML750–ML927 General: history and construction; music and playing
MT259–MT338 String instrument techniques
See also individual instruments (violin, etc.)

Suites

M9 Organ
M24; M203 Piano; piano 4-hands
M220 Violin and piano
M232 Violoncello and piano
M1003 Orchestra
M1103 String orchestra

M1203; M1254 Band or wind ensemble
History and criticism
    ML646 Organ
    ML746 Piano
    ML896 Violin
    ML1158 Chamber music
    ML1258 Orchestra, string orchestra
MT64.S8 Composition techniques

Trombone

M90–M94 Trombone alone
M262 Trombone and piano, original
M263 Arrangements for trombone and piano
M1032 Trombone with orchestra (full score)
M1033 Trombone with orchestra (piano reduction)
M1132 Trombone with string orchestra (full score)
M1133 Trombone with string orchestra (piano reduction)
ML128.T76 Trombone music–Bibliography
ML128.W5 Wind instrument music–Bibliography
ML156.4.T7 Trombone music–Discography
ML965–ML968 General: history and construction; music and playing
MT460–MT472.8 Trombone techniques
MT801.T67 Instruction and study for children

Trumpet

M85–M89 Trumpet alone
M260 Trumpet and piano, original
M261 Arrangements for trumpet and piano
M1030 Trumpet with orchestra (full score)
M1031 Trumpet with orchestra (piano reduction)
M1130 Trumpet with string orchestra (full score)
M1131 Trumpet with string orchestra (piano reduction)
ML128.T78 Trumpet music–Bibliography
ML128.W5 Wind instrument music–Bibliography
ML156.4.T8 Trumpet music–Discography
ML960–ML963 General: history and construction; music and playing
MT440–MT448 Trumpet techniques
MT801.T7 Instruction and study for children

Tuba

M95–M99 Tuba music
M264–M265 Tuba and one other instrument
(e.g., piano)
M557.4 Tuba with brass ensemble
M1034.T8 Tuba with orchestra (or large ensemble; full score)
M1035.T8 Tuba with orchestra (or large ensemble; piano reduction)
M1205 Tuba with band (full score)
M1206 Tuba with band (piano reduction)
ML128.T8 Tuba music–Bibliography
ML970–ML973 General works; History and
criticism; Construction; Music and playing
MT480–MT488 Tuba technique
MT801.T8 Instrumental techniques for children

United States Music

M1628–M1677.8 Popular music (including
folk, rock, jazz, etc.)
    M1630.18 Popular music collections
    M1659.7–M1667 Political/patriotic songs
    M1668–1671 Ethnic songs (African-
    American, etc.)
M1940–M1973 Students' songs (alma maters,
etc.)
M2115–M2146 Hymnals
ML1 Periodicals published in the U.S.
ML13–ML19 Directories/almanacs
ML106.U Biographical dictionaries
ML200 Music (general)–History and criticism
ML476 Instrumental music–History and
criticism
ML1111 Chamber music–History and criticism
ML1211 Orchestral music–History and
criticism
ML1311 Band music–History and criticism
ML1411 Vocal music (general)–History and
criticism
ML1511 Choral music–History and criticism
ML1611 Secular vocal music–History and
criticism
ML1711 Dramatic vocal music–History and
criticism
ML2511 Secular songs (general)–History and
criticism
ML2611 Secular part-songs
ML2811 Secular solo songs
ML2911 Sacred vocal music–History and
criticism
ML3011 Roman Catholic

ML3111 Protestant
ML3211 Oratorio
ML3311 Program music
ML3411 Dance music
ML3551–ML3562 Popular music
MT3.U... and MT4 Music education/school
music

Viola

M45–M49 Viola alone
M224–M226 Viola and piano, original
M227–M228 Arrangements for viola and piano
M1014 Viola with orchestra (full score)
M1015 Viola with orchestra (piano reduction)
M1114 Viola with string orchestra (full score)
M1115 Viola with string orchestra (piano
reduction)
ML128.V36 Viola music–Bibliography
ML128.S7 String instrument music–Bibliography
ML132.V36 Viola music–Graded lists
ML156.4.V48 Viola music–Discography
ML900–ML905 General: history and construction; music and playing
MT280–MT298 Viola techniques
MT760–MT778 Instruction and study for children

Violin

M40–M44 Violin alone
M217–M221 Violin and piano, original
M222–M223 Arrangements for violin and
piano
M1012 Violin with orchestra (full score)
M1013 Violin with orchestra (piano reduction)
M1112 Violin with string orchestra (full score)
M1113 Violin with string orchestra (piano
reduction)
ML102.V4 Encyclopedias
ML102.V45 Violin and keyboard instrument,
Encyclopedias
ML128.V4 Violin music–Bibliography
ML128.S7 String instrument music–Bibliography
ML132.V4 Violin music–Graded lists
ML800–ML897 General: history and construction; music and playing
MT260–MT279.7 Violin techniques
MT760–MT778 Instruction and study for children

Violoncello

M50–M54 Violoncello alone
M229–M233 Violoncello and piano, original
M235–M236 Arrangements for violoncello and piano
M1016 Violoncello and orchestra (full score)
M1017 Violoncello and orchestra (piano reduction)
M1116 Violoncello and string orchestra (full score)
M1117 Violoncello and string orchestra (piano reduction)
ML128.V5 Violoncello music–Bibliography
ML128.S7 String instrument music–Bibliography
ML910–ML915 General: history and construction; music and playing
MT300–MT318 Violoncello techniques (including orchestral excerpts)
MT785–MT798 Instruction and study for children

Vocal Music

M1500–M1508 Operas (*see* entry for "Opera")
M1528–M1529.5 Duets, trios, etc. of solo voices (secular)
M1611–M1624.8 Songs (secular)
    M1611–M1618 Orchestral or ensemble accompaniment
    M1619–M1622 Piano accompaniment or unaccompanied
    M1623–M1624.8 Accompanied by one instrument (not piano)
M2000–M2007 Oratorios (*see* entry for "Oratorio")
ML48–ML54 Libretti
ML102.V6 Vocal music–Dictionaries
ML128.S2 Sacred vocal music–Bibliography
ML128.S3 Songs–Bibliography
ML128.V7 Vocal music–Bibliography
ML156.4.V7 Vocal music–Discography
ML1400–ML1460 General: by period, by region or country
ML1600–ML2881 Secular vocal music–History and criticism
    ML1700–ML2400 Dramatic music–History and criticism
    ML2500–ML2881 Songs and part-songs–History and criticism

ML2900–ML3275 Sacred vocal music–History and criticism
MT820–MT949 Singing and voice culture
For children's vocal music *see* "Children and music."
For choruses *see* "Choral music (sacred)" and "Choral music (secular)."
For liturgical or church music *see* "Liturgy and religious music."
For popular, folk, etc. music *see* "Popular music."

Wind Instruments (includes brass and woodwinds)

M60–M111 Solo wind instrument music
M240–M271 Piano and one wind instrument
M288–M289 Duets of wind instruments
M355–M359; M455-M459, etc. Trios, quartets, etc. of wind instruments
M1020–M1035 Solo wind instrument with orchestra (or two or more like wind instruments, e.g., flute trio and orchestra)
M1120–M1135 Solo wind instrument with string orchestra
ML128.W5 Wind instrument music–Bibliography (For individual wind instruments, *see* the instrument)
ML930–ML990 General: history and construction; music and playing
MT339–MT538 Wind instrument techniques
See also individual instruments (clarinet, trumpet, etc.)

Notes

1. Library of Congress, Cataloging Policy and Support Office, Library Services, *Library of Congress Classification, M. Music* (Washington, DC: Library of Congress, Cataloging Distribution Service, 2007).

2. The idea for this guide originated with Jeannette Drone when she was music librarian at Memphis State University. To help guide students, she inserted LC Classification summaries into the card catalog there in the 1970s. We have used a version of the guide for many years on the George F. DeVine Music Library website at the University of Tennessee. I am indebted to Margaret Kaus, original cataloger at Kansas State University Libraries, for checking and revising this Library of Congress Classification information in October 2007.

Appendix 4

Bibliographies by Topic in ML128

This alphabetical list of subject bibliographies in music is available as a quick guide. Check here for the topic, write down the specific LC classification, and go to the shelves to find them.

By topic, A–Z	ML128.A–Z
Accordion	ML128.A3
African American music	*see* ML128.B45
African American spirituals	*see* ML128.S4
Alleluia	ML128.A45
Analysis	*see* ML128.A7
Appalachian dulcimer	ML128.A67
Appreciation. Analysis	ML128.A7
Bagpipe	ML128.B17
Ballets	ML128.B2
Band music	ML128.B23
Bandora	ML128.B235
Baritone. Euphonium	ML128.B24
Bassoon	ML128.B26
Big band music	ML128.B29
Biography	ML128.B3
Black music. African American music	ML128.B45
Blind, Music for	ML128.B47
Blues	ML128.B49
Brass instruments, general works	ML128.B73
For individual brass instruments, *see* separate classes	
Campaign songs	ML128.C13
Cantatas	ML128.C15
Carnatic music	*see* ML128.K37
Catholic Church music	ML128.C2
Chamber music	ML128.C4
Children's music	*see* ML128.J8

Chorales	ML128.C46
Choruses	ML128.C48
Church music, general works	ML128.C54

    For church music of individual denominations, *see* separate classes
    For specific types of sacred music, *see* separate classes

For sacred music	*see* ML128.S17
For Catholic Church music	*see* ML128.C2
For Hymns	*see* ML128.H8
For Protestant church music	*see* ML128.P7
For Sacred vocal music	*see* ML128.S2
Clarinet	ML128.C58
Community music	ML128.C59
Competitions	*see* ML128.P68
Computer music. Computers and music	ML128.C62
Concertina	ML128.C8
Concertos	ML128.C84
Cornet	ML128.C86
Dance music	ML128.D3
Bibliography of discographies	ML128.D56
For discographies	*see* ML156–158
Dömbra	ML128.D58
Double bass	ML128.D6
Easter music	*see* ML128.L2
Elche, Festa de	ML128.E38
Electronic music	ML128.E4
English horn	*see* ML128.O2
Ethnomusicology	ML128.E8
For musicology	*see* ML128.M8
Euphonium	*see* ML128.B24
Festa de Elche	*see* ML128.E38
Festivals	ML128.F47
Flute	ML128.F7
Folk music	ML128.F74
Folk songs	ML128.F75
Funeral music	ML128.F8
Gongs	ML128.G6
Ground bass	*see* ML128.O7
Guitar	ML128.G8
Harp	ML128.H3
Harpsichord	ML128.H35
Horn	ML128.H67
Humor	ML128.H75
Hymns	ML128.H8
Incidental music	ML128.I6
Instruction and study	ML128.I64
Instrumental music, general works	ML128.I65

    For individual forms and types of instrumental music, look up specific words

Instruments, general works	ML128.I66
Jazz	ML128.J3
Jewish music	ML128.J4
Includes sacred and secular music, music by Jewish composers, etc.	
Juvenile music	ML128.J8
Includes music for children to perform or listen to	
Karnatic or Carnatic music	ML128.K37
Keyboard instruments, general works	ML128.K5
For individual keyboard instruments, look up specific instruments	
Ku Klux Klan in music	ML128.K8
Lenten music. Easter music	ML128.L2
Librettos	ML128.L5
Lute	ML128.L88
Madrigals	ML128.M2
For part-songs in general	see ML128.P13
Mandolin	ML128.M23
Marches	ML128.M25
Medical and physiological aspects of music	ML128.M27
Medieval music	ML128.M3
Military music	ML128.M4
Motets	ML128.M67
Motion picture music	ML128.M7
Music competitions	see ML128.P68
Music theory	see ML128.T5
Music therapy	ML128.M77
Musical revues, comedies, etc.	see ML128.M78
Musicals. Revues	ML128.M78
Musicology	ML128.M8
For ethnomusicology	see ML128.E8
National music. Patriotic music	ML128.N3
Notation	ML128.N7
Oboe. English horn. Oboe d'amore	ML128.O2
Oboe d'amore	see ML128.O2
Operas	ML128.O4
Oratorios	ML128.O45
Orchestra. Orchestral music	ML128.O5
Organ	ML128.O6
Ostinato. Ground bass	ML128.O7
Part-songs, general works	ML128.P13
For madrigals	see ML128.M2
Pastoral music (Secular)	ML128.P15
Patriotic music	see ML128.N3
Percussion instruments	ML128.P23
Performance practice	ML128.P235
Periodicals	ML128.P24
Peru in music	ML128.P26
Piano	ML128.P3

Polonaises	ML128.P6
Popular music	ML128.P63
Presidents. Presidential candidates	ML128.P66
Prizes, competitions, etc.	ML128.P68
Program music	ML128.P69
Protestant church music	ML128.P7
Rap	ML128.R28
Recorder	ML128.R31
Revues	*see* ML128.M78
Rock music	ML128.R6
Rockabilly music	ML128.R65
Sacred music	ML128.S17
Sacred vocal music	ML128.S2
Salsa	ML128.S24
Sardanas	ML128.S244
Saxophone	ML128.S247
School music	ML128.S25
Scores	ML128.S29
Singers	ML128.S295
Songs	ML128.S3
Sound recordings	*see* ML156–158
For bibliography of discographies	*see* ML128.D56
Spirituals	ML128.S4
Star-spangled banner	ML128.S6
Stringed instruments, general works	ML128.S7
For individual stringed instruments, look up specific instruments	
Students' songs	ML128.S75
Symphonies	ML128.S9
Television music	ML128.T4
Thematic catalogs	ML128.T48
Music theory	ML128.T5
Trombone	ML128.T76
Trumpet	ML128.T78
Tuba	ML128.T8
Twelve-tone system	ML128.T9
Viol	ML128.V35
Viola	ML128.V36
Viola d'amore	ML128.V38
Violin	ML128.V4
Violoncello	ML128.V5
Vocal music	ML128.V7
Wars	ML128.W2
Wedding music	ML128.W4
Wind instruments, general works	ML128.W5
For individual wind instruments, look up specific instruments	
Women in music	ML128.W7
Zither	ML128.Z

Bibliography

The symbol ** indicates the title is highly recommended.

Chapter 1. The Research Process

**Barzun, Jacques, and Henry F. Graff. *The Modern Researcher*. 6th ed. Belmont, CA: Thomson Learning/Wadsworth, 2004.

**Booth, Wayne C., Gregory G. Colomb, and Joseph M. Williams. *The Craft of Research*. 3rd ed. Chicago Guides to Writing, Editing, and Publishing. Chicago: The University of Chicago Press, 2008.

Chapter 2. Starting-Point Resources: Reference Books

Bibliographies for the Discipline of Music

**Duckles, Vincent H., and Ida Reed. *Music Reference and Research Materials: An Annotated Bibliography*. 5th ed. Advisory editor, Michael A. Keller. Indexed by Linda Solow Blotner. New York: Schirmer Books, 1997.

Mixter, Keith E. *General Bibliography for Music Research*. 3rd ed. Detroit Studies in Music Bibliography, 75. Warren, MI: Harmonie Park Press, 1996.

**Sampsel, Laurie J. *Music Research: A Handbook*. New York: Oxford University Press, 2008. Companion website at http://www.oup.com/us/musresearch.

Bibliographies of General Reference Books

Balay, Robert, and Vee Friesner Carrington. *Guide to Reference Books*. 11th ed. Chicago: American Library Association, 1996.

Blazek, Ron, and Elizabeth Aversa. *The Humanities: A Selective Guide to Information Sources*. 5th ed. Library and Information Science Text Series. Englewood, CO: Libraries Unlimited, 2000.

Union Catalogs

**OCLC. *WorldCat*. Dublin, OH: OCLC, 1971–. http://www.oclc.org.

General Dictionaries or Encyclopedias: ML100

**Finscher, Ludwig, ed. *Die Musik in Geschichte und Gegenwart: Allgemeine Enzyklopadie der Musik* (MGG). 2d ed. Kassel: Barenreiter, 1994–2007.
    Sachteil (Subject volumes). 9 vols. 1994–1998. Includes a print index (vol. 9) and index on CD-ROM, 1999.
    Personenteil (Biography volumes). 17 vols. 1999–2007. Index on CD-ROM, 2005.
Griffiths, Paul. *The Penguin Companion to Classical Music*. London: Penguin Books, 2004.
Kennedy, Michael. *The Concise Oxford Dictionary of Music*. 5th ed. New York: Oxford University Press, 2004.
———. *The Oxford Dictionary of Music*. 2d ed., revised. New York: Oxford University Press, 2006. http://www.grovemusic.com. Part of *Oxford Music Online*.
Latham, Alison. *The Oxford Companion to Music*. Oxford: Oxford University Press, 2002. http://www.grovemusic.com. Part of *Oxford Music Online*.
**Macy, Laura, ed. *Grove Music Online*. Oxford: Oxford University Press, 2006. http://www.grovemusic.com. Part of *Oxford Music Online*.
Nettl, Bruno, and Ruth M. Stone, eds. *The Garland Encyclopedia of World Music*. 10 vols. Founding editors, James Porter and Timothy Rice. New York: Garland Publishing, 1998–2002. Each volume is accompanied by an audio compact disc.
1.   Stone, Ruth M. *Africa*. 1998.
2.   Olsen, Dale A., and Daniel E. Sheehy, eds. *South America, Mexico, Central America, and the Caribbean*. 1998.
3.   Koskoff, Ellen. *The United States and Canada*. 2001.
4.   Miller, Terry E., and Sean Williams. *Southeast Asia*. 1998.
5.   Arnold, Alison. *South Asia, the Indian Subcontinent*. 2000.
6.   Danielson, Virginia, Scott Lloyd Marcus, and Dwight Fletcher Reynolds. *The Middle East*. 2002.
7.   Provine, Robert C., Yoshihiko Tokumaru, and John Lawrence Wizlebenm. *East Asia: China, Japan, and Korea*. 2002.
8.   Rice, Timothy, James Porter, and Chris Goertzen. *Europe*. 2000.
9.   Kaeppler, Adrienne Lois, and Jacob Wainwright Love. *Australia and the Pacific Islands*. 1998.
10.   Stone, Ruth M. *The World's Music: General Perspectives and Reference Tools*. 2002.
———, eds. *The Garland Encyclopedia of World Music Online*. Alexandria, VA: Alexander Street Press, 2007. http://glnd.alexanderstreet.com.
**Sadie, Stanley, and John Tyrrell, eds. *The New Grove Dictionary of Music and Musicians*. 2d ed. 29 vols. London: Macmillan, 2001.

National Dictionaries: ML101

Hitchcock, H. Wiley, and Stanley Sadie, eds. *The New Grove Dictionary of American Music*. 4 vols. London: Macmillan, 1986.

Kallmann, Helmut, Gilles Potvin, and Kenneth Winters, eds. *Encyclopedia of Music in Canada*. 2d ed. Toronto: University of Toronto Press, 1992.

Marcondes, Marcos, ed. *Enciclopédia da Música Brasileira: Popular, Erudita e Folklorica*. 4 vols. São Paulo, Brazil: Art Editora, 2000.

Rodicio, Emilio Casares, José López-Calo, and Ismael Fernández de la Cuesta, eds. *Diccionario de la Música Española e Hispanoamericana*. 10 vols. [Spain]: Sociedad General de Autores y Editores, 1999–2002.

Subject Dictionaries: ML102

Boldrey, Richard. *Guide to Operatic Roles & Arias*. Dallas: Pst...Inc, 1994.

Kernfeld, Barry, ed. *The New Grove Dictionary of Jazz*. 2d ed. 3 vols. New York: Grove's Dictionaries of Music, 2001. http://www.grovemusic.com.

Larkin, Colin. *The Virgin Encyclopedia of Jazz*. Rev. & updated ed. London: Muze UK, 2004.

———. *The Encyclopedia of Popular Music*. 4th ed. New York: Oxford University Press, 2006. Part of *Oxford Music Online*, http://www.oxfordmusiconline.com.

Loewenberg, Alfred, comp. *Annals of Opera, 1597–1940*. New York: Rowman & Littlefield, 1978.

Osborne, Charles. *The Dictionary of the Opera*. New York: Welcome Rain Publishers, 2001.

Palmieri, Robert. *The Piano: An Encyclopedia*. 2d ed. Encyclopedia of Keyboard Music. New York: Routledge, 2003.

Reid, Cornelius L. *A Dictionary of Vocal Terminology: An Analysis*. New York: Joseph Patelson Music House, 1983.

Sadie, Stanley, ed. *The New Grove Dictionary of Opera*. 4 vols. New York: Grove's Dictionaries of Music, 1992. http://www.grovemusic.com.

Santelli, Robert. *The Big Book of Blues: A Biographical Encyclopedia*. New York: Penguin Books, 2001.

Taylor, Steve. *The A to X of Alternative Music*. New York: Continuum, 2004.

Biographical Dictionaries: ML105–107

**Biography and Genealogy Master Index*. Farmington Hills, MI: Gale Group 2001–. http://infotrac.galegroup.com/menu. Available via institutional subscription.

Burns, Kristine H. *Women and Music in America since 1900: An Encyclopedia*. 2 vols. Westport, CT: Greenwood Press, 2002.

Floyd, Samuel A. *International Dictionary of Black Composers*. 2 vols. Chicago: Fitzroy Dearborn, 1999.

International Who's Who in Classical Music. 23rd ed. London: Europa Publications, 2007.

International Who's Who in Popular Music. 9th ed. London: Europa Publications, 2007.

Sadie, Julie Anne, and Rhian Samuel. *The Norton/Grove Dictionary of Women Composers*. New York: Norton, 1994.

**Slonimsky, Nicolas, and Laura Kuhn, eds. *Baker's Biographical Dictionary of Musicians*. 6 vols. Centennial Edition (9th ed.). New York: Schirmer Books, 2001. Online from Alexander Street Press, http://www.alexanderstreet.com or from Gale, http://gale.cengage.com.

Term Dictionaries: ML108–109

Fradkin, Robert A. *The Well-Tempered Announcer: A Pronunciation Guide to Classical Music*. Bloomington: Indiana University Press, 1996.

Hoffman, Miles. *The NPR Classical Music Companion: Terms and Concepts from A to Z*. Boston: Houghton Mifflin, 1997. Available in print and as an electronic book from NetLibrary.

Latham, Alison, ed. *The Oxford Dictionary of Musical Terms*. New York: Oxford University Press, 2004.

Leuchtmann, Horst. *Terminorum musicae index septem linguis redactus*. [*Polyglot Dictionary of Musical Terms: English, German, French, Italian, Spanish, Hungarian, Russian*]. Budapest: Akadémiai Kiadó, 1978.

**Randel, Don Michael. *The Harvard Dictionary of Music*. 4th ed. Cambridge, MA: Belknap Press of Harvard University Press, 2003. Online from Credo Reference, http://corp.credoreference.com.

Thomsett, Michael C., comp. *Musical Terms, Symbols and Theory: An Illustrated Dictionary*. Chicago: St. James Press, 1989.

Chapter 3. Starting-Point Resources: Journals

Lists of Periodicals

Directory of Open Access Journals (*DOAJ*). Lund, Sweden: Lund University Libraries, 2002–. http://www.doaj.org.

**Fellinger, Imogen, Julie Woodward, and others. "Periodicals." In *Grove Music Online*. Edited by L. Macy. London: Oxford University Press, 2006. http://www.grove music.com.

Fidler, Linda M., and Richard James. *International Music Journals*. New York: Greenwood Press, 1990.

Ulrich's Periodicals Directory. New Providence, NJ: R. R. Bowker, 2000–. http://www.ulrichsweb.com/ulrichsweb/

Databases for Music

***International Index to Music Periodicals* (*IIMP*) or *International Index to Music Periodicals Full Text*. Alexandria, VA: Chadwyck-Healey, 1996–.http://iimpft.chadwyck.com/. This title may be available jointly with *International Index to the Performing Arts* (*IIPA*) under the title *Music & Performing Arts Online*.

***Music Index Online: A Subject-Author Guide to Periodical Literature, 1975–2007*. Warren, MI: Harmonie Park Press, 1979–. http://www.hppmusicindex.com/.

***RILM Abstracts of Music Literature*. New York: RILM, 1967–. http://www.rilm.org/.

RIPM Online: International Index to Nineteenth-Century Music Periodicals. Baltimore, MD: RIPM, 1997–. Online from EBSCO, NISC, OCLC, and Ovid. http://www.ripm.org.

Full-Text Archives

Directory of Open Access Journals (DOAJ). Lund, Sweden: Lund University Libraries, 2002–. http://www.doaj.org.
JSTOR. Music Collection. New York: JSTOR, 2003–. http://www.jstor.org.
Project MUSE: Scholarly Journals Online. Baltimore, MD: Johns Hopkins University Press, 1995–. http://muse.jhu.edu.

Databases for Music Education

Asmus, Edward P. *Music Education Search System.* Miami: University of Miami, 1998–. http://www.music.miami.edu/mess.
University of Texas at San Antonio Department of Music and Institute for Music Research. *CAIRSS for Music (Computer-Assisted Information Retrieval Service System).* San Antonio: University of Texas, 1994–. http://imr.utsa.edu/CAIRSS.htm.
University of Victoria Faculty of Education. *Music Education Resource Base.* Victoria, BC: University of Victoria, 1995–. http://www.merb.org.

Databases for Related Disciplines: Humanities/Performing Arts

Arts & Humanities Citation Index. Philadelphia: Institute for Scientific Information (ISI), 1976–. http://scientific.thomson.com/products/wos/.
Humanities Abstracts. New York: H. W. Wilson, 1984–. http://vnweb.hwwilsonweb.com/hww/.
International Index to the Performing Arts (IIPA) and *International Index to the Performing Arts Full Text.* Alexandria, VA: Chadwyck-Healey, 1998–. http://iipa.chadwyck.com/. This title may be available jointly with *International Index to Music Periodicals* under the title *Music & Performing Arts Online.*

Databases for Related Disciplines: Education

Education Full Text. New York: H. W. Wilson, 1983–.
** Educational Resources Information Center (U.S.). *ERIC.* Washington, DC: Institute of Education Sciences (IES) of the U.S. Department of Education, 1993–. Available from various database vendors; for free access: http://www.eric.ed.gov.

Databases for Related Disciplines: Other

"Google Scholar." Mountain View, CA: Google, Inc., 2004–. http://scholar.google.com/.

For listings of other subject databases, see pages 26–27. Then check your library's list of databases for availability of appropriate ones.

Chapter 4. Starting-Point Resources: Bibliographies

Bibliographies for the Discipline of Music: ML113

**Duckles, Vincent H., and Ida Reed. *Music Reference and Research Materials: An Annotated Bibliography*. 5th ed. New York: Schirmer Books, 1997.

Mixter, Keith E. *General Bibliography for Music Research*, 3rd ed. Detroit Studies in Music Bibliography, 75. Warren, MI: Harmonie Park Press, 1996.

**Sampsel, Laurie J. *Music Research: A Handbook*. New York: Oxford University Press, 2008. Companion website at http://www.oup.com/us/musresearch.

Bibliographies in Series

Bibliographies in American Music. Sponsored by The College Music Society. Warren, MI: Harmonie Park Press, 1974–. Classed separately according to topic. Use subject headings to search for them.

Detroit Studies in Music Bibliography. Warren, MI: Harmonie Park Press, 1961–.

Garland Composer Resource Manuals. New York: Garland Publishing, 1981–2000.

MLA Index and Bibliography Series. Lanham, MD: Scarecrow Press, 1964–.

Music Research and Information Guides. New York: Garland Publishing, 1987–2001.

Routledge Music Bibliographies. New York: Routledge, 2000–.

Musical Sources: ML113

Benton, Rita, ed. *Directory of Music Research Libraries*. 5 vols. International Inventory of Musical Sources (RISM). Series C. New York: Barenreiter, 1967–1985.

Boorman, Stanley, John A. Emerson, David Hiley, David Fallows, and others. "Sources, MS." In *Grove Music Online*. Edited by L. Macy. London: Oxford University Press, 2006. http://www.grovemusic.com.

International Inventory of Musical Sources (RISM). Series A/I. Einzeldrucke vor 1800. Kassel: Barenreiter, 1971–81; corrections, 1986–99.

International Inventory of Musical Sources (RISM). Series B. Munich: Henle, 1960–.

International Inventory of Musical Sources (RISM) Online. Cambridge, MA: International Inventory of Musical Sources (RISM) Office, Harvard University. 1997–. http://www.rism.harvard.edu/cgi-bin/zform.CGI?A2.

Dissertations and Theses: Online or ML128

Dissertation Abstracts Online. Ann Arbor, MI: ProQuest Information and Learning Company, 2000–. http://wwwlib.umi.com/dissertations/.

Dissertations in Progress. Urbana, IL: Council for Research in Music Education, School of Music, University of Illinois at Urbana-Champaign, 1999–. http://www2.music.uiuc.edu/sonorities/article01.html.

Doctoral Dissertations in Musicology Online: DDM-Online. Edited by Thomas J. Mathiesen, Andreas Giger, and Cecil Adkins. Bloomington: School of Music, Indiana University, 1996–. http://www.chmtl.indiana.edu/ddm/.

Networked Digital Library of Theses and Dissertations (NDLTD). ETD Union Catalog. Blacksburg, VA: NDLTD, 2001–. http://www.ndltd.org/browse.en.html.

****ProQuest Dissertations and Theses—Full Text (PQDT).* Ann Arbor, MI: ProQuest Information and Learning Company, 2002–.

Song Indexes in Print: ML128

Ferguson, Gary Lynn. *Song Finder: A Title Index to 32,000 Popular Songs in Collections, 1854–1992.* Music Reference Collection, 46. Westport, CT: Greenwood Press, 1995.

Goleeke, Tom. *Literature for Voice: An Index of Songs in Collections and Source Book for Teachers of Singing.* 2 vols. Metuchen, NJ: Scarecrow Press, 1984–2002.

Goodfellow, William D. *Where's That Tune? An Index to Songs in Fakebooks.* Metuchen, NJ: Scarecrow Press, 1990.

Song Indexes Online: ML128

California Library Systems. *Cooperative Song Index.* Fresno, CA: San Joaquin Valley Library System, 2000–. http://www.sjvls.org/songs.

Popular Song Database. Seattle, WA: The Library, University of Washington, 1997–. http://db.lib.washington.edu/PopSong/.

Song Index. Mesa: Arizona State University Libraries. http://www.asu.edu/lib/resources/db/songindx.htm.

UT Song Index: An Index to Songs in over 1500 Song Anthologies. Knoxville: George F. DeVine Music Library, University of Tennessee, 1995–. http://www.lib.utk.edu/music/songdb/.

Analysis Indexes: Online or ML128

Diamond, Harold J. *Music Analyses: An Annotated Guide to the Literature.* New York: Schirmer Books, 1991.

UT Analysis Index. Knoxville: University of Tennessee Music Library, 1980–. http://www.lib.utk.edu/music/analysis/index.html.

Wenk, Arthur. *Analyses of Nineteenth- and Twentieth-Century Music, 1940–2000.* MLA Index and Bibliography Series, 34. Lanham, MD: Scarecrow Press and Music Library Association, 2007.

Music in Print: Online or ML128

Farish, Margaret. *Orchestral Music in Print.* Roslyn, PA: emusicquest, 2002.

Reese, Donald. *Music-in-Print Series.* Roslyn, PA: emusicquest. 2000–2007. http://www.emusicinprint.com.

Music: Repertoire Lists: ML128

Cohn, Arthur. *The Literature of Chamber Music.* 4 vols. Chapel Hill, NC: Hinshaw Music, 1997.

Gillaspie, Jon A., Marshall Stoneham, and David Lindsey Clark. *The Wind Ensemble Catalog*. Music Reference Collection, 63. Westport, CT: Greenwood Press, 1998.

Goodfellow, William D. *Wedding Music: An Index to Collections*. Metuchen, NJ: Scarecrow Press, 1992.

Hinson, Maurice. *Guide to the Pianist's Repertoire*. 3rd ed. Bloomington: Indiana University Press, 2000.

Koshgarian, Richard. *American Orchestral Music: A Performance Catalog*. Metuchen, NJ: Scarecrow Press, 1992.

Kvet, Edward J. *Instructional Literature for Middle-Level Band*. Reston, VA: Music Educators National Conference, 1996.

Laster, James H. *Catalogue of Choral Music Arranged in Biblical Order*. Lanham, MD: Scarecrow Press, 1996. *Supplement*, 2002.

Scott, William, comp. *A Conductor's Repertory of Chamber Music: Compositions for Nine to Fifteen Solo Instruments*. Music Reference Collection, 39. Westport, CT: Greenwood Press, 1993.

Villamil, Victoria Etnier. *A Singer's Guide to the American Art Song, 1870–1980*. Metuchen, NJ: Scarecrow Press, 1993.

Music: Graded Lists: ML132

Dvorak, Thomas, L., and Richard L. Floyd. *Best Music for Beginning Band: A Selective Repertoire Guide to Music and Methods for Beginning Band*. Brooklyn, NY: Manhattan Beach Music, 2000.

Hopkin, J. Arden. *Songs for Young Singers: An Annotated List for Developing Voices*. Lanham, MD: Scarecrow Press, 2002.

Bibliographies of Individuals: ML134

Smialek, William. *Frédéric Chopin: A Guide to Research*. Garland Composer Resource Manuals, 50. New York: Garland Publishing, 2000.

Wentzel, Wayne C. *Samuel Barber: A Guide to Research*. Routledge Music Bibliographies. New York: Routledge, 2001.

Bibliography of Thematic Catalogs: ML113

**Brook, Barry S., and Richard J. Viano. *Thematic Catalogues in Music: An Annotated Bibliography*. 2d ed. Annotated Reference Tools in Music, 5. Stuyvesant, NY: Pendragon Press, 1997.

Discographies: ML156–ML156.4

Blyth, Alan, ed. *Choral Music on Record*. New York: Cambridge University Press, 1991.

Canning, Nancy. *A Glenn Gould Catalog*. Discographies, 50. Westport, CT: Greenwood Press, 1992.

Cuscuna, Michael, and Michel Ruppli. *The Blue Note Label: A Discography*. Discographies, 88. Westport, CT: Greenwood Press, 2001.

Green, Jeff. *The Green Book of Songs by Subject: The Thematic Guide to Popular Music*. 5th ed. Nashville, TN: Professional Desk References, 2002.

Lowrey, Alvin. *Lowrey's International Trumpet Discography*. Columbia, SC: Camden House, 1990.

Smoley, Lewis M. *Gustav Mahler's Symphonies: Critical Commentary on Recordings since 1986*. Discographies, 66. Westport, CT: Greenwood Press, 1996.

Tommasini, Anthony. *Opera: A Critic's Guide to the 100 Most Important Works and the Best Recordings*. New York: Times Books, 2004.

Whitburn, Joel, ed. *Joel Whitburn's Top Pop Singles, 1955–2002*. Menomonee Falls, WI: Record Research, 2003.

Indexes to Record Reviews: ML156.9

Myers, Kurtz, ed. *Index to Record Reviews: Based on Material Originally Published in* Notes, The Quarterly Journal of the Music Library Association *between 1949 and 1977*. 5 vols. Boston: G. K. Hall, 1978–1980.

———. *Index to Record Reviews: Based on Material Originally Published in* Notes, The Quarterly Journal of the Music Library Association *between 1978 and 1983*. Boston: G. K. Hall, 1985.

———. *Index to Record Reviews: Based on Material Originally Published in* Notes, The Quarterly Journal of the Music Library Association *between 1984 and 1987*. Boston: G. K. Hall, 1989.

Palkovic, Mark, and Paul Cauthen, comps. *Index to CD and Record Reviews, 1987–1997: Based on Material Originally Published in* Notes, The Quarterly Journal of the Music Library Association *between 1987 and 1997*. New York: G. K. Hall, 1999.

NOTE: There are no bibliographic entries for **Chapter 5**.

Chapter 6. Scholarly Writing

Style Manuals for Multiple Styles

**Hacker, Diana. *A Pocket Style Manual*. 4th ed. Boston: Bedford/St. Martin's, 2004.

Style Manuals: APA

American Psychological Association. *Concise Rules of APA Style*. Washington, DC: American Psychological Association, 2005. http://www.loc.gov/catdir/toc/ecip053/ 2004026327.html.

American Psychological Association. *Publication Manual of the American Psychological Association*. 5th ed. Washington, DC: American Psychological Association, 2001.

Style Manuals: Chicago Style

***The Chicago Manual of Style*. 15th ed. Chicago: University of Chicago Press, 2003.

Turabian, Kate L., John Grossman, and Alice Bennett. *A Manual for Writers of Term Papers, Theses, and Dissertations*. 6th ed. Chicago: University of Chicago Press, 1996. [Based on the Chicago style]

Style Manuals: MLA

Gibaldi, Joseph. *MLA Style Manual and Guide to Scholarly Publishing*. New York: Modern Language Association of America, 1998.

Style Guides for Writing about Music

Cowdery, James R., Carl Skoggard, and Barbara Dobbs Mackenzie, eds. *How to Write about Music: The RILM Manual of Style*. 2d ed. New York: Répertoire International de Littérature Musicale, 2006.

**Holoman, D. Kern. *Writing about Music: A Style Sheet from the Editors of 19th-Century Music*. Berkeley: University of California Press, 1988. Also available electronically from NetLibrary.

"Names and Terms." Chap. 8 in *The Chicago Manual of Style*. 15th ed. Chicago: University of Chicago Press, 2003.

"Spelling, Distinctive Treatment of Words, and Compounds." Chap. 7 in *The Chicago Manual of Style*. 15th ed. Chicago: University of Chicago Press, 2003.

Copyright Information Sources: Books

Fishman, Stephen. *The Public Domain: How to Find & Use Copyright-Free Writings, Music, Art & More*. 3rd ed. Berkeley, CA: Nolo, 2006.

Frith, Simon, and Lee Marshall, eds. *Music and Copyright*. 2d ed. New York: Routledge, 2004.

**Krasilovsky, M. William, Sidney Shemel, John M. Gross, and Jonathan Feinstein. *This Business of Music: The Definitive Guide to the Music Industry*. 10th ed. New York: Billboard Books, 2007.

"Rights and Permissions." Chap. 4 in *The Chicago Manual of Style*. 15th ed. Chicago: University of Chicago Press, 2003.

Copyright Information Sources: Websites

"Checklist for Compliance with the TEACH Act." Indianapolis: Copyright Management Center, IUPUI. http://www.copyright.iupui.edu/teachlist.htm.

"Copyright." Washington, DC: U.S. Copyright Office at the Library of Congress, 2007. http://lcweb.loc.gov/copyright/.

"Copyright Advisory Center." New York: Columbia University. http://www.copyright.columbia.edu/.

"Copyright for Music Librarians." Middleton, WI: Music Library Association, 2006–. http://www.lib.jmu.edu/org/mla/.

"Copyright Resource Center." New York: Music Publishers Association, 2004–. http://www.mpa.org/copyright_resource_center/.

"Fair Use Checklist." New York: Columbia University, Copyright Advisory Office, 2007. http://www.copyright.columbia.edu/fair-use-checklist.htm.

Harper, Georgia. "Crash Course in Copyright." Austin: University of Texas System, Intellectual Property Section. http://www.utsystem.edu/ogc/IntellectualProperty/cprtindx.htm.

Chapter 7. Writing Samples

Badke, William B. *Research Strategies: Finding Your Way Through the Information Fog.* New York: IUniverse, 2004.

Boyle, David J., Richard K. Fiese, and Nancy Zavac. *A Handbook for Preparing Graduate Papers in Music.* 2d ed. Houston, TX: Halcyon Press, 2004.

Helm, E. Eugene, and Albert T. Luper. *Words & Music: Form and Procedure in Theses, Dissertations, Research Papers, Book Reports, Programs, Theses in Composition.* Rev. ed. Totowa, NJ: European American Music, 1982.

Henry, Michele L., and Laurel E. Zeiss. "Musicians as Authors: Teaching the Art of Writing Program Notes." *College Music Symposium* (2004): 121–132.

Irvine, Demar, and Mark A. Radice. *Irvine's Writing about Music.* 3rd ed., revised and enlarged. Portland, OR: Amadeus Press, 1999.

Leedy, Paul D., and Jeanne Ellis Ormrod. *Practical Research: Planning and Design.* 8th ed. Upper Saddle River, NJ: Pearson Merrill Prentice Hall, 2005.

NOTE: There are no bibliography entries for **Chapter 8**.

Chapter 9. Databases: Structured for Searching

WorldCat

Online Computer Library Center (OCLC). *WorldCat.* Dublin, OH: OCLC, 1992–. http://www.oclc.org/worldcat. Free version, *WorldCat.org* is also called *Open WorldCat* and is available at http://World Cat.org.

Reference Books for Composition Titles

Berkowitz, Freda. *Popular Titles & Subtitles of Musical Compositions.* 2d ed. Metuchen, NJ: Scarecrow Press, 1975.

Hodgson, Julian. *Music Titles in Translation: A Checklist of Musical Compositions.* Hamden, CT: Linnet Books, 1976.

Room, Adrian. *A Dictionary of Music Titles: The Origins of the Names and Titles of 3,500 Musical Compositions.* Jefferson, NC: McFarland, 2000.

Uniform Title Tutorial

Fenske, David E., R. Michael Fling, Brenda Nelson Strauss, and Shirlene Ward. *Making the Most of the Music Library: Using Uniform Titles.* Bloomington: Indiana University, 2006. http://library.music.indiana.edu/collections/uniform/uniform.html.

Chapter 10. Subject Searching in Library Catalogs: Controlled Vocabulary

Controlled Vocabulary

**Library of Congress. Cataloging Policy and Support Office. *Library of Congress Subject Headings*. 30th ed. 5 vols. Washington, DC: Library of Congress, Cataloging Distribution Service, 2007.

Chapter 11. Subject Searching in Indexes and Abstracts

Music Indexes and Abstracts

**International Index to Music Periodicals (IIMP)* or *International Index to Music Periodicals Full Text*. Alexandria, VA: Chadwyck-Healey, 1996–.
http://iimpft.chadwyck.com/. This title may be available jointly with *International Index to the Performing Arts (IIPA)* under the title *Music & Performing Arts Online*.
**Music Index Online: A Subject-Author Guide to Periodical Literature, 1975–2007*. Warren, MI: Harmonie Park Press, 1979–. http://www.hppmusicindex.com/.
**RILM Abstracts of Music Literature*. New York: RILM, 1967–. http://www.rilm.org/.

NOTE: There are no bibliography entries for **Chapter 12**.

Chapter 13. Related-Record Searching and Citation Indexes

ISI Web of Science. Philadelphia: Institute for Scientific Information (*ISI*), 1970–. http://isiknowledge.com/wos. Includes: *Arts & Humanities Citation Index (A&HCI)*, *Science Citation Index (SCI),* and *Social Sciences Citation Index (SSCI).*

Chapter 14. Other Discovery Methods: Experts and the Internet

Print Directories

**College Music Society. *Directory of Music Faculties in Colleges and Universities, U.S. and Canada*. Missoula, MT: College Music Society, 1996–. http://www.music. org/Pubs/FacDirsearch/FacDirsearch.html.
International Who's Who in Classical Music. 23rd ed. London: Europa Publications, 2007. Published annually. [ML106] See directory sections.
International Who's Who in Popular Music. 9th ed. London: Europa Publications, 2007. Published annually. [ML106] See directory sections.
**Musical America*. Great Barrington, MA: Billboard Publications, 2005. Published annually. [ML13]

Online Directories

"AT&T Directories." San Antonio, TX: AT&T, 2003–. http://www.att.com/directory/.

Directory of Music Faculties for U.S. and Canadian Institutions. Missoula, MT: College Music Society, 2007. http://www.music.org/cgi-bin/showpage.pl?tmpl=infoserv/facdir/facdirhome&h=63.

"Yahoo! Phone Numbers and Addresses." Sunnyvale, CA: Yahoo! Inc., 1994–. http://dir.yahoo.com/Reference/Phone_Numbers_and_Addresses/.

Internet Search Engines

"Ask.com." Oakland, CA: IAC Search & Media, 1996–. http://www.ask.com.

"Google." Mountain View, CA: Google, Inc., 1996–. http://www.google.com.

Metasearch Engines

"Clusty." Pittsburgh, PA: Vivisimo, Inc., 2000–. http://www.vivisimo.com/.

"Ixquick." Zeist, The Netherlands: Surfboard Holding BV, 1998–. http://www.ixquick.com/.

Music Subject Directories

"DW3 Classical Music Resources." Duke University Libraries, Music Library and Music Media Center, 2007. http://www.lib.duke.edu/dw3/.

"Online Internet Resources for Music Scholars." Harvard College Libraries, Loeb Library, 2007. http://hcl.harvard.edu/research/guides/music/resources/index.html.

General Subject Directories

"Infomine: Scholarly Internet Resource Collections." Riverside, CA: Infomine, The Regents of the University of California, 1994–. http://infomine.ucr.edu/.

"Intute: Arts & Humanities." San Mateo, CA: The Intute Consortium, 2006–. http://www.artifact.ac.uk/.

"Librarians' Internet Index." San Mateo, CA: The Califa Library Group, 1997–. http://lii.org/.

Deep Web

"Google Scholar." Mountain View, CA: Google, Inc., 2004–. http://scholar.google.com/.

Evaluation Criteria

"Evaluating Web Pages." Berkeley: University of California, Berkeley Library, 2005. http://www.lib.berkeley.edu/TeachingLib/Guides/Internet/Evaluate.html.

Kirk, Elizabeth E. "Evaluating Information Found on the Internet." Baltimore, MD: Johns Hopkins University, The Sheridan Libraries, 1996. http://www.library.jhu.edu/researchhelp/general/evaluating/index.html.

Chapter 15. Using Thematic Catalogs

**Brook, Barry S., and Richard J. Viano. *Thematic Catalogues in Music: An Annotated Bibliography*. 2d ed. Stuyvesant, NY: Pendragon Press, 1997.

Chapter 16. M: The Music—Scores and Recordings

Musical Editions

Robinson, Sydney Charles, George R. Hill, Norris L. Stephens, and Julie Woodward. "Editions, historical." In *Grove Music Online*. Edited by L. Macy. http://www.grove music.com.

Critical Editions and Their Indexes: ML113

Heyer, Anna Harriet. *Historical Sets, Collected Editions, and Monuments of Music: A Guide to Their Contents*. 2 vols. 3rd ed. Chicago: American Library Association, 1980.

Hill, George R., ed. *Index to Printed Music: Collections & Series (IPM)*. Baltimore, MD: National Information Services Corp., 2004–. Electronic database.

Hill, George R., and Norris L. Stephens. *Collected Editions, Historical Series & Sets, & Monuments of Music: A Bibliography*. Berkeley, CA: Fallen Leaf Press, 1997.

Sound Recording Databases

Classical Music Library. Alexandria, VA: Alexander Street Press, 2004–. http://www. alexanderstreet.com.

DRAM (Database of Recorded American Music). New York: Anthology of Recorded American Music, 2001–. http://www.dramonline.org/.

Naxos Music Library. Franklin, TN: Naxos of America, 2004–. http://www.naxosmusic library.com.

Naxos Music Library Jazz. Franklin, TN: Naxos of America, 2005–. http://www.naxos musiclibrary.com/jazz.

Smithsonian Global Sound. Alexandria, VA: Alexander Street Press, 2005–. http://www. alexanderstreet.com.

Chapter 17. ML: Music Literature

Texts and Translations: ML49–54.8

Castel, Nico, in conjunction with various opera singers. Geneseo, NY: Leyerle, 1993–.
The Complete Puccini Libretti. 2 vols. 1993–1994.
The Complete Verdi Libretti. 4 vols. 1994–1996.
Schubert's Complete Song Texts. 2 vols. 1996.

The Libretti of Mozart's Completed Operas. 2 vols. 1997–1998.
French Opera Libretti. 2 of 3 vols. published. 1999–.
Italian Bel Canto Opera Libretti. 3 vols. 2000–2002.
Italian Verismo Opera Libretti. 1 of 2 vols. published. 2000–.
Four Strauss Opera Libretti. 2002.
Ring des Nibelungen. 2003.
German Miscellaneous Opera Libretti. 2005.
Jeffers, Ron. *Translations and Annotations of Choral Repertoire.* Vol. 1. *Sacred Latin Texts.* Vol. 2. *German Texts.* Corvallis, OR: Earthsongs, 1988–2000.
Phillips, Lois. *Lieder Line by Line, and Word for Word.* Rev. ed. New York: Oxford University Press, 1996.
Rohinsky, Marie-Claire. *The Singer's Debussy.* New York: Pelion Press, 1987.

Music History and Chronology

Glenn, Stanley. "Historiography." In *Grove Music Online.* Edited by L. Macy. http://www.grovemusic.com.

History Surveys: ML160

**Burkholder, J. Peter, Donald Jay Grout, and Claude V. Palisca. *A History of Western Music.* 7th ed. New York: Norton, 2006.
Crocker, Richard. *A History of Musical Style.* New York: McGraw-Hill, 1966.
Lang, Paul Henry. *Music in Western Civilization.* New York: Norton, 1941.

History Series: ML160 or Classified by Period or by Region

Norton Introduction to Music History. New York: Norton, 1978–2005.
  Medieval Music. Richard H. Hoppin, 1978.
  Renaissance Music: Music in Western Europe, 1400–1600. Allan W. Atlas, 1998.
  Baroque Music: Music in Western Europe, 1580–1750. John Walter Hill, 2005.
  Romantic Music: A History of Musical Style in Nineteenth-Century Europe. Leon Plantinga, 1984.
  Classical Music: The Era of Haydn, Mozart, and Beethoven. Philip G. Downs, 1992.
  Twentieth-Century Music: A History of Musical Style in Modern Europe and America. Robert P. Morgan, 1991.
The Oxford History of Western Music. 6 vols. Edited by Richard Taruskin. New York: Oxford University Press, 2005. Online in 2009 from *Oxford Music Online,* http://oxfordmusiconline.com.
  v. 1. *The Earliest Notations to the Sixteenth Century*
  v. 2. *The Seventeenth and Eighteenth Centuries*
  v. 3. *The Nineteenth Century*
  v. 4. *The Early Twentieth Century*
  v. 5. *The Late Twentieth Century*
  v. 6. *Resources: Chronology, Bibliography, Master Index*
The Prentice-Hall History of Music Series. 7 vols. Upper Saddle River, NJ: Prentice Hall, 1991–2002.

History by period:
Music in the Renaissance. 2d ed. Howard Mayer Brown and Louise K. Stein, 1999.
Baroque Music. 3rd ed. Claude V. Palisca, 1991.
Music in the Classic Period. 4th ed. Reinhard G. Pauly, 2000.
Nineteenth-Century Romanticism in Music. 3rd ed. Rey M. Longyear, 1988.
Twentieth-Century Music: An Introduction. 4th ed. Eric Salzman, 2002.
History by region:
Folk and Traditional Music of the Western Continents. 3rd ed. Bruno Nettl and Gerard Béhague, 1990.
Music Cultures of the Pacific, the Near East, and Asia. 3rd ed. William P. Malm, 1996.
Music in India: The Classical Traditions. Bonnie C. Wade, 1979.
Music in Latin America: An Introduction. Gerard Béhague, 1979.
Music in the United States: A Historical Introduction. 4th ed. H. Wiley Hitchcock and Kyle Gann, 2000.

Chronology: Classified by Topic (General Works, Period, Country)

Hall, Charles J. *A Chronicle of American Music: 1700–1995.* New York: Schirmer Books, 1996.
Kendall, Alan. *The Chronicle of Classical Music: An Intimate Diary of the Lives and Music of the Great Composers.* London: Thames & Hudson, 1994, 2000.
**Slonimsky, Nicolas, and Laura Kuhn, eds. *Music since 1900.* 6th ed. New York: Schirmer Reference, 2001. Online from Alexander Street Press, http://alexander streetpress.com.

Music Iconography: ML85–89

Besseler, Heinrich, and Max Schneider, eds. 26 vols. *Musikgeschichte in Bildern.* Leipzig: Deutscher Verlag für Musik, 1961–. Published in four series:
Band I. *Musikethnologie* [Music in Societies and Cultures of the World]
Band II. *Musik Altertums* [Music of Antiquity]
Band III. *Musik des Mittelalters und der Renaissance* [Music of the Middle Ages and Renaissance]
Band IV. *Musik der Neuzeit* [Music of Modern Times]
Kinsky, George. *A History of Music in Pictures.* Reprint. New York: Dover Publications, 1951.
Seebass, Tilman, and Tilden Russell. *Imago musicae: International Yearbook of Musical Iconography.* Basel: Bärenreiter-Verlag, International Repertory of Musical Iconography, 1984–.

Outline Histories: ML161

Miller, Hugh Milton, and Dale Cockrell. *History of Western Music.* 5th ed. New York: Harper Perennial, 1991.
Wold, Milo. *An Outline History of Western Music.* 9th ed. Boston: WCB McGraw-Hill, 1997.

Source Readings for General Music History: ML160

**Strunk, W. Oliver, and Leo Treitler, eds. *Source Readings in Music History*. Rev. ed. New York: Norton, 1998.

Weiss, Piero, and Richard Taruskin. *Music in the Western World: A History in Documents*. New York: Schirmer Books, 1984.

Source Readings for Special Topics: Classed by Subject

Harrison, Frank. *Time, Place and Music: An Anthology of Ethnomusicological Observations c.1550 to c.1800*. Source Materials and Studies in Ethnomusicology, 1. Amsterdam: Frits Knuf, 1973.

MacClintock, Carol. *Readings in the History of Music in Performance*. Bloomington: Indiana University Press, 1982.

Mark, Michael. *Music Education: Source Readings from Ancient Greece to Today*. 2d ed. New York: Routledge, 2002.

Neuls-Bates, Carol. *Women in Music: An Anthology of Source Readings from the Middle Ages to the Present*. Rev. ed. Boston: Northeastern University Press, 1996.

Southern, Eileen. *Readings in Black American Music*. 2d ed. New York: Norton, 1983.

Indexes to Biographies and Musicians' Necrology

Biography and Genealogy Master Index. Detroit, MI: Gale Research, 1993–. http:// www .galegroup.com.

Gaylord Music Library, Washington University Libraries. *Necrology*. http://www.library .wustl.edu/units/music/necro/ (accessed 3 December 2007).

Greene, Frank, comp. *Composers on Record: An Index to Biographical Information on 14,000 Composers Whose Music Has Been Recorded*. Metuchen, NJ: Scarecrow Press, 1985.

Biographies in Series

The Master Musicians. New York: Oxford University Press. 1948–.

The New Grove Composer Biography Series. Publishers vary. London: Macmillan Reference or Oxford University Press. New York: Palgrave or Norton.

Performance Practice: Reference Books

Jackson, Roland John. *Performance Practice: A Dictionary-Guide for Musicians*. New York: Routledge, 2005.

———. *Performance Practice, Medieval to Contemporary: A Bibliographic Guide*. New York: Garland Publishing, 1988.

Vinquist, Mary, and Neal Zaslaw. *Performance Practice: A Bibliography*. New York: Norton, 1971.

Performance Practice: General Books: ML457

Butt, John. *Playing with History: The Historical Approach to Musical Performance*. New York: Cambridge University Press, 2002.

**Donington, Robert. *The Interpretation of Early Music*. New rev. ed. New York: Norton, 1989.

Duffin, Ross W. *A Performer's Guide to Medieval Music*. Bloomington: Indiana University Press, 2000.

**Neumann, Frederick, and Jane R. Stevens. *Performance Practices of the Seventeenth and Eighteenth Centuries*. New York: Schirmer Books, 1993.

Schultz, Timothy. *Performing French Classical Music: Sources and Applications*. Hillsdale, NY: Pendragon Press, 2001.

Performance Practice: Early Music Revival and "Authenticity"

Haskell, Harry. *The Early Music Revival: A History*. Reprint. Mineola, NY: Dover Publications, 1996, 1988.

Music Theory and Composition: ML and MT

Treatises

Reaney, Gilbert, ed. *Corpus Scriptorum de Musica (CSM)*. Neuhausen, Switzerland: American Institute of Musicology, 1950–.

Thesaurus Musicarum Italicarum (TMI). Utrecht University, Institute of Information and Computing Sciences. http://euromusicology.cs.uu.nl/.

Thesaurus Musicarum Latinarum (TML). Project director, Thomas J. Mathiesen. Bloomington: Indiana University, 1990–. http://www.music.indiana.edu/tml/.

Music Industry: ML3790–3795

**Krasilovsky, M. William, Sidney Shemel, and John M. Gross. *This Business of Music: The Definitive Guide to the Music Industry*. 9th ed. New York: Billboard, 2003.

Guides to Research and the Discipline for Musicology: ML3797

Clarke, Eric F., and Nicholas Cook. *Empirical Musicology: Aims, Methods, Prospects*. New York: Oxford University Press, 2004.

Duckles, Vincent, and others. "Musicology." In *Grove Music Online*. http://www.grove music.com.

Kivy, Peter. *New Essays on Musical Understanding*. Oxford: Clarendon, 2001.

Korsyn, Kevin Ernest. *Decentering Music: A Critique of Contemporary Musical Research*. New York: Oxford University Press, 2003. Also available as an electronic book from NetLibrary.

Williams, Alastair. *Constructing Musicology*. Aldershot, UK: Ashgate, 2001.

Guides to Research and the Discipline for Ethnomusicology: ML3797.6–3799

Clayton, Martin, Herbert Trevor, and Richard Middleton, eds. *The Cultural Study of Music: A Critical Introduction*. New York: Routledge, 2003.

Myers, Helen. *Ethnomusicology: Historical and Regional Studies*. New Grove Handbooks in Music. New York: Norton, 1993.

Chapter 18. MT: Instruction and Study

Instruction and Study in the Schools: MT1–5

General Works: MT1

North, Adrian C., and Hargreaves, David J. *Musical Development and Learning: The International Perspective.* New York: Continuum, 2001.

By Region or Country: MT3.A–Z

Labuta, Joseph A., and Deborah A. Smith. *Music Education: Historical Contexts and Perspectives.* Upper Saddle River, NJ: Prentice Hall, 1997.
**Mark, Michael L., and Charles L. Gary. *A History of American Music Education.* 3rd ed. Reston, VA: MENC, 2007.

Guides to Research and the Discipline for Music Education: MT1

**Colwell, Richard. *Handbook of Research on Music Teaching and Learning: A Project of the Music Educators National Conference.* New York: Schirmer Books, 1992.
**Colwell, Richard, and Carol Richardson. *The New Handbook of Research on Music Teaching and Learning: A Project of the Music Educators National Conference.* New York: Oxford University Press, 2002.
Phelps, Roger P., Ronald H. Sadoff, Edward C. Warburton, and Lawrence Ferrara. *A Guide to Research in Music Education.* 5th ed. Lanham, MD: Scarecrow Press, 2005.
Rainbow, Edward L., and Hildegard C. Froehlich. *Research in Music Education: An Introduction to Systematic Inquiry.* New York: Schirmer Books, 1987.

Pedagogy: Individual Instruments, Voice, Ensembles

Baker, Martha. *Practical Piano Pedagogy: The Definitive Text for Piano Teachers and Pedagogy Students.* Miami, FL: Warner Brothers, 2003.
Colwell, Richard J., and Thomas W. Goolsby. *The Teaching of Instrumental Music.* 3rd ed. Upper Saddle River, NJ: Prentice Hall, 2002.
Fraser, Alan. *The Craft of Piano Playing: A New Approach to Piano Technique.* Lanham, MD: Scarecrow Press, 2003.
Phillips, Kenneth H. *Directing the Choral Music Program.* New York: Oxford University Press, 2004.

Ballet, Opera, Theater Music, and Production: MT950–960

Boland, Robert, and Paul Argentini. *Musicals! Directing School and Community Theatre.* Lanham, MD: Scarecrow Press, 1997.
Clark, Mark Ross, and Lynn V. Clark. *Singing, Acting, and Movement in Opera: A Guide to Singer-getics.* Bloomington: Indiana University Press, 2002.
Radice, Mark A., ed. *Opera in Context: Essays on Historical Staging from the Late Renaissance to the Time of Puccini.* Portland, OR: Amadeus Press, 1998.

Author–Title Index

Subject Index

abstract:
    definition, 24
    sample, 73
adjacency operators, 139, 143–44, 145
    chart for music databases, 145
analysis indexes, 39–40
annotated bibliography. *See* bibliographies
annotation, 67
argument, 3, 5, 6, 7, 10, 53, 67, 81, 92, 170
authenticity in music, 202

ballet, 205, 211
bibliographic essay, 67, 72, 181
bibliographic management software, 9, 53,
    58
bibliographic record, 38, 97, 106, 109, 110–
    11, 125, 128, 140, 156
bibliographies, 4, 31–44
    of analysis indexes, 245
    annotated, 32, 34, 37, 67, 78–81
        writing, 67, 78–79
        sample, 79–81
    of bibliographies, 32
    in case study, 48–49
    of composers, 42, 246
    definitions of, 32, 54
    descriptive catalogs, 42
    of discipline of music, 14, 239, 244
    discographies, 32, 42–44, 246–47
    of dissertations and theses, 38–39,
        244–45
    of general reference books, 14, 239
    of graded lists (repertory), 41, 246
    in journal databases, 35–36
    LC Classification numbers for, 33
    of music in print, 40, 245
    of musical sources, 38, 244
    as reference books, 36–44

of repertory, 41, 245–46
of reviews (recordings), 44, 247
in series, 37–38, 244
of song indexes, 245
of sound recordings. *See* discographies
subject headings for, 33–34
thematic catalogs, 42, 246
by topic, 235–38
types and LC Classification, 33
biographies, 199–201
Boolean connectors. *See* Boolean operators
Boolean operators, 141–42
    in search engines, 164–65
Boolean searching. *See* keyword searching
browsing, 94–100
    effective practices, 100
    use of classification to start browsing,
        96–98, 217–22, 221–36 (instru-
        ments, genres, topics)
    use of subject headings to start brows-
        ing, 98–100
business of music, 206, 256

catalog record. *See* bibliographic record
catalog searching, 105–9
    advanced search, 146–47
    basic search, 107–8
    Boolean search, 141–47
    metasearch (integrated), 147–48
catalogs, library, 103, 105–6
    field searching in, 106–9
    keyword searching in, 145–47
    subject searching in, 118–28
    uniform titles in, 109–13
catalogs, union:
    WorldCat, 8, 13, 15, 50, 103, 104, 105,
        153, 249
    in case study, 50

About the Author

Pauline Shaw Bayne is assistant dean of libraries and professor at the University of Tennessee, Knoxville, where she has long been associated with music libraries and service to music students and faculty. She received her Master of Science in Library Science degree from the University of North Carolina, Chapel Hill, in 1973 and her Master of Music degree in Music History and Literature from Northwestern University in 1971. At Millikin University, she earned the Bachelor of Music degree in piano and music education. This book is based on the experiences of more than 17 years of teaching music bibliography and research methods to graduate students at the University of Tennessee School of Music.

As an active member of the Music Library Association, Bayne served as fiscal officer and member of the Board of Directors from 2003 to 2005. She chaired the MLA Committee on Basic Music Collections to produce the content for *A Basic Music Library: Essential Scores and Books* in 1978 and 1983. The first edition was named an Outstanding Reference Book in 1978 by the American Library Association. She authored *The Gottfried Galston Music Collection and the Galston-Busoni Archive* in 1978 and co-authored *The David Van Vactor Collection: A Catalog* in 1993. Two web-based resources, the *UT Song Index* and *UT Analysis Index*, were initially created by her and are maintained by staff of the George F. DeVine Music Library, which she managed for more than 34 years. She has also written articles on moving library collections, digital audio reserves, delivering instructional media electronically, and computer-based training for library staff.